Succeeding Sane

MAKING ROOM FOR JOY

IN A CRAZY WORLD

Bonnie St. John Deane

SIMON & SCHUSTER

SIMON & SCHUSTER
Rockefeller Center
1230 Avenue of the Americas
New York, NY 10020

SIMON & SCHUSTER and colophon are registered trademarks
of Simon & Schuster Inc.

Designed by Chris Welch

Manufactured in the United States of America

1   3   5   7   9   10   8   6   4   2

Library of Congress Cataloging-in-Publication Data
Deane, Bonnie St. John.
Succeeding sane: making room for joy in a crazy world /
Bonnie St. John Deane.
p.   cm.
1. Life skills—United States.   2. Success—United States.
I. Title.
HQ2039.U6D43   1998
158—dc21   97-35103   CIP
ISBN 0-684-81853-1

Acknowledgments

This book took hold of me like a tree putting down roots and spreading its branches as I watched in awe. It began with a simple desire to know how to be successful in a particular way, a way compatible with goodness. How can we be our best and brightest if success leads to corruption? The idea turned out much bigger than I thought.

After interviewing almost thirty phenomenally successful people it became clear to me that many, many people are as passionate about this as I am. I thank each of you who spoke with me for answering questions about your personal life and for sharing what you have learned by trial and error. Whether you were old friends or new acquaintances, it was amazing to go behind the scenes of your famous, powerful, and exalted lives.

You all taught me that achieving both success in a worldly sense and goodness in a personal sense is within reach for all of us. It seems so unusual only because people who succeed sane do it with less fanfare than the superstar nutcases. I want to thank my role models cited in this book for showing me the way forward.

I also want to acknowledge all the support and faith from others that has made my dream of being an author become a reality—a reality that exceeded my wildest dreams:

Jan Miller, my agent, who believed in me 100 percent and challenged me to write a far better book than what I originally envisioned. (Tony Robbins, too, who convinced her to believe in me.)

Dominick Anfuso, my editor at Simon & Schuster, who gave me lots of latitude and enthusiastic support to write my own book. I still wonder at such faith in a novice author.

All my established writer friends who took me in and treated me like a professional writer from the beginning. You know who you are, lunch bunch.

Ruby, my mother, who was always there with a new idea or article to banish writers' block, who took classes with me, who took Darcy away for the weekend when I needed to write, and who didn't balk at some of the things I wrote about. A rare mom, indeed!

April, my sister, the only person who volunteered to do close, time-consuming editing at no charge. She loves books as much as I do.

Wayne, my brother, who gave me the courage to become a writer by his example and creed: "A writer is a person who writes." I come from a family of writers.

Alissa Richardson, my gifted nanny, who took the job from hell (working part-time, with two babies in a house with mothers underfoot!) and made it heaven.

Susanne Scherman who keeps me sane and successful by not only sharing my business responsibilities but also sharing my life as a mother, a cook, and a gardener. She understood the concept of blending long before the book was written. (To Greg and Rachel: thanks for sharing her!)

My husband, Grant, who bought a computer for me to write my book during the first year of our marriage. He has always encouraged me—not to do what he thinks I should do, but to find out who I want to be.

Darcy, my daughter, who forced me to slow down the writing process, to think leisurely, and to feel a lot more.

To my Mom, Ruby,
who gave me life.

To my husband, Grant,
who encouraged me to experience more life.

To my daughter, Darcy,
who is life.

Contents

Part III   How to Hit Your Targets with Three Times the Punch!

Part IV   Finding Fulfillment on the Road to Success

Introduction

Are you as successful as you could be?
Are you as sane as you could be?
Why not?

Many times I have felt forced to choose between a full life and success. My decision to stop ski racing after the Olympics filled me with an immense, physical pain. Unable to continue ski racing and complete my college studies, I knew I had to choose. The night I decided to stop skiing I walked down to the frozen Charles River and sat feeling the cold air on my cheeks. Tears erupted in waves. Who would I be if I didn't ski?

For years skiing had been my life. I lived on a glacier every summer and in winter moved to small towns in Vermont, Nevada, and Colorado. How could I live without the sound of my ski boot clicking into the binding and all the adventure such a sound promised? I knew I would miss running my fingers along the sides of my ski to test the sharpness of the edge. Being an Olympic skier was my identity.

Yet it wasn't enough for me. Although I didn't want to give it up, spending the rest of my life going up and down a frozen slope seemed so pointless, like a hamster in a wheel going round and round.

I have joined and left some of the most elite competitive arenas in the world: Wall Street, Oxford, the White House. Glamorous as they may be from the outside, they all contain talented people intensely focused on doing the same thing over and over. When asked what was on her mind during her historic vault at the 1996 Olympic Games, Keri Strug said, "I had practiced that vault over 1,000 times, so when I stepped up I was positive."

Whether it's one more 500-million-dollar deal, a Superbowl, or the latest political crisis, top performers rush into the game with confidence based on hundreds of repetitions. Life spins at a frenetic pace but the view seldom changes.

Originally this book was intended to share my experience of competing. "I can teach people to win," I thought. As I began writing, however, I realized the hypocrisy of what I was doing. I left sports. I left academia. I left big business and big politics. Each of these worlds was not rewarding enough to justify the craziness of the hamster-on-a-wheel lifestyle. How could I give directions to others to go somewhere I didn't want to be?

I had escaped the fast track once again in April 1994 when I left my job at the White House. Starting a business as a writer and a speaker was my bid to be successful and make a contribution with less stress. I thought I would have a cushy life as my own boss, working at home, and raising a family.

To my surprise it was not an easy life. Even though I didn't have the pressure of a large organization, running a small business was tough. I found that professional speakers who earn a decent living are constantly traveling, marketing, and developing new material. Writing, too, consists of many hours bent over a computer. Furthermore, managing a business demanded knowledge of accounting, taxes, and personnel management. Thus even the business of writing and speaking threatened to derail my quality of life.

Changing jobs—from sports to politics to writing—didn't change anything. No profession made it easy to stay sane. To get quality of life, I had to change myself. But how?

As succeeding sane became the central problem in my life, I realized it should be the subject of this book. Sacrificing the quality of my work was not a solution I wanted to try. I wanted my sanity *and* my success. I wanted to know how to achieve excellence without being eaten up by the hard work, the ego trip, and the fast crowd. I researched the answers fueled by a personal desire to know.

At first I wondered if anyone could do it. When top performers are plagued by drugs, failing marriages, bad financial decisions, and health problems, they start to accept these problems as necessary side effects of achievement. In intensely competitive worlds it's considered normal, even admirable, to sacrifice one's marriage, health, or ethics for the sake of winning. Whether you want to be an Olympic medalist, a Nobel prizewinner, an elected official, or a Fortune 500 CEO, "You have to pay the price," people will tell you as though that excuses any sort of behavior.

On the other hand, moving in those same circles I had met certain people doing it differently. Being less flamboyant, more at peace, and less prone to publicity-seeking, these people were less noticeable than their more driven peers. They bounced from success to success with less effort and more joy. Their achievements were rooted in their own growth, health, and well-being. Their lives enriched those around them and made the world a better place.

They were (and are) singularly successful people leading a good life. I chose about thirty role models for *Succeeding Sane* from the people I had known and worked with. Those were the people I began to interview and write about. I began to see a pattern that cut across seemingly different worlds.

Whether you are in sports, medicine, business, or academia, our society condones getting on the fast track and becoming more machine than human. Those who retain the power of their minds, bodies, and spirits despite intense specialized training are hailed as superhuman heroes. For example, what we find so amazing about a superb young golfer like Tiger Woods is that he has developed his mind and heart in addition to his body. Too many young athletes trained to a high level of excellence end up narrow-minded, self-centered, and barely literate because they didn't get enough coaching for values or brains, only body.

It was that narrow approach to excellence I had never accepted. I was not satisfied with being *just an athlete* because I wanted to finish college and stretch my mind. I was not satisfied with being *purely academic* because I wanted to get out of the ivory tower. Wall Street money or power politics didn't hold enough allure either. None of these careers would develop mind, body, *and* spirit. Or so I thought.

But now I see it was not the careers that fell short, it was me. No matter how many hours I put into a job, I wasn't putting in my total humanity—my mind, body, and spirit. There is no meaning inherent in collecting ski medals, college degrees, money, or votes. It is only through the way we live that we put meaning into these things.

In this book you will learn how to shape your life to succeed more, to tap more of your humanity and to have more meaning in your life. There are many examples in the pages that follow of lives lived to the fullest.

There are athletes like Florence Griffith-Joyner who put mind, body, and soul into sports. She inspires others through her foundation. She teaches people the value of health and fitness as a co-chair of the President's Council on Physical Fitness. She expresses her vitality through wild outfits and fingernails. She isn't *just an athlete*. Flo Jo puts meaning into sports.

Certain academics, like Laura Tyson, put body and soul into theory and numbers. Given an opportunity, she is willing to step out of the ivory tower, go to Washington, and use her mind to improve the lives of working Americans. She isn't *just a number-crunching economist*. She cares about people.

In business, too, there are many who compete with their whole self. Bob Chappelle of the Saturn Corporation is an example you will hear more about. He is doing more than *just making money*. He is infusing every transaction, every personal contact, with his values.

And there are many examples around us of people competing with mind, body, and spirit who are not highlighted in this book. Once you know about this new approach to life, you'll see as many examples of people succeeding sane as succeeding crazy. Yet they can't explain to others how to do it. There was no book for them on competing with their full humanity. They did it through trial and error.

Succeeding Sane is truly a new concept in the self-help literature. I know because I have tried many of the major lifestyle and success trends.

I have:

- **Achieved** my goals with focus, positive attitude, and refusal to believe in obstacles
- **Downshifted** my goals in search of life quality and simplicity
- **Balanced** career, husband, home, time at the gym, and community service

None of these lifestyles was right for me. You may think, "What else is there?" If you don't want pure goal setting or pure quality of life, if having it all is too much of everything and balance leaves you with too little of anything . . . what else is there?

Succeeding Sane is a new answer. It isn't balance. It isn't pulling back the throttle or changing professions. It isn't necessarily downsizing, simplifying, or moving to the country. I have applied the principles I have learned in the process of writing this book and carved out a life that allows me to compete as a nationally recognized speaker and writer and still put energy into the things that are personally important to me: relationships, community service, health, and personal growth. Using the philosophy of *Succeeding Sane* I blend the parts of my life and make them reinforce one another better.

Succeeding Sane also involves looking for a unique lifestyle to fit you. I'm not "having it all" because I don't want to. Having it all reminds me of those Sunday breakfast buffets where you get a little bit of everything, eat too much, and feel sick afterward. Rather, I have designed a life that particularly suits me. I have learned from my role models without simply doing what they do. And now you can, too.

I finally found a profession with which I am satisfied. Once again I have attained the hallmarks of excellence in my field. My literary agent works with many best-selling authors who are my role models. My editor is one of the best nonfiction/self-help editors at one of the largest publishers in the country. As a speaker I travel throughout the country, receive high fees, and am often acclaimed with standing ovations. I work hard to be among the best. However, these things alone don't make me happy.

I would never be satisfied if I wasn't putting myself into my writing and my speaking. Between these pages lies my soul, my pain, my joy, and everything I know about how to be a better person. Many readers will find new ways to have more success and happiness at the same time. Those who grapple with the philosophy and apply it in their own way can unlock personal greatness. That is what satisfies me about being a writer.

As a speaker I work hard to learn about each audience, to perform at my best, and to connect as a human being. I never leave a speech unchanged by it. By the end of the year, I am a collection of the knowledge, feelings, and opinions of those groups to whom I have spoken. I make friends. It is because the audiences force me to grow at least as much as I help them that I find this work satisfying. I could write well, speak eloquently, and make money without really putting mind, body, and soul on the line. But what would be the point? When I put in more, I get more out of it.

The biggest reason that I am finding real satisfaction in my life, however, is that I have finally gotten my professional life aligned with my personal goals. As I travel the country, speaking, I am reconnecting with friends, serving my community, and growing as a person. I know that my business won't prosper unless I invest in my health, my family, and my ethics. I surround myself with people who respect those principles.

In sum, what makes me sane makes me successful and what makes me successful makes me sane. People say, "That's great, but it takes a lot of hard work and time to get your life into that position." That's true. But it also takes a lot of hard work and time to create a successful life that destroys you. Surviving without being very successful is hard work, too. If you're going to work hard for the next ten years, why not do it in a way that makes you more successful and more sane at the same time?

You can climb your mountains on a path that is compatible with who you are and what is meaningful to you. That way you don't arrive at the top of the heap feeling empty, bored, or just plain burned out.

You can resist the pressure to compete on one level, in one way. Every occupation has pressure to conform which can steal your individuality. If you want success and sanity you have to meet challenges and learn discipline, yet dare to be different. Dare to be you. After all, how can you be a superstar if you follow the crowd? When you harness the power of your unique mind, body, and spirit, you tap into the hidden time and energy you need to become a superstar. You have to put your whole self into the game. And this book shows you how.

CHAPTER 1

The Balance Trap

This book will change your life because it gives you a new paradigm —a new way of thinking—that will redefine your limits. Writing this has been no idle journey of curiosity for me. I have an urgent need to know in my own life. Feeling that I don't belong among the win-at-any-cost crowd I have already tried to pull back the throttle in several ways.

First I tried leading a *balanced* life. I tried working a nine-to-five job instead of seventy- to eighty-hour weeks. I went to the gym, took vacations, and made more time for friends and family. I planned to use my maternity leave, start raising a family, and enjoy all the richness that a balanced life promised. I downshifted before it became trendy.

I was not long in the world of balance, however, when I discovered it was at least as stressful as (but far less rewarding than) the world of achievement. The balanced people I saw—especially Moms and Dads —were neither enjoying their work nor their personal lives. What good is a balanced life if it involves rushing from work to daycare, to gym, and/or to night school while grabbing a McLean Burger on the road?

Balance looked to me like the worst of both worlds. Many people who share my contempt for the so-called balanced life have responded by dropping out altogether. They've decided to give up power and position, the big salary, and the big house in favor of simpler pleasures and more time. Many more women would like to do so. The popularity of books like *Simple Abundance* and *From Briefcase to Diaper Bag* shows that many people are dropping out, considering dropping out, or enjoying the fantasy of dropping out.

In some ways I wish I could drop out, too. But I can't do it. Perhaps I am still too much of an achievement junkie. I like telling people at cocktail parties what I do and hearing them say, "Oooh," as their eyes get big as saucers. I know it's shallow, but it's true.

Even in my less shallow moments I still can't let go of the thrill I get when I do my best at something. I love to work flat out for weeks at a time and accomplish the impossible at least once a year. I can't imagine a life in which I don't continue growing , learning, and reaching down inside myself to bring out my best. I can't just enjoy being.

Workaholism is not my problem. I enjoy the simple pleasures in life: swimming with my daughter, watching videos with my husband and rubbing his feet, or walking in the forest. But I know these things alone are not enough for me.

When I pull back on the throttle and relax, I don't feel comfortable. I get restless. But at the same time I don't feel comfortable in the win-at-any-cost world. Where do I belong? Limiting my choices to workaholism, dropout, or balance is so damaging, destructive, and plain wrong. It makes me angry.

Figure 1. **THE SEESAW VIEW OF LIFE**

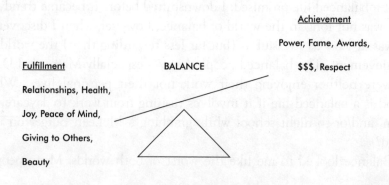

Achievement

Power, Fame, Awards,

Fulfillment   BALANCE $$$, Respect

Relationships, Health,

Joy, Peace of Mind,

Giving to Others,

Beauty

Seeing only these alternatives—all work, all home, all balance—is what I call "seesaw thinking."

It's as though life is a child's teeter-totter. At one end lies external achievements such as power, money, recognition (fame, awards), and respect of one's professional peers. The other end represents personal fulfillment through loving relationships, health, joy, peace of mind, giving to others, and appreciating beauty for its own sake.

I made my decisions as though I had to choose one end or a precarious balance somewhere in the middle. I believed that each hour in the day had to be devoted to one set of goals or the other. I could work sixteen hours a day and be wildly successful or I could come home at 5 P.M. and have less achievement but more fulfillment. "That's just the way it is," I thought. "There are only twenty-four hours in a day."

The Alternative to Balance: Blending

As I thought about the problem and studied my role models I realized they didn't look at success as a yes or no question. They didn't accept the fast track as the only way to the top. They were not afraid to do things differently from those around them. I call this modified approach *blending*. My role models were finding unique and creative solutions that allowed them to make success and personal fulfillment mutually reinforcing.

To me blending does not come naturally. The concept is so alien I had to spend two years researching and writing about it in order to explain it to myself. My tendency is to compartmentalize each part of my life and then try to optimize each part. If you are like me in this respect, this book can help you undo years of conditioning from "experts" who have encouraged us to run our lives as though everything had to be separate and perfect. The experts on exercise, religion, children, or education always encourage us to set aside an hour or more, go to a particular location, and do it "the right way." After regular work we are supposed to have personal trainers to create a perfect hour in the gym, weekly services to give us our quality time with God, night school for learning, and quality time with our children somewhere in between.

No wonder we are frazzled. Each piece of our lives may be at optimal level, but the overall picture is a shambles. Why has this happened? It is easier for specialists to advise you on perfecting one activity than it is for them to help you maintain overall life quality because they don't know you, your interests, and your limitations. Besides, experts can charge more for providing a "best solution" that is one-size-fits-all. They don't want to tell you to listen to your instincts.

The philosophy of blending reverses this approach and asks you to sacrifice some quality of individual activities in order to create more overall quality. Blending some activities together often makes them less than perfect, but it reduces the stress of balancing.

What is even more exciting than reducing stress, is that blending sometimes pays off in unexpected ways. When you look at all the pieces of your unique life and try to fit them together a little better, sometimes the whole becomes greater than the sum of the parts: Your community service work brings you more business; your exercise provides networking opportunities; your children learn values from helping you at work; or other effects spill over. In my life, all of these synergies and more are pulling together to move me forward professionally and personally. When all the pieces of your life are mutually reinforcing instead of being at war, you, too, are on the road to *Succeeding Sane*.

The Success Grid opposite illustrates how happily successful people see more options than seesaw thinkers. Achievement and fulfillment are not opposing goals in this new paradigm. You are free to choose both achievement and fulfillment, either one of them, or neither. It's up to you. Where do you belong in this grid? Where would you like to be?

BOX A: HIGH ACHIEVEMENT, LOW FULFILLMENT

This box includes a wide range of people who have chosen to devote their lives to the pursuit of fame, fortune, and power with less focus on personal enrichment, ethics, relationships, health, community service, and all that other soft stuff. If life is a seesaw, they know which end they are on. People in this category range from the honest but insensitive workaholic, to the unscrupulous schemer driven by raw ambition. Also included are "staminacs," or achievement junkies like me who go from one triumph to the next addicted to the high.

Figure 2. **THE SUCCESS GRID: WHERE DO YOU BELONG?**

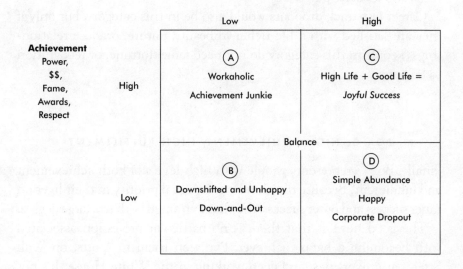

Fulfillment
Relationships, Health, Joy,
Peace of Mind, Giving to Others, Beauty

BOX B: LOW ACHIEVEMENT, LOW FULFILLMENT

This square covers various people who are not successful either person-ally or professionally. This might include people like me who have tried to downshift but find themselves restless, unhappy, and in the worst of both worlds. An extreme case might be a down-and-out bum who says, "I can't remember whether I started drinking because my wife left me, or whether my wife left me because I started drinking." For whatever reason, he's down-and-out.

BOX D: LOW ACHIEVEMENT, HIGH FULFILLMENT

This box encompasses the diverse group of people who have chosen to place personal development, relationships, or service to others ahead of professional ambitions. These are the unsung heroes of the world. At the extreme corner of the box you might encounter a full-time mom, a priest, a white-robed guru, or a community volunteer. Some nurses, teachers, policemen, nuns or secretaries might be good examples if they have bypassed fame, fortune, and power in favor of people, love, and peace. Ideally, they lead a life that serves others and makes the world a better place.

Career fast-track dropouts would also be in this category, but only if they are satisfied with a life richer in beauty, nature, or close relationships. People in this category do not need fame, fortune, or recognition to be happy.

BOX C: HIGH ACHIEVEMENT, HIGH FULFILLMENT

Finally, Box C represents people with high levels of both achievement and fulfillment. Because they have put an equal priority in their lives on inner success and outer success, they have attained both to a large degree.

The good news is that there is no particular profession associated with becoming a happy achiever. I've seen them in sports, on Wall Street, at universities, and even working in the White House. It's not what they do that matters. It's not how many hours they do or do not work. It is the way they go about it.

Although it seems obvious that everyone should want both, I've learned it isn't so. Some unsung heroes (as in Box D) do not want the fuss of the fast lane. If offered the chance to be famous and sought after, they would say, "No thank you!" Similarly, there are achievers (as in Box A) who get little joy from family, art, or service to others. When asked whether they want more personal activities blended into their work life, they might say, "Why?"

If you, on the other hand, are the sort of person who desperately wants both high achievement and a highly fulfilling life, this is the book for you. Whether you're starting from Box A, B, or D—or a combination of boxes— on the Success Grid, the ideas and exercises in this book can help you shift into Box C.

The Success Grid represents a very different perspective on life from the seesaw. There are more choices that look appealing. While the seesaw view tends to make everyone think balance is the best option, the Success Grid shows you that balance, fulfillment, achievement, and joyful success are all viable (but different) options.

When I realized I had been limiting myself to a seesaw view of the world I became really angry. I had been forcing myself to choose between high achievement and enjoying the simple pleasures of life. I could have had both, but I settled for less!

Lately when people start talking to me about balance it really irritates me if I see it is based on seesaw thinking. I sense they are fighting the same illusory struggles I have fought.

"I used to be really driven," a highly successful saleswoman says to me, "but now I think balance is more important. Being number one doesn't mean as much to me anymore. It's hard though, coming home at the end of the day and trying to switch gears. Trying to really listen to my daughter without letting my mind wander to problems at work."

As she continues talking I hear the anguish in her voice. I see the tug-of-war between her goals. I can only take this for so long. I blurt out, "Balance is a crock!" That gets her attention.

If you define balance as standing precariously near the middle of a moving teeter-totter, why bother? It isn't very satisfying. You have given up on using your talents to their utmost. You have given up maximum enjoyment of your family, your daily existence, your spirituality, and service to others. Seesaw thinking means you have decided to live somewhere between Simple Abundance and Achievement Junkie. You have already written off the chance to be your best self inwardly and outwardly at the same time.

I wasted so much of my life trying to find the right spot on the teeter-totter that I can't stand watching others do it. I was always searching. "Maybe if I just move three more inches to the left I'll be happy. . . ." Arrgh! But the best answer for me wasn't on the seesaw at all.

To get off the seesaw, first you have to start believing that your personal and professional goals can be mutually reinforcing.

Sorry to say, I can't tell you exactly what the answer is for you. I can't tell you how to allocate your time from moment to moment. But I can show you the right questions to ask to find your own path.

○

Changing the Way You Think: From Seesaw to Blending

Instead of asking: How much of this should I give up to get that? you ask questions like: How can I make this and that go together better?

For example, a seesaw mind-set leads to questions like:
   "Can I justify leaving work for an hour to play racquetball?"
   "Will it mean I have to stay later at work and see less of my family?"
From a blending mind-set you ask:
   "How can I make my exercise time reinforce my work and/or family time?"
   Creative options begin to emerge when you ask new questions. You could:

- *Start a challenge night at the racquet club for clients and colleagues.*
- *Switch to a new sport or a new gym that is more popular among your clients and colleagues.*
- *Spend more active time with your family, either swimming, walking, or even playing croquet.*
- *Offer to teach free lessons (such as racquetball, tennis, or golf) to a valued client.*

○

Once you start thinking this way, you immediately reduce the intensity of the conflict between your need for exercise, work, and family time. You still have to decide how much time to devote to what, but you feel less stress about leaving work to exercise, for example, when you know you are meeting a client.

To get off the seesaw and into joyful success, you have to look for creative solutions. Because your personal life is unique and your talents, ambitions, and desires are unique, the best way for you to blend them is necessarily unique. The more creative you get and the more ideas you try, the better you get at it. Every once in a while you find great combinations that are not just a compromise between two things, but actually better than the sum of the parts.

Unfortunately, nothing stays the same. Sometimes, just when you find a great combination, your life changes again and you have to find a new blend. For example, one of the best blenders I found was inviting people to network with me by strolling in the park with my daughter in the pram. What could be more spiritually fulfilling than seeing a baby laugh and play, feeling the sunshine, and getting to know a new person? We could do a little business and stretch our legs, too. But now that my daughter's a little older, she won't sit still in the pram for long. I have to find other ways to combine my activities.

Like the patterns of a kaleidoscope, the unique jewels in our lives create fleeting mosaics. The designs of rich color and shape depend on our interests, talents, resources, and relationships. As with the kaleidoscope, these change quickly and cannot be preserved or recreated. That's why I can't tell you the right answers for you. But I can help you change the way you ask the questions so that new alternatives emerge. I can show you examples of the creative solutions others have found to give you an idea of what you're looking for.

Let me digress for a moment to explain something that convinced me immediately how ridiculous seesaw thinking is. If you think outward success is the opposite of inner success then you know getting rich won't make you happy. But if you turn that around it says getting poorer will make you happy. What a ridiculous idea!

I see so many people jumping on the bandwagon of downshifting, simplicity, and antimaterialism. But it won't work for everyone. *Your happiness is not determined by how much stuff you have!* Whether it's a lot of stuff or very little stuff, stuff is the wrong focus.

In the Success Grid you can see that having low ambition in the outer world leads to ordinary poverty or the frustration of talent just as easily as it leads to simple joy. (The seesaw is deceptive in that it implies giving up your stuff automatically leads to some idyllic state of bliss. Common sense tells you that isn't realistic.)

There is no guarantee that giving up ambitions will give you a more fulfilling life. You get a more personally fulfilling life the same way you get a more wildly successful life: by devoting more time and attention to it.

The core of the problem, then, is how do you have enough time and energy to focus on both personal and professional goals equally without giving up a little of each (or a lot of each)? Blending is the answer.

Finding creative ways to make your goals line up so this reinforces that can help end the war for your time and energy.

Recently I learned the lesson of blending again. As a speaker I enjoy going to youth groups and community groups for free as well as being an extremely highly paid keynote speaker at conventions. At first I thought that free speeches at Rotary clubs, churches, and women's groups would help publicize my name and lead to more paid events. I thought that the charity speeches would reinforce speaking to business groups. I soon learned, however, that charity speaking only leads to more charity speaking. So I began limiting myself to one or two charity speeches a month and actively pursuing paid business. I still did free speeches, but only at major showcase events with potential clients in the audience.

But I didn't feel right. And my business wasn't developing as rapidly as I wanted it to. I felt I was losing my sense of purpose and just chasing after dollars. Ironically, I was working on some of the exercises in this book at the same time and realized that I wasn't applying my own principles in my speaking. I was limiting the community service speaking because I saw it as competing for my time and energy. When I asked myself, "How can I put more spirit power into my work?" I came up with this creative idea: I offer a pro bono speech as a bonus to each paying client. While speaking for their company, group, or convention, I will throw in another speech for a nonprofit group of their choice.

The client wins: They take me to their Kiwanis club as a breakfast speaker, to their child's school or a community group like the Urban League, free of charge.

I win: I get to do more community service events, all across the country, for all kinds of groups. I don't even spend extra time away from my baby daughter and husband. I get paid for the event that brought me there, to boot. Adding the bonus makes me feel better about my work and has directly resulted in more business as a speaker. Instead of asking, "What is the right mixture of free and for-fee events?" I began asking, "How could I make charity and for-profit speaking reinforce each other?"

Because I got off the seesaw I found a way to make my life personally and professionally richer at the same time. In this book you'll hear so many more stories like that.

I wrote this book to be read in different ways by different kinds of people. Start from wherever you like. Regardless of where you start, you can always go back to read more. I also wanted this book to serve as a convenient reference over time, a book you would reread and consult for ideas on a regular basis. Tools such as the table of contents and the index make it easy to find anything you need in a hurry. Chapter 18, the ideas inventory, provides a wide range of examples to help you complete the exercises in the book and offers a handy source of blending ideas to be used as a reference long afterward.

Here's an overview of what's in each section of the book and what you should get out of it:

- Part I is about me: Many people have been inspired by my story of an amputee, African-American girl from San Diego who becomes an Olympic ski champion, Rhodes scholar, businesswoman, wife, and mother. Here, for the first time, I get to tell my story more fully than ever before.

- Part II is about you: Where do you stand? What do you need most? Getting from where you are today to joyful success is a very personal journey. What you have to do may be the exact opposite of what someone else should do. Because I do not offer a one-size-fits-all solution, I have to show you how to customize your secrets of success.

- Part III is about achievement: How can you apply what you've learned about yourself and the principles of blending to become more successful in the real world today? You should pick and choose which chapters in Part III cover subjects that interest you. Each chapter has exercises that help you to immediately apply more mind, body, and spirit to achieve astounding results without losing your sanity.

- Part IV is about fulfillment: enriching every moment of the present. In Part IV the exercises show you how to take the life you have now and make small changes that will help you to keep growing. Over the long haul, it is these small changes that will determine whether you are happy with yourself as well as your achievements. There are tips for finding the hidden time and hidden energy in your life.

Conclusion

Success is getting what you want.
Happiness is wanting what you get.
—*Anonymous.*

Is it possible to achieve at the highest levels without losing your mind, body, and soul? I am happy to say that after two years of researching books and interviewing people, the answer is a resounding YES! I can show you the proof from my life and many others. I can show you step-by-step how to make small changes in your life that lead to lasting, satisfying success.

When you finish this book and the exercises, you will have created a customized plan for your success both personally and professionally. You will have a clearer idea of your personal strengths and weaknesses. You will have new ideas on how to tap hidden resources of talent, time, and energy to perform better right away. You will have a list of bite-size changes to make in your day-to-day schedule that will have profound effects over the long haul. You will have a map for living both successfully and happily ever after.

PART I

My Succeeding Sane Story

How I Escaped the Suffering Success Track

I had to learn to tap into the strength of my mind, my body, and my spirit. As a child I coped with serious problems, including sexual abuse, divorce, and disability. Like many children in my position I used the power of my mind to transcend reality and to master my emotions of insecurity and fear. Yet I went too far, living through books and suppressing all my emotions.

In my teens and early twenties I poured my energy into building body power as an athlete. I chased success as measured by external standards garnering ski medals, scholarships, and prestigious jobs. I moved outside my mind and lived in the world. But once again, I went too far. I acquired things, experiences, and accolades as voraciously as I had previously read books. I became an achievement junkie.

Now in my thirties, I am still an infant in the realm of spirit power. Developing my inner sense of meaning, values, and self-esteem is like learning to walk. As a wife, a mother, a writer, and a speaker I am forced to grow. It is terrifying.

I know all of these struggles and wrong turns were not wasted effort because blending requires me to use it all. As you read my story, you may think about your own struggles to grow in mind, in body, and in spirit. Building a creative life that reflects your personal standards of greatness demands every ounce of imagination, hard work, and passion you can muster. You must reclaim the strengths you may not believe you have.

CHAPTER 2

Surviving Tragedy with Mind Power

M y story opens on what seemed like a typical day in my four-year-old life. In our dining room a shapely young woman stood with her hands on her hips yelling loudly at an equally short, white-haired Italian man who was forty years older than she. He stood immobile, as though weathering the verbal blows like an experienced sea captain. Only his eyes blinked, slowly. His impassive silence seemed to fuel her desire to make him hurt as she hurt.

The young woman was Ruby, my hot-blooded, twenty-nine-year-old mother. She married Paul, the older man, after divorcing my real father before I could remember. Since Paul was strict to the point of cruelty, I feared and sometimes hated him. But he was the only father I ever knew.

Unlike other days, however, this argument began to escalate to new levels. Mom headed for the kitchen and removed a plate from the kitchen cabinet. Glaring fixedly at Paul, she threw the plate on the linoleum, shattering it into pieces. I hid behind my brother, Wayne, and my sister, April, as another dish crashed to the floor. We heard Paul opening and closing his dresser drawers. He packed his clothes and left while my mother destroyed every plate, cup, and bowl in the house.

I was four years old; Wayne was six and April, seven. We didn't understand how long Paul would be gone or what it meant, but Mom cried for days afterward.

At night, I stared out at the stars. I invented a game of wiggling my eyes to make the stars zigzag like luminous ribbons blowing in the wind. I felt frightened about the future.

As I lay in bed, I thought about my mother's hot temper. I imagined my own emotions like regal, Arabian horses: yellow for joy, red for anger, purple for fear, and blue for love. Emotions had power and majesty, but without reins to control them they ran wild, trampling everything. I vowed never to trust my emotions to run free. I promised myself to learn to harness their power and direct it with my mind. I never wanted to experience my mother's pain.

Just as suddenly as the catastrophe had struck, it was over. Although I know not why or how, my stepfather returned. We were once again a happy family in our little house in San Diego. Or so it seemed.

Through her strength of will and imagination, my mother gave my brother, my sister, and me the sort of childhood she didn't have growing up in a New York City ghetto. She supported us on her teacher's salary and still got home at about the same time we did. Unlike the tenement she grew up in, we had a real house with a well-kept front lawn and a backyard where we grew fruit trees and a vegetable garden.

Our home was filled with smells like homemade peach and berry jams, spaghetti sauce simmering for hours, and cornbread baking on holiday mornings. She made every Christmas a model of what she hadn't had: cookies baking, lights outside the house, a beautiful tree with all the trimmings, and mountains of presents on Christmas Day. During the year, activities like scouts, music lessons, sports, crafts, and hobbies kept us out of trouble.

Life was never dull. In the evening Mom read poetry to us or sang songs in Yiddish that she learned from being a governess in a Jewish household. Going to coffee shops in the middle of the night or the beach to see the sunrise were as much a part of our childhood as Sunday School.

Although my stepfather, Paul, persisted in periodically deserting us for months at a time with no explanation, Ruby had found the courage to live with or without him. But it wasn't easy for her.

We might eat out at an expensive restaurant one week and then not have enough money to buy eggs and milk the next. However, there was always food on the table, clothes on our backs, and a roof over our heads. Now that I have a child and a job, I marvel at how she did it all.

She triumphed by learning to use the strength of her heart and her mind to shape her own destiny rather than let others shape it for her. She collected a library of books on positive thinking by such people as Dale Carnegie, Claude Bristol, Sondra Ray, and Arnold Patent. I took it for granted as a child that she would go to Keith's all-night diner with her friend Rosemary and spend hours writing "affirmations." These positive thoughts she practiced over and over helped her conquer the despair that threatened to engulf her.

I remember being dragged along to inspirational speeches by Patricia Fripp and Terry Cole Whittaker. Our family enrolled in Transcendental Meditation training together. I couldn't help but learn something about the power of the mind in my childhood.

In the 70s my mother wasn't the only one to turn to the new positive thinking literature for support. In the aftermath of sixties' idealism, America had to face up to Watergate, the oil crisis, spiraling inflation, and unemployment levels not seen since the depression. Positive thinking, affirmations, and meditation were as fashionable as flowered pants, *Laugh-In*, Twiggy, and bouffant hairdos.

These New Age ideas worked for my mother. Through guts and optimism she not only survived but went on to transform the lives of thousands of students during her long educational career. My mother earned a doctorate in education after four years of research and night classes while holding down a job as a high school vice principal and looking after three kids.

As a principal she turned around schools that were on the brink of disaster. One of these schools was an inner city, mostly black school, which reminded her of the shabby school house to which blacks were relegated in her childhood. Fixing the windows, painting the graffiti, and breathing a new attitude of enthusiasm into the school was a way to heal her own childhood wounds.

She has won national awards as an educator, has spoken around the country, has been written about in newspapers, and has appeared on television. People in San Diego still come up to her on the street to thank her for her influence in their lives or their children's lives. It's like walking around with Gandhi or something. She is a truly amazing human being.

Though my mother raised us well without a reliable father, it still left an indelible mark on me. I worried about growing up and being deserted by some man, left to raise a pack of kids on my own. My mother had already been through one divorce with my natural father. She seemed headed for divorce with my stepfather. Every time my parents fought, every time Paul walked out, I thought the world would cave in again. I never felt secure.

"When you need them most, people disappear," I thought. "If you love someone, they can hurt you."

I liked staring out windows. On school buses I preferred to watch the countryside whir backward rather than join in the rowdy activities among the other kids. Being separated from life by a cool, transparent sheet of glass felt safe somehow, as though I couldn't be harmed if I kept my distance.

I felt guilty, too. What if Paul kept leaving because we kids didn't follow all his rules? He had a lot of rules.

I presented a facade of cheerful obedience to try to please my parents, keep them happy, and keep them together. Inside my stomach churned with acid from the tension of wondering what would become of me. I cleaned my room, ate all the food on my plate, washed the dishes, took out the garbage, and did whatever else might hold my world together. To me, marriage seemed like a wild and implacable god tormenting its prisoners regularly.

At four years old, playing the pleaser made me an easy mark for my stepfather. While Mom was at work and my older brother and sister were in school, he would play games with me in my bedroom—sexual games. Always the obedient and obliging child, I cooperated willingly for fear of punishment. He told me not to tell, and I did not. In a way, I enjoyed the affection from Paul since he was the only father I ever knew. His closeness was a warm and comforting security in an otherwise cold and scary world.

For many years afterward I did not even remember what had happened. Only later did I see the scars left on my self-esteem and my already crippled ability to have relationships with men. First he showed me how much he could hurt my mother by leaving her. Then he taught me to connect affection and approval with sex. I still find damage and scars I didn't know I had.

To think about it now makes my blood run cold. It sickens me to contemplate what sort of man could wear ordinary clothes, buy groceries, and sleep with his wife while molesting a four-year-old child after her half-day kindergarten class. When the image comes to mind of laying on my back on my bed and his giant, wizened, eighty-year-old body hovering over mine, I automatically push it away as my eyes begin to sting with tears. I feel angry, repulsed, tainted, and dirty. I feel guilty because I didn't fight. I feel guilty because I didn't tell my mother. Behind his silhouette I see light and air coming through the billowing pink curtains of a child's room. My mother always wanted pink for her little girls. Pink dresses, pink carpet, pink curtains.

How can you compare the severity of damage from child abuse to the difficulty of growing up physically disabled? Invisible handicaps are just as real. Yet people focus on my amputated leg and say, "What a difficult life you have had."

The growth in my right leg was stunted from birth for reasons never discovered. The more I grew, the more apparent the difference between my legs became. To start walking I wore a heavy metal brace with high-top, white orthopedic shoes. How I hated that brace! It dragged around behind me and prevented me from running with other kids. How I hated that brace and those ugly shoes! I knew I was a misfit (though no one told me) because everyone stared and kids called me names.

At age five the doctors told me that they would cut off my leg and make a new one for me. I thought things would be different with the new leg.

"Will I be able to wear normal shoes?" I asked.

"Yes. Of course," the doctor said.

"Any color? Any style?"

"Yes . . ."

"Okay," I said happily, "cut it off!"

Months and months passed on the third floor of the Shriner's Hospital for Crippled Children in Los Angeles. My world was narrowed to three long dim corridors with white (graying) walls, medicinal smells, wheelchairs, and the twenty other crippled girls on the ward. We were rarely allowed to go outdoors and play. On Sundays, I was allowed to go over to the boys' ward and look through a chain-link fence at my brother and sister who were three floors down on an outdoor playground we couldn't use.

For a five-year-old, six months feels like forever. Halloween, Thanksgiving, my birthday, and Christmas all passed in the hospital with no home-cooked meals, no sister and brother, and no parents unless the holiday fell on a Sunday (none did).

When my mother and stepfather tried to sneak upstairs to give me a cake for my birthday on a Saturday, the hospital unceremoniously threw them out. As punishment, they were barred from the regular visiting day on Sunday. No one told the ward nurses or me what happened, so Sunday morning I dressed up like the other kids, let the nurses primp up my hair, and waited for my parents to come. Since my sixth birthday was the day before, I just knew they would bring me a present and maybe a cake. We all waited eagerly with eyes wide, like puppies in the pound hoping to be claimed by the next passerby. As each parent came in to claim a waiting child I watched and watched.

"Maybe the next one," I kept thinking. Until finally, visiting time ended. I was exhausted from hours of waiting, straining on the edge of my bed, and hoping for my parents to come and celebrate my birthday. All the loneliness, isolation, and pain of surgery welled up and poured out in a torrent of tears. I lay in my hospital bed, a sodden heap of primped-up curls on my head and a cold hollow spot inside. Once again, I learned that having feelings and caring about people meant getting hurt. I wanted to stop feeling anything.

The physical pain of surgery and therapy was almost a welcome distraction from the routine loneliness and boredom. The amputation left me with a rounded stump of a leg, which was a bit longer than the thigh of my other leg. Sharp stabbing pains, called phantom pains, shot through my nonexistent foot. Nothing could be done to alleviate these phantom pains since the foot wasn't really there anymore. By day I seemed to be able to ignore it. Some nights, however, I would wake up being shaken by a nurse to stop me from screaming in my sleep.

To cope with the depressing realities of my life I not only controlled my emotions, I escaped into other worlds through books and stories. In the hospital at age five I powered through the entire set of Dick and Jane readers and polished off two or three spelling chapters a week while the hospital's schoolteacher sat back aghast.

Physical therapy took place in a pleasant, sunny room with brightly colored pillows, stuffed animals, toys, and games. Yet the bright surroundings couldn't make it any easier to toughen up the end of my leg that had been chopped off. Agonizing hours were spent in that lovely room trying to use my stump of a leg to push on a scale that sat on a big pile of phone books.

"Push harder! You have to push harder," the nurses would say. Waves of pain were matched by echoing waves of nausea. How would I ever walk on this tender mass of nerve endings? But eventually I did. Finally, I was allowed to go home with one less foot, new shoes, and a new wooden leg.

And it was better than before. At least I wasn't dragging around that heavy metal brace anymore or wearing ugly white lace-up shoes. My first pair of real shoes were made of blue suede with red stitching around the edges and black, waffle soles. I had picked them out myself. They were, I still believe, the most beautiful shoes ever made. For hours I looked at the two of them on my feet, which were both touching the ground for the first time.

However, my differentness didn't end: Kids now chanted "wooden leg, wooden leg" when I walked by. Throughout elementary school I rode in a special, door-to-door school bus for the disabled. This convenience prevented me from joining with the other kids after school, walking home together, playing, and perhaps visiting each others' houses. Excluded from their afternoon games, I was always the outsider.

By second grade, I had already learned that I was ugly and undesirable to the opposite sex. The boys would chase all the girls except me. I was made to feel sort of neuter: "the wooden child."

On the playground I read books in a far corner to avoid the looks and jeers that rang in my ears for hours afterward. Not only was I unable to play jump rope and hopscotch with the others, but I felt ugly with my thick glasses, chubby body, and my kinky hair wrestled into untidy ponytails. I looked down when people talked to me and seldom smiled. From a distance I watched the other girls. My heart climbed in my throat as they gracefully dodged the spinning jump ropes or spun in circles on the bars while boys watched their blonde hair and pink panties.

Escaping into my books, however, I could imagine myself as Lancelot slaying dragons, Nancy Drew catching crooks, and Scheherazade seducing sultans. In my fantasies I was cool and confident, not the nerdy kid with a squeaky voice and butterflies in her stomach. I had little attachment to the real world in which I didn't fit.

At twelve and entering junior high, I knew that I shouldn't bother aspiring for a number of things. Being a cheerleader was out of the question since I couldn't perform the athletic, acrobatic steps. Besides, my heavy wooden leg would look stupid in those short, twitchy skirts.

Nor could I dream of becoming Miss America with a wooden leg! Can you imagine me in the bathing suit contest?

I also knew without being told that taking ballet lessons like my taller, slimmer sister, April, was a laughable idea. Slim, pink, satin toe shoes would not fit on a plastic foot that did not bend. April went to charm school and modeled in fashion shows; I did arts and crafts. April dreamed of being the perfect bride in the white flowing gown, but I did not. I guess when you see that you are excluded from all the other idealized images of femininity, bridal grace and beauty seems out of reach, too.

Later on as a teen I would hear that great saying, "He'll go after anything with two legs," and cringe inside. Yeah, he'll take anyone but me. I could never aspire to be (or even choose to reject) the image of a girlie-girl.

As a tomboy, I didn't fare much better: When I signed up for judo in summer school the teacher had me removed from class after one day because he was afraid I might hurt the other kids with my wooden leg. Trying out for school sports was just one more laughable idea for the handicapped kid. Although I was proud of being able to join the regular PE classes in school, I was regularly humiliated as the absolute last pick for teams in every sport.

With so much misfortune, it isn't so surprising that I hid myself. I felt like an ugly, unwanted guest at a two-legged party, waiting for someone to cast me out if I caused problems.

Anxieties about divorce, sexual abuse, and having my leg cut off robbed me of a normal childhood with the love and security that builds a foundation of confidence and healthy self-respect. Whether I was more of an emotional or physical cripple is hard to say. Unable to trust people, unable to trust my body, my mind became my safe haven, my strength, and my answer to any problem. Only in schoolwork could I excel without impediment. The power of my mind grew and developed by default. It seemed natural to use my mind to solve my emotional problems, too.

I coped by using my mother's positive thinking techniques to suppress all my negative emotions and reprogram my reactions. Day by day I gave myself inner pep talks to rein in my wild horses of fear, anger, loneliness, and hurt.

"What do you want to be when you grow up?" my mother asked.

"Happy," I answered.

"Don't you want to accomplish anything?" Mom asked me.

"Of course, Mom. I wouldn't be happy if I didn't."

Among Mom's positive thinking tapes and books I heard it said that anger, unhappiness, and frustration were habits of thinking. A person could get in the habit of being happy more often than not. I saw my moods as a curve bobbing up and down. I vowed to shift the curve up a few notches.

Sometimes when I felt sad and pep talks failed, I stopped fighting and just let myself fall into the mud of unhappiness and wallow in it. Curled up on my bed, I would eat chocolate and suffer. As I sank deeper into feeling sorry for myself I inevitably reached a point where the whole thing seemed comical. Was I starving? No. Was I cold? No. In fact I had friends at school, a nice home, clothes, and a really fun mom. Eventually my habit of happiness won out.

Sure, things hurt me. Standing against the wall while other girls got asked to dance, having kinky black hair, and looking funny at the beach with one leg made me die a thousand deaths in high school. But when I read a book, sat alone in a garden, or wandered among strangers in the city I could fly away and be someone different in my imagination. It also helped to imagine myself twenty years in the future looking back at the situation that upset me. I saw myself as a wealthy jet-setter with many male admirers. Powerful and free, I could look back at being snubbed by the popular girls in school and laugh. Immediately my energy was redirected into becoming powerful and free instead of stewing in my own juices.

Controlling my mind and suppressing my feelings was how I survived. I became so good at redirecting my emotions that often I didn't realize I was upset until it exploded beyond my control. Even today I still tend to suppress my feelings to a dangerous degree. Some control of your emotions is essential to success. However, when taken to excess, you have no idea what you are feeling at all.

Writing this section of the book has been absolute torture for me because I am so used to denying my own suffering. When I began writing, I focused only on my achievements and the wonderful things that have happened because of my disability. After the first draft, however, a good friend of mine urged me to dig a little deeper and acknowledge some of the pain.

"It sounds so Pollyanna, for christsakes. Ugh," she grimaced. "Like drinking syrup through a straw! If you want to inspire people you have to be one, you know." Her words were harsh but she was right. "What made you cry? What helped you get by? Write about that."

I knew she was right. My "hey, having one leg is fun" attitude is the result of my methods of coping, not the reality. To tell others "It was easy for me. You can do it" insults people by disrespecting the agonies they have lived through.

Each section of this book has been extracted like pulling a tooth without Novocain. Willingly reliving that past has not been fun. It is part of the process, however, of healing my deepest wounds and really letting them go.

CHAPTER 3

Fighting Back with
Body Power

My life changed when I turned fourteen. Perhaps my hormones
kicked in and woke me up. Or maybe, when my parents' relationship finally deteriorated to the point where Mom changed the locks, I
realized I didn't need to appease the gods of tranquillity anymore. Paul
never moved back home again, and I decided to stop avoiding the
world around me. I wasn't sure what life was, but I wanted it. I wanted
all of it. I decided to burst through the glass bubble in which I had
been living.

Everything had to change. I stopped going to church and quit reading fiction. I scorned my mother's mumbo-jumbo positive thinking,
meditation, and affirmations. These things, I decided, had little to do
with reality. I decided to do less thinking and more doing. In the real
world, I thought, success is measured by external standards like money,
power, and prestige. If people suffered, rich or poor, I reasoned, I might
as well suffer in comfort. My vision of the future included a jet-setting
executive job, lots of money, and travel.

My earliest hopes and dreams were borrowed from ads on TV like
the Enjoli perfume commercial. I cheered and sang along with the
woman who wore a tight, pin-striped suit and held a leather briefcase:

I can bring home the bacon . . .
. . . and fry it up in a pan . . .
and never, never, never, never let you forget you're a man.
Cause I'm a woman.   Enjoli!

Clearly this woman didn't need anyone to support her, feed her, or make her happy. Men needed her, but she didn't need them. I admired that. I wanted a pin-striped suit and a briefcase of my own.

You could say I was cynical. Causes like saving the environment, fighting hunger, or world peace made me yawn. I was less concerned with the way things ought to be than with dealing with life "as is."

I didn't want to have children. Children seemed impractical for a lifestyle of travel and power. Besides, I assumed that I would end up married and divorced like all the adults I knew. Thus, I would only end up struggling with single motherhood and alimony fights. That was not for me. At my most sentimental moments, I hoped I might have a second or third marriage that made me happy.

Can you blame me for being so callous? Behind my tough stance lay a mass of fears. I was afraid no one would ever fall in love with the one-legged black girl. If I did somehow find love, would I end up divorced anyway?

Also, I heard about unemployment, racial discrimination, and rising costs of college. I was afraid I would never be able to afford college. Even if I did get through somehow, would I ever get a job? Life didn't look like no crystal stair.

Whereas I had spent the first part of my life escaping my fears with books and imagination, I now wanted to face them. I wanted to take action in the real world to vanquish my demons. I shifted my energy away from my inner world and into the outer world.

First I tried things randomly like a starving person at a smorgasbord, gorging on everything within reach. I started a business selling hand-made Indian crafts. I signed up for travel with the student exchange club and ended up in Chicago for a semester. I tried water skiing and horseback riding. I wanted to find out about everything.

The docile, reserved, goody-goody child became a confident, cynical hustler. Lying about my age allowed me to get a Burger King job and pay for contact lenses, new clothes, and a treatment to straighten my frizzy black hair. Like Superman entering a nearby phone booth, I ditched the nerdy glasses, ponytails, and clothes. I transformed myself physically.

As my chubby childhood figure turned into big breasts and curvy hips, I found clothes to emphasize my figure and hide my leg. I learned to wear makeup. With a new sense of power I walked taller, breathed deeper, and looked others straight in the eye. For the first time, I experienced body power.

Male heads turned as I whizzed around on a fire-engine red moped in a low-cut, tropical bikini and sarong. The Eagles played "Life in the Fast Lane" as I sped past swaying palm trees and honked at good-looking guys. For the first time in my life I began to smile.

Then, one day at school, bursting with smiles and energy, a friend of mine named Barbara Warmath presented me with a coupon for my birthday, which changed my life forever. It read:

Good for one week of skiing in Mammoth over Christmas vacation.

It was an invitation to join her family at their cabin in Mammoth.

"Wow," I gushed. "But I don't know how to ski."

"It's okay," she answered. "It's easy." Her dark eyes sparkled. Her easy manner told me, "You can do it." Not only did she believe in my ability to ski despite my handicap, she didn't care whether it would cause her any inconvenience.

I had no idea whether it would really work. "How hard is skiing for an amputee?" I wondered. "Where could I get special equipment? Would it be expensive?" For weeks I called disabled organizations in the white pages, ski shops, and clubs. I asked every adult I knew and asked them to ask their friends.

Finally, I got through to a retired military officer, Jerry Dalquist, who served as the president of Amputees in Motion (AIM), a San Diego club for athletic amputees.

"I want to ski with my friend's family in three weeks. Is it hard?"

"Only when you start. It gets easier eventually." He hesitated, trying not to discourage me. "Tell you what, I can loan you some outriggers and . . ."

"What are outriggers?" I interrupted.

"Outriggers are ski poles with ski tips on the bottom. I can give you a copy of the *Guide to Amputee Skiing* by Hal O'Leary. The book shows you how to get on and off chairlifts, how to stand, and how to fall."

"I need lessons in standing and falling?" I asked.

"It's not like walking around. I wish I could take you out and show you how to do it, but our club isn't planning another trip before Christmas."

"Gosh. Do you think I can do it with just a book?"

"Well," he paused, "I don't want to say no. Why don't you give it a try?"

It was horrible. I fell and fell and fell again. Barb's brothers would ski by, pick me up, and offer words of encouragement: "You're doing great. Try it again."

When you start on one leg, you can't slow down or stop because you can't snowplow (forming a wedge with two skis). Over and over, I stood up, wobbled, and then flew kamikaze-style down the hill until I crashed. To make matters worse, I was dressed all wrong. What does a San Diego kid know about snow? I wore jeans, knit mittens, and several sweaters with a windbreaker over the top. With all the falling, my clothes got very wet and then froze solid. I was bruised, cold, and miserable.

But I did it. I skied with Barbara Warmath and her family over Christmas. Sure, I fell a lot. I just kept getting up off the snow—and I kept getting better. By the third day I learned to stop without crashing. By the fifth day normies (two-legged skiers, that is) watched in awe as I cruised down intermediate slopes at high speeds. Once an amputee learns to turn and stop, she skis better than a normie who is still snowplowing, crossing her tips, and crashing. Amputees become perfect parallel skiers much more quickly.

In the end, it was like a fantasy come true. I felt good at it. I enjoyed sitting in the gently swinging lift chairs with a breathtaking panorama of snow-covered mountains, deep cleft valleys, and tall dark pines. The skiers in their fire-engine red or fuchsia pink ski suits dotted the hill like Christmas ornaments on a tree. It was nothing like San Diego.

I experienced exhilarating speeds and freedom without my wooden leg. The air felt crisp and cold. I smelled fresh air and fir trees. In the evening I felt warm and cozy inside drinking hot chocolate by a roaring fire. This San Diego girl was hooked. Why escape into books when you can live the fantasy?

I began racing and won six medals at my first national ski competition. This early success resulted in lots of local press coverage and encouraged me to aim higher: the U.S. Disabled Ski Team.

Applying the power of my mind as well as my body to a physical goal gave me a tremendous edge over other disabled skiers. I convinced ski companies like Rossignol, Nordica, Lange, and Marker to sponsor my equipment. The Rotary Club of San Diego paid my way to the nationals.

I applied to an elite ski school in Vermont, Burke Mountain Academy, and was accepted as a student. For three months I searched for grants, scholarships, and sponsors to no avail. I will never forget the moment when I told the headmaster I couldn't afford the tuition and I had failed to find sponsors. He said, "Come anyway." I knew this opportunity would change my life. Not, however, in the ways I expected.

What I had thought would be a great lark—attending a cool, private ski-racing school—turned out to be the most hellish year in my life. On the first official day of school I broke my leg—my real leg—while playing on a skateboard.

As the only kid there with one leg, I had so badly wanted to show them I could run obstacle courses, jump rope, and play soccer. Instead, walking on crutches with my artificial leg I could barely get from my room to dinner without tripping on stones in the path. Being so thoroughly inept among a crowd of super athletes hurt more than my injuries. At night I cried in my pillow to keep my roommate from hearing.

When the doctor cut off my cast after six weeks, my luck did not turn. Less than a week out of the cast, my artificial leg broke in half. When you think things can't get any worse, you're wrong. For three weeks my prosthesis roamed the country lost in the U.S. Postal Service.

When I tell this story about Burke Mountain Academy and how difficult it was for me, people ask, "Why didn't you quit and go home?" I suppose the easy answer is that I couldn't have afforded the airline ticket. But seriously, I thought often that I would have to go home. I kept waiting for someone to say to me, "Okay, you have no money and you've busted up your legs. It's time for you to go." I thought my mother would call and tell me to come home immediately. I kept waiting to be shown the door. But it never happened!

If none of these adults thought I had to go, I certainly wasn't going to bring up the idea. I had fought and scrapped to get where I was.

Some outside force or external circumstance might stop me, but how could I be stopped by anything from within?

This is one of the most important lessons I can share: Don't stop yourself from reaching your goals. Circumstances may stop you, other people may stop you, but for crying out loud, don't stop yourself. Once you've decided not to stop yourself, it is surprising how much you really can do.

I spent most of fall on crutches. As a result I trained less and worked with Burke's fund-raiser hunting for grants to defray my tuition costs and training expenses. A lucky break came through in early January of 1982 when I received a response on the phone. "This is Ben Finley," he said in a voice bubbling with laughter. "I am President of the National Brotherhood of Skiers." It was one of the many organizations I had contacted for help. "We sponsor promising young black skiers," he said. "That sounds like you."

"Well, thanks. I could sure use some help," I said in shock. My prayers and hard work had paid off!

"Can we interest you in a trip to Park City, Utah? We're having a meeting out here and I'd like to present you to the board of directors. I think you can get some funding support out of this . . ."

The opening ceremony for the NBS Summit convention at Park City, Utah, was held at the foot of the mountain. Over 400 of the 1200 convention participants were gathered on the patio at the edge of the lodge and shops. The mountain peaks, covered with snow, fir trees, and gently curving ski trails, provided an otherworldy backdrop for the podium.

Speakers included African-American movie stars, politicians, and club officials. They told inspirational and humorous stories to kick off the largest ski convention in the country. How can it be that the largest ski convention in the United States each year is comprised of African-Americans? Why do thousands of NBS members drop what they're doing to attend this outrageous week of skiing and celebrating?

NBS members are not into segregation or isolation. They probably didn't make their money or learn how to ski without learning to "hang with the white folks." Most NBS members spend most of the year completely surrounded by white people except for this one week of the year when the tables are turned and whites are in the minority.

Furthermore, this group has a lot more in common than the color of their skin—and a lot to celebrate. Typically, Summit attendees are successful and wealthy or they couldn't afford to be at the week-long ski convention. Most are well educated and have diverse interests, of which skiing is only one. None of them are hindered by myths like "black people can't ski" or "black people don't like cold weather." These are people willing to take risks and able to leap through stereotypes in a single bound. This is not just any group of black people; it is a group of champions. As much as my disabled ski groups helped me enjoy being handicapped, the Brotherhood of Skiers forced me to grow into my identity as an African-American.

The NBS helped me survive at Burke. The NBS made it possible for me to enter ski races with the other Burkies by paying my race fees and providing spending money for meals and lodging as we traveled across the Northeast. In addition, the NBS found more ski clothes for me and paid thousands of dollars toward my tuition at Burke. A personal touch came when Gertrude, an NBS member from Boston, came to visit me at Burke and gave me a much-needed shoulder to lean on.

Succeeding (okay, surviving) at Burke was worth it. In that Spartan training camp, the coaches and the other kids taught me the discipline of physical conditioning, showed me ski technique, and turned me into a real athlete. In addition they taught me to loosen up, have a good time, and appreciate people more for what is in their hearts rather than judging them for the intellectual content of their conversations.

The high school graduation ceremony at Burke took place in a barn that had been converted for a local theater group. Sixteen of us received diplomas on the tiny stage. My mother couldn't afford to come. I made a short speech to explain how much the year at Burke had meant to me and to thank Warren Witherell in particular. Before, I was a mushy city kid with big dreams. After Burke Mountain Academy, I was real Olympic material. Standing up in front of the school proved too much—I choked on my tears before I could finish. My year at Burke had been an ordeal of both agony and triumph.

After leaving Burke, the NBS continued to raise money for my ski training, coaching, and other race expenses. I left Vermont to train on a glacier in Oregon for the summer.

In the fall I relocated to Boston where I began college at Harvard. I was seventeen years old. Soon after starting college, I realized I would have to take a leave of absence to continue my ski training or forgo my chance at the Olympics altogether. I completed one semester, then left for a year.

Moving from Nevada to Oregon and Colorado as the seasons changed, I organized my own apartments, coaches, and equipment. The NBS provided partial financial support. I waited tables or worked in gift shops to make ends meet. Being independent, traveling, living in ski resorts, and making a bid for the Olympic ski team fulfilled the part of me that wanted to lead an alluring, adventurous lifestyle. At the same time, I waited anxiously to find out whether I would qualify for the Olympic team. Three winters and a summer of training led up to this one chance at the U.S. team.

I was worried. Only three amputee women would be chosen from the entire country. Other women had more training and experience in international competition. I knew I could ski well, but my performance at the last National Championships had been less than stellar. Finally the phone call came through: I made it, but barely. As third pick, I had received the last slot for an amputee woman on the U.S. team!

With more hard work over summer and fall, I got the kinks out of my skiing and went to the 1984 Olympics in Innsbruck, Austria, feeling stronger and faster than ever before. On the flight over to Europe I celebrated with my teammates on the U.S. Disabled Ski Team. Having my red team sweater and my snow jacket with U.S.A. on the back was the fulfillment of the dream I had kept alive over so many years. I felt relaxed and happy, having reached my goal. Winning wasn't something I thought much about.

You can imagine my surprise, then, to find myself in first place after the first run of the slalom race. Although the last pick on the team, I had the fastest time in the world! I was starting the second run in the lead. All I needed was one more good run to grab a gold medal in my first Olympics! My mother, who came to watch the races, was so excited that my brother rolled her in the snow to cool her off.

I returned to the top of the hill to gather my concentration and wait for my turn in the second run. Waiting among the other racers, I heard a rumor that all the racers were falling on an especially vicious patch of ice near the bottom. "If only I stand up and finish the race," I thought, "I have the gold medal!" Despite the chill in the January air, beads of perspiration rolled down the back of my neck.

In the starting gate at last, I wedged my outriggers in the snow preparing for the initial push across the starting line. The announcer sounded the countdown: "Five. Four. Three. Two. One. Go!"

As always, my stomach lurched as though in a falling elevator as I jumped down the starting bump and into the course. Soon I forgot about gold medals and crowds of spectators by focusing on the snow, the blue and red poles, and each new turn. As the finish line appeared before me and came nearer, new energy surged through my tired leg and aching arms. I began to feel relief and excitement about finishing a good run.

And then it happened. My ski slid on the infamous ice patch. I struggled to stay in balance, leaning on my outriggers and twisting my body to stay over my wandering ski. To no avail. Wham! My hip landed hard in the icy snow. My hopes for a gold medal jeered at me from only a few feet away on the other side of the finish line. For a split second, I cursed myself and thought seriously about skiing off the course with my tail between my legs. Years of training, however, took over. I choked back my tears, gathered up my outriggers and pushed quickly back into the course and over the line.

Thank goodness I finished the race! Despite the lost seconds, I ended up with the bronze medal. All of the best racers who took the tightest line slipped and fell on the treacherous spot. I learned the importance of getting up and finishing, no matter what.

I learned another lesson from the Austrian woman who took the gold medal. I knew she couldn't ski slalom faster than I could because I had beaten her soundly in the first run. In the second run she, too, had slipped and fallen. So how did she beat me? At the end of the day, she won the Olympic gold medal, not for skiing faster, but for getting up faster. The Austrian skier taught me that winners aren't people who never make mistakes. Winners are those who get up and finish. Gold medal winners get up the fastest.

Despite the disappointment, I remained ecstatic about winning even a bronze medal in my first Olympic competition. I won another bronze in giant slalom and placed seventh in the downhill. Overall, my performance earned a silver medal and the title of the second-fastest amputee woman in the world on one leg. I felt fantastic.

During the closing ceremonies my family and friends cheered as my name was called among the overall world winners. I puffed up my chest and stepped up to the second-place platform. The U.S. national anthem played, and the stars and stripes unfurled behind me. The Queen of Sweden hung the silver medal around my neck, handed me a bouquet of tulips and daffodils, and shook my trembling hand. Through misty eyes I saw reporters swarm and cameras flash. At that moment, I knew I had made my country and my family proud.

The kid with thick glasses and orthopedic shoes had come a long way. *Hour Magazine* and *Sunday Morning with Charles Kuralt* filmed television segments about me. I was interviewed on *Good Morning America* and *CBS Morning News*. My picture ran on the front page of the *New York Times* and the *Christian Science Monitor*.

Within a week after the Olympics I was back in classes at Harvard. I maintained my commitment to succeed in the "real" world by studying politics and economics. History, literature, and science were inadequate tools for addressing what I thought was the central question: How can I make sure that I end up hanging around with the rich and powerful instead of the down-and-out?

Competing with college juniors from across the United States, I got the summer job of my dreams on Wall Street. In 1985 greed was still good. Wall Street was *the* place for smart, hardworking, and ambitious Ivy League graduates. The allure of investment banking remained un-sullied by Black Monday, Michael Milken's junk bonds, and insider trading scandals. Masters of the universe still reigned, and I had a key to the inner sanctum.

On my very first day at Morgan Stanley & Co. I was asked to help prepare a client presentation involving millions of dollars. We slaved over hot calculators until three o'clock in the morning. Using the prices from that day's stock market close, we produced by morning a custom printed and bound analysis of the clients' options for debt and equity deals. Only perfect accuracy was acceptable since so much money was at stake.

The total dedication, talent, and efficiency of our team dazzled me. People who operated the copying machines were as dedicated to their jobs as the senior partners. I dug into the work with gusto. I wanted to be a Wall Street millionaire.

After my summer job was over, I returned to college where I moved from one battle to the next without questioning my choices or my values. I was consumed with problems such as: How will I pay my tuition? How will I pass my exams? Should I take on more bartending jobs? Can I finish my thesis and graduate with honors? How will I pay for my airline ticket to the Rhodes interview? When will I get another date? I met one challenge after another without pause.

Finally, in 1986, my fast track took a sudden detour. Winning the Rhodes scholarship meant two or three years of study at Oxford University, all expenses paid. Being removed from my country, my peers, and my familiar financial pressures forced me to take stock of my life and my choices, whether I wanted to or not.

CHAPTER 4

Spirit Power and
the Meaning of Life

Returning to my Oxford dorm room, I felt deflated and tired after the glamorous dinner reception at the Rhodes House. I slipped out of my inky-purple strapless evening dress and hung it in the closet. Turning to face the mirror in my slip, I looked deep into my own black eyes for an answer. "What's with you?" I thought. "Everything you've always wanted is at the tips of your fingers. . . ."

The Rhodes House reception welcomed the new Rhodes scholars—thirty-two from America and thirty-five from other countries—into one of the world's most exclusive clubs. After sherry in the garden, we adjourned to the main dining room, a grand hall with glowing, grainy wood paneling covering the walls and cathedral ceiling. Elephant-sized crystal chandeliers seemed to hang miles above our heads in this hall that dwarfed its guests with grandeur and history. Ornate carvings, pre-Raphaelite tapestries, and portraits of the founders still left the large hall uncluttered.

I had been looking forward to meeting my fellow Rhodes scholars. Handpicked from around the world for brains, athletic ability, leadership, and community service, our class of scholars was bound to include future senators, Nobel Prize winners, artists, and others who would leave their imprint on the world. Cecil J. Rhodes had, of course, designed this scholarship program to identify and train the future leaders of the English speaking world.

The purpose of this reception, however, was not merely to encourage Rhodes scholars to mingle. No, the Warden of Rhodes House had arranged the evening as our debut in English society. At dinner, each of us was seated between lords and ladies, college presidents, captains of industry, or minor royalty.

Not surprisingly, all the Rhodes Scholars chatted amiably with this crowd. After all, we were selected in part for our performance at cocktail parties the night before our interviews. Furthermore, in the interviews we were tested on our ability to converse on subjects ranging from symphony to current events, literature, or science. We were prepared to walk in circles of power confidently. And we had arrived there.

"Wasn't that what you wanted?" I asked the mirror again. "Money, power, and swarms of charming men?" Goosebumps were showing along my shoulders. Despite the warm and sunny fall days, the nights were already damp and chilling to the bone. Shaking off the memories of the evening, I found my red flannel night gown and climbed under my goose down duvet.

Everyday life at Oxford had the rhythm of centuries past without the glamour of mingling with the beautiful and powerful at Rhodes House. Dinner at Trinity College was served formally every evening at 7:30 sharp. Simpson, the college butler, shut the doors to the dining hall and clapped his hands twice for everyone to stand.

Wearing black cotton academic gowns, the students stood while the faculty members, also wearing gowns, entered in a line at the front of the long, narrow hall. A faculty member called one of the students forward to recite the blessing in Latin. We sat on long wooden benches, and the faculty sat at an elevated table in front called "the high table." Servants brought out and cleared each course. This was a far cry from Harvard's trays and jeans cafeteria-style dining.

My scholarship to Oxford gave me a feeling of financial security for the first time in my life. I relaxed a notch or two. I began the process of learning to build relationships with others and with myself. Not only did I acknowledge the importance of the power of the mind and the power of the body, but also the power of the spirit.

It was then that I met Grant.

From the beginning, it was clear that he was different from most men I had been attracted to. When I asked him about his career goals he said only, "I want to keep developing and challenging myself."

My cynical side was not impressed. "Who is this loser?" I thought. "Is he going to be a doctor, lawyer, MBA, or a freeloader?" The less cynical side of me, on the other hand, thought: "Wow . . . he's like, really deep."

In response to his questions about my parents and my childhood, I let the cynic in me toss out my usual flippant answers. "My parents split before I was two, so I don't remember my real dad at all. My stepfather was a jerk. My leg was cut off when I was five." My suffering and my nonchalant toughness visibly moved him. Even though we were in a restaurant on our first date, he almost began to cry. He felt my pain and showed compassion at levels I was not yet capable of showing to myself. But I began to learn from him.

One rainy day Grant came knocking on my door. "Cup of tea?" I asked him opening the door wide. He smiled and made himself comfortable in front of the electric hearth. As I puttered around filling the kettle and getting the cups and milk Grant noticed that my shoes and socks were pretty wet.

"Bonnie, I'll make the tea," he said kindly while jumping up. "You go get yourself comfortable in dry socks. Did you just come in?" I realized from the way he said it that most people probably worried about things like dry feet. I hadn't noticed they were wet and had been indoors for over an hour. Without answering I went to the bedroom and changed my socks and shoes. Gosh, dry warm socks were comfortable though! I realized how accustomed I'd become to ignoring my own discomforts. I suppose it's how I cope with wearing an artificial limb— ignoring the sores, blisters, and calluses that develop when I walk.

Grant cared for me more than I cared for myself. Grant accepted me more than I accepted myself. The fact that I had one leg and he had two was as unimportant to him as the fact that we were different races and different nationalities. He saw no barriers.

I, on the other hand, wasn't sure what to think. I decided to consult my best girlfriend. Sherry and I always met on Wednesdays for afternoon tea at Rosie's cafe on the High Street. Sometimes we discussed her research on politics in Britain and Africa or my economics research on British business contracting. Other times we complained about the weather, the stuffy old men, or the insufferable young men.

On every occasion, however, we enjoyed the best of what Britain offered: freshly baked scones smothered with chunky strawberry jam and topped with a dollop of clotted Devonshire cream. Depending on our mood, the small white china teapot held upright Earl Grey, homey English breakfast, or smoky Indian Darjeeling. Today, a heavy-scented and bittersweet Lapsang souchong matched my mood.

"Sherry," I said, "I don't understand why I feel so blue sometimes. This Rhodes scholarship is a ticket to everything I've always wanted: money, power, career, and tons of gorgeous athletic men. Yet, the longer I'm here, the less I feel like I know what I want out of life."

"Don't worry," she answered quickly, "it's this foul English weather." She flung her arms into the air as though worshipping a nonexistent sun. "You just need some sunshine, California girl." Sherry's flamboyant gestures, dark skin, and American accent were drawing attention from the more reserved, British patrons of Rosie's. Sherry's long colorful scarves matched her extravagant gestures and emotional outbursts. The silk seemed to linger in the air behind her for a few moments whenever Sherry turned a corner.

"Be serious!" I said. "It isn't just the weather; I'm confused."

"About what?"

"Sherry, you and Ian have been dating for years, but I'm not used to being attached." I wrinkled my nose. "With Grant I feel soft and feminine, but it's strange. It makes me feel weak . . . or vulnerable." No one had ever made me feel so swept off my feet, so damsel-like. I felt like I needed him and it bothered me.

"You in love, girlfriend?" asked Sherry.

"Maybe I am." I sighed. "But he's not my type. I want excitement and adventure . . . all he does is work on computers, watch movies, and play squash."

"So why do you love him?" She cut to the heart of the matter.

I thought for a long time and finally answered almost against my will in a soft whispery voice: "He's kind. He's always there for me. He wants to be with me all the time and hear about what I do every day, no matter how boring it is." The light began to dawn for me. "All my life men have come and gone, especially Dads. But his love makes me feel more safe and secure than I ever have . . ." Relying on someone else was a decidedly new sensation.

Sherry spoke, pulling me back from my misty-eyed reverie. "That sounds pretty special to me." She sipped her tea. "Not as special as my Ian, mind you, but pretty special."

We laughed and then dug into the scones and jam with a comfortable break in the conversation. In our minds we reminisced about the special points of our men.

"Listen Bonnie," Sherry said at last, "You're probably spending too much time by yourself in the library studying all that math and economics. Why don't you get out and join a club or volunteer for something? Stop thinking about yourself for a while. Whaddaya say?"

"Okay. I will," I answered. The conversation continued until we asked for our check and left.

The very next day I signed up to help the Disabled Riding Association teach children to ride horses. Since I had stopped skiing two years ago, I missed being outdoors. Working with horses in the British countryside sounded like the perfect antidote for musty libraries and endless statistics.

Each week I bicycled to the outskirts of Oxford and into the ancient, family-run Hickory Stables. The main house had the charm of an English pub with a thatched roof and flower boxes at the windows. The fifteen stables in the back were made not of wood, as in America, but of tawny yellow Cotswold stone from the surrounding countryside. The matriarch of the family, a gnomish, gnarled, and incredibly strong woman, ran the stable almost single-handedly. She showed me how to bridle and saddle the horses before the children arrived.

As the van pulled up with six children and several therapists, we led the horses into the training ring. Some of the children had mental disabilities, which prevented them from uttering more than a few words or grunts. Other physically disabled children chattered nonstop as their horse walked around the ring. Either way, all the children showed their delight by laughing, smiling, or bouncing up and down in the saddles.

Watching these handicapped children smile and play taught me to look back at the disabled child I had been with more love and affection. Although a strong disdain for weakness had driven me to overcome my problems, it was not too late to learn some compassion, even for myself. I no longer needed to deny my pain to keep going. For the first time in my life I had the strength to cry for the child I was. Finally the respite from the fast track gave me space and time to nurture myself and begin developing some spiritual qualities.

After the children left, I took the gear off of the horses and brushed them down while enjoying the pungent warmth of their bodies and the smells of hay, fresh air, and freedom. The horses reveled in the attention and ate carrots out of my hand. Occasionally I took a riding lesson myself. I learned to feel more balanced and connected to the horse as we strode outside the training ring and across vast green meadows by the river Thames.

Horses and children, however, were still easier for me to trust than men. I guarded my heart from Grant with an armor of steel. About a month after our first date, I made a casual remark indicating I didn't take him seriously.

"You're going back to New Zealand and I'm heading to America, so let's have fun while it lasts," I said easily. We were sitting on a grassy hill eating lunch at a picnic with other friends. Grant stopped eating, put down his plate, and turned to look me straight in the eyes.

"If I wanted to, I would follow you to America," and after a pause for emphasis, "so don't count on it."

Grant was, and is, a remarkable human being. Not only was he totally unafraid of showing compassion or making a commitment, he didn't worry about silly problems like money, work visas, and immigration papers.

If you had seen the look in his eye, you would have no doubt that Grant could scale mountains should his damsel require it. Grant redefined for me the meaning of bravery and risk taking. Wall Street traders who risked millions of dollars daily looked timid and insecure compared to this man prepared to cross oceans and bare his feelings for me.

Trusting my own feelings felt like venturing out on a suspension bridge above a deep ravine with rushing water below. Others may fear skiing fast or traveling alone, but relationships seem far more scary to me.

Within six months Grant proposed.

"Marriage is a scary thing," I answered while hiding behind a chair.

"I'll hold your hand all the way through it," he promised. "Why wait?" he kidded.

We married before a year went by. Our wedding was in San Diego. I wore a flowing, white wedding dress: the perfect picture of bridal grace and femininity after all.

After chasing external rewards for so long I had begun to yearn for a more personal kind of happiness. What remained a mystery, however, was just how my professional ambitions were supposed to fit in with my plans to be a wife and mother.

CHAPTER 5

Putting It All Together

Returning to America with a new husband, I set out in search of the "balanced" lifestyle. Finding a sales job at IBM San Diego seemed ideal. Although the salary wasn't near what my friends earned at big consulting firms like McKinsey, the hours and benefits were much more family friendly. IBM's highly acclaimed training program for new employees was another advantage. Besides, Grant had been offered a prestigious position as a Mellon Fellow at the Scripps Institution of Oceanography in La Jolla, California. And my mother lived in San Diego, too.

My job satisfied my thirst to understand the world of business. Selling computer systems to hospitals, banks, aerospace manufacturers, distributors, and even software companies taught me about their customers, business operations, and investment decision-making processes.

I began finding ways for our customers to improve the quality and competitiveness of their business, not only with computers, but also by reorganizing their work to suit the needs of their customers. Soon I was not only selling computers, but also my services to lead reengineering workshops for our customers' employees. I enjoyed getting the workers, executives, and companies excited about being the best they could be. For some reason, I could help groups to leap through boundaries and push the limits of their potential. I drew from my ski racing stories to inspire them as we worked. I strived to do better at teaching them to reach higher.

I could see, however, that my career and family plans were still on a collision course. At work I saw lots of unhappy and harried working parents. One mother who came back to work after her child was born confessed to me, "I'm up at six, off to day care by seven, and then lucky if I get home and eat dinner by seven at night. During the week I see my baby for about twenty minutes before she's ready for bed." She soon quit her job altogether.

"What difference does it make whether you work twelve hours or eight hours each day if you still never see your kids?" I thought.

Another mother worked part-time, three days per week, after her first child was born. When I asked her how it was working out her feelings were mixed. "There's always pressure on me to work extra days because things need finishing. So I often do. Bottom line is I get crummy pay, less authority over my work, and no benefits while working *nearly* as hard as I used to."

Downshifting from the fast track didn't seem very family friendly after all. Who wanted to stay in a dead-end job? To me work had to be challenging and continually moving forward to keep my interest. People say I am ambitious, but I just like to stretch myself a little more every day. If a stagnant career at IBM wasn't all that compatible with a young family, a growing career would have an even worse impact. It was becoming clear that moving up to management or consulting jobs within IBM would involve relocation, travel, and—you guessed it— working long, long hours.

"If I'm going to work twelve-hour days," I thought, "I might as well go back to Wall Street where I'd pull down the big bucks. If I wanted to work my guts out for less money, I could go into teaching like my mother."

Any time Grant brought up the subject of children we would have these tortuous conversations about day care options, maternity leave, and our careers.

"I just don't see how it's going to fit together," I said over and over, year after year. "I have yet to see a woman balancing it all in a way that will work for me. I don't get it!"

I continued looking for examples of women who raised a family without giving up a career with challenge, growth, and moneymaking potential. Did anyone do it? Just as I became increasingly restless about my future at IBM, an opportunity to work in the White House arose. I flew to Washington for an interview and was offered the job as one of the Directors for the National Economic Council.

"If I don't take this," I thought, "I may never have another chance." For the next few days, Grant and I spent many hours talking about our future, the family we wanted, and his career options. But we both kept coming back to one inescapable conclusion.

"You may regret it the rest of your life if you turn down a presidential appointment," said Grant with a rueful smile, "and I don't want to be married to a bitter woman." Grant knew it wasn't a choice between our relationship and my work. Part of our relationship is supporting each other's growth. Knowing that he wants me to grow in my own way makes me feel more committed than ever to the relationship.

Together we made our decision. I would move to D.C. to work on Clinton's economic team while he stayed in San Diego pursuing his career in science. Together we saw it through.

We planned ways to keep our relationship close across thousands of miles. Rather than investing money in new furniture for my apartment, we spent it on airfares and marathon telephone calls to keep in touch. We even went to movies together, virtually, by picking the same movie and going alone. Anything to make us feel connected to each other helped. We should have done an AT&T commercial. "If you love someone, let them go. But don't stop calling."

The experience challenged—and strengthened—our relationship at its roots. We proved that we could work together, plan, and pull off a complicated task. We showed each other that our relationship was strong enough to support each of us as individuals without smothering us.

Many people ask, "What was it like to work in the White House?" Although the toll on my personal life was high, it was the most exciting, high-pressure, and glamorous job I have ever had. From my first days on the staff, I was pulled into urgent response teams for the President. Last minute decisions for big speeches, travel, press conferences, or a TV interview with Larry King sent loyal members of his staff into a stampede of preparation for every possible detail. I remember clearly the first time I was drafted: "Gene wants you in the NEC conference room, *now*," said Sandy, my assistant, poking her head into my office door and then disappearing.

At 5:30 P.M. in the White House the day's scheduled meetings usually wound down to a close. The dignitaries, lobbyists, and Capitol Hill staffers filed out through the iron security gates into their waiting limos and taxis. At the end of the day, most of the staff of the executive office of the president, including me, usually started on the stacks of reading and memo writing that couldn't be tackled during the business day. Tonight, obviously, was going to be different.

I walked down the dimly lit corridor of the Old Executive Office Building (OEOB), glancing at the vice president's office down the hall. The president's senior advisers and their staff worked here as it was only a stone's throw from the Oval Office in the West Wing of the White House. Like a general's headquarters, the NEC conference room buzzed with activity. Gene Sperling, deputy assistant to the president for economic policy, spoke to David and Dorothy in a huddle. As a few others and I arrived, Gene gathered everyone around to brief us on the project.

"The POTUS announces a preliminary list of military base closures tomorrow," said Gene. We called him the POTUS, meaning President of the United States, to distinguish him from all the other presidents running around the building such as presidents of corporations and foreign countries. "He said that in places on the list every mayor, congressman, and governor needs good answers when the flood of phone calls comes in. As a former governor, he knows what it's like."

"Dorothy. David." Gene leaned toward them with hands out-stretched. "People are going to ask how they can stop the bases from closing. Local officials have to be able to explain the base closure process as it rolls out from here." They nodded and moved off to one of the computers in the room. "Make it clear that the president can't arbitrarily decide to keep certain bases open," he called after them. Turning back to the others, he continued, "Tom, is there technology money in our budget they can use to redevelop the bases into airports, shopping centers, or industrial parks? Can you find some examples? Great." Tom, too, took his assignment and dug in.

"Bonnie, list any of our training initiatives that will put laid-off civilians into new jobs. Explain how. And put down the money. They want to know how much money they'll get as a consolation for pulling out the base." I stopped to check with the others on the format of the

document to which I would be contributing as Gene continued hand-
ing out assignments.

At last, Gene gave the final order: "Sandy, call Domino's. We're
going to be here awhile." Pizza was the lifeblood of an administration
that worked long nights on a tight budget.

The intensity, expertise, and dedication of our team awed me. Gene's
ability to assemble the expertise in order to respond to the president's
request overnight was part of the rationale for keeping the NEC staff
as a small, tight-knit group of less than twenty. Together we could
cover all facets of a domestic economic issue. As the evening wore on
Gene reviewed the work. "Simple. It has to be easy to understand. I
know you are an expert, but they aren't. What does this mean? Say it
in one sentence." As each one of us finished our section we proofed
one another's work, editing, clarifying, and checking the facts. A few
others remained to wrap up the final version of the document after I
left exhausted at 2:30 A.M.

After working in Washington, I'm less concerned about Democrats
and Republicans and more proud of being an American. I saw firsthand
how the media overlooked all the good things we did in their zeal to
become the-reporter-who-uncovered-the-next-Watergate. There were
hundreds of things we did every day to make the country better that
nobody noticed. No matter who is in the White House, rest assured
that many hard-working people are busting their buns to do the best
job they know how for our president.

Of course, I was also drunk with the glamour of being in the so-
called center of the world. Working side by side with power brokers
and cabinet members exhilarated me. Not since Wall Street had I been
part of a super-qualified team prepared to hit the decks at a moment's
notice, handle millions of dollars, and work all night to get the details
just right.

I love being the best. I'm addicted. I admit it.

At the same time, however, I had to admit that working sixty to
eighty hours per week was not at all conducive to starting a family. A
career in Washington, though exciting, wasn't going to get me where I
wanted to be in life, if I could ever figure out exactly where *that* was.
What I wanted out of life seemed irreconcilable. Money, excitement,
family, contribution to community, and flexibility. Yep. That's it. Was
I asking too much? I couldn't find an example of a working mother
who had it all.

Then one day, a voice on the radio caught my ear. "I'm Mariel Hemingway," cooed the voice. "As a wife, mother, manager of a restaurant, and an actress, I keep pretty busy."

"Not nearly as busy as your average mother working for IBM San Diego!" I thought to myself. Mariel probably doesn't spend an hour every day driving kids to day care or weekends doing laundry and grocery shopping. Like a ton of bricks hitting me on the head, I realized how wrong my thinking had been. I got the answer.

Suddenly I realized that choosing between success and sanity was not a zero-sum game. This idea of "balancing" is a hoax. Lowering my career goals, I realized, wouldn't maximize my family time. Less success wouldn't ensure greater sanity. After years of frustrated searching, questioning myself and others, I finally had a vision of a working mother that I could be excited about.

Mariel Hemingway doesn't limit her professional goals—she gives more and gets more in return. She doesn't see her choices on a seesaw with a driven, ninety-hour-a-week job at one end and stay-at-home motherhood on the other end. Mariel creates her own unique blend of work and mothering. That was the first inkling of understanding I had about the importance of *blending* rather than *balancing* my goals. It made me change the way I thought about my own career decisions.

After a year in the White House, the personal cost of working six-day weeks of twelve-hour days and having a coast-to-coast marriage had become too high. I'd felt I had made a respectable contribution to my country and fellow teammates at the NEC. It was time to go. At last, I understood that I didn't have to choose between all work, all family, or an uneasy truce. I could create my own special blend. With Grant I developed a plan to return to San Diego, start a family, and start a business as an inspirational speaker and writer.

Of course, starting a business and having a baby at the same time is easier said than done. At one point I was working about ten to fifteen hours per week on writing and speaking while nursing Darcy, changing diapers, and adjusting to all the other joys of motherhood: more laundry, cooking, and cleaning; less sleep and time for myself.

I felt so discouraged by the slow progress in putting together a marketing campaign that I began to doubt my abilities. "Has having a baby permanently affected my brain?" I wondered.

"Give yourself a break," said Grant. "Most small business owners work ten to fifteen hours each day, not each week." Putting it into perspective that way made me feel better. I realized it was taking me a month to do what another entrepreneur would do in a week. A rigorous month's work would take me four or five months. I felt better about my performance as an entrepreneur, but I still found it difficult to be content with snail-like momentum. I was accustomed to working long hours and using innovative ideas to stay ahead of the crowd. In the past, working harder and smarter had always done it.

Not this time. For the first time in my life, I was forced to go beyond my comfort zones of mind and body resources. I had to extend myself spiritually in several ways. First of all I had to accept that I couldn't do it all by myself. I needed someone to help with booking speeches, answering the phone, and handling the mail, especially when I was on the road. I thought it would be a good opportunity for someone with a child who wanted a part-time, home-based job. We could even share a nanny.

My vision materialized even faster than I expected. One day I met a friend from my gym to stroll in the park with our babies. As we pushed our prams past streams and park benches I told her about the business I was building. "I use my experiences to motivate people," I explained. "From executives to disadvantaged children, they get excited by my story of triumph over disability. I teach techniques for peak performance under less-than-ideal conditions. However, I can't do it alone. I need someone else who wants to work part-time from home. Someone to answer the phone and deal with the mail while I am on the road.

"We can blend together our work and our mothering," I proposed to her. Susanne was so excited about the idea she began immediately and never once looked back.

Even with two of us, things still moved forward slowly. Susanne's daughter, Rachel, is only three weeks older than my daughter, Darcy. We both nursed for nine months and were responsible for the majority of their care. There were times when the babies were screaming, the nanny was sick, and work felt like trying to empty a swimming pool using thimbles.

Today, two years later, we have built the business of our dreams. I speak across the country for executives, national associations, and community groups. My first book has been published by Simon & Schuster, the biggest publisher in the country. We have created audio tapes, videos, and booklets on peak performance, teamwork, self-motivation, vision, and even work-family issues. These products are all selling well, changing lives, and improving organizational performance.

At the same time, we blend work and kids in mutually reinforcing ways. We treasure being able to have lunch with the girls, give hugs throughout the day, and take off work entirely if they need us for an emergency. We have home offices at both my house and Susanne's so we can choose to be close to the girls or farther away for uninterrupted focus on work. It came as a surprise to me how much the arrangement benefited our daughters, too. They get so much love and security from each other. Now that they can walk and talk, they greet each other with smiles and hugs in the morning. In sum, we have created a place where we influence the nation, nurture our children, stretch ourselves every day, and earn a living, too.

Getting to this special place in my life would not have been possible without drawing on my spirit power as well as mind and body power. From the very beginning I leaned on Grant financially and emotionally as I detoured from the conventional fast track. It was hard for me to quit a high-paying, prestigious White House job. Knowing my self-worth without getting a paycheck was awkward territory for me. I was forty pounds overweight and without a business card. When I told people I was writing a book but hadn't sold it yet, they nodded knowingly. They treated me like a housewife.

Many times along the way I resented Darcy for slowing me down. With 20/20 hindsight, however, I see that being forced to slow down also pushed me to focus on higher quality performance as a speaker and a writer. Drawing on spiritual resources helped me to be patient. I don't think I would have had the patience to spend nine months rewriting the proposal for this book if I hadn't been pregnant. I probably would have given up and gotten a job or shifted my attention to speaking opportunities. "I can't write it," I would have concluded after two or three months. "I'll never sell it." But writing takes time. Editing, publishing, and distributing takes even longer. From beginning to end, this book will have taken almost four years from the time I left the White House. I have learned patience.

Establishing myself as a speaker has been a long, hard process as well. In the speaking business, building a reputation takes time. Word of mouth, articles, and high-profile speeches can sometimes take six months or a year to pay off. Someone once said the definition of a professional speaker is someone who has stuck with it long past the point of what is reasonable or rational.

Had I been single and started my business, I would have raced around accepting speeches right and left to get exposure. With a family, however, I carefully considered each speech and accepted only a few each month. As a result I crafted each speech meticulously, researched the organizations and people in the audience, and put more heart into it. Clients who hired me then—and now—didn't get an exhausted speaker delivering the same speech for the thirty-second time. When I speak I make sure that it is a special event for everyone in the room, including me.

My career does not follow the optimal path of progression for a professional speaker. Yet, by using more mind, body, and spirit, I can achieve at the highest levels regardless.

Conclusion

No one, I'm convinced, starts on the road to success with all the right luggage. We all have an extra cross or two to carry along or emotional baggage that we should have left behind. Embracing our mind, body, and spirit usually requires each of us to reconnect with a piece of ourselves we have tried to put aside.

I'm on a journey to reclaim the spiritual side of myself. I don't know where this journey leads, but I know that speaking, writing, and inspiring others puts me on the right track. Writing this book, for example, forces me to reconnect with my severed memories and suppressed emotions. Letting go of the pain from child abuse, amputation, and loneliness allows me to begin to feel joy and love for the first time.

The flexibility of my job also gives me time and space to build my family and personal relationships. Having a daughter has been a sort of crash course in spirituality since I am definitely not cut out of maternal fabric. Nurturing myself and others rather than simply slashing my way through obstacles is another part of my spiritual journey. Most of all, I am learning to rejoice in myself for who I am, rather than for the accolades I've collected.

Explaining my life to others in writing and speeches helps me to crystallize my creed for living and become a better role model. Telling my stories heals me as much as it helps anyone else.

That was my life story. What about yours? Whether you need to work on mind, body, or spirit, this book can help you. This book helps you chart your own path. Which part of the journey are you on? Is it time to start taking action in the world, to push your physical limits and tackle problems with energy and drive? Is it time for you to develop more imagination, mental strength, and self-discipline? Or, like me, are you learning about quality, values, and personal relationships?

PART II

Basic Ideas, Personal Assessment Quiz, and Definitions

This section covers the basic building blocks for blending. In chapter 6 you get an overview of why and how blending helps you become more successful and a better person at the same time. At the end of chapter 6 there is a personal assessment quiz to help you diagnose your strengths and weaknesses. Chapters 7, 8, and 9 define the terms mind, body, and spirit in specific ways that will allow you to understand your strengths and tap the resources in your weakest area.

CHAPTER 6

Two Roads to the Top

Total Commitment: The Traditional Path

To succeed, people say, you need to "give it all you've got!" But what does that mean? I grew up believing it means working late into the night, giving up personal life, and eliminating everything not directly related to your goal. Now I call that the *total commitment* philosophy.

This way of thinking is based on what I described as the seesaw paradigm in the introduction. People act as though their life is a seesaw with achievement on one end and personal happiness on the other. A person can choose to tip the seesaw (1) toward achieving more money, power, or fame; (2) toward family, spiritual growth, or serving others; or (3) to be balanced somewhere in the middle and settling for less of each.

Those who believe in total commitment see the world this way and choose to tip the seesaw toward achieving things. According to this philosophy, putting aside family, friends, values, health, and enjoyment of life is necessary if you really want to be the best. Belief in this warped sense of total commitment is so widespread that many people willingly pay for their success with their relationships, health, and happiness.

If you believe in total commitment you say things like:

No pain, no gain.
Quitters never win, winners never quit.
Perfection is our goal, excellence is acceptable.
Excuses are like assholes, everyone has them and they all stink.
Winning isn't everything, it's the only thing.

When I think of total commitment, I think of Katrina (not her real name) who I met at an elite training camp for Olympic skiers. Several weeks after breaking my one and only ankle, the doctor recommended that I join Katrina for a therapy session. First we plunged our feet into a bucket of ice, then we took clay packs out of boiling water and applied them to the injury. Hot. Cold. Hot. Cold. Katrina asked the doctor, "How long in the ice?"

"As long as you can stand it," the doctor answered.

Katrina could stand an awful lot. Taking him at his word, she kept her foot in the ice for so long that she had frostbite after two days of therapy. Imagine someone so programmed to tolerate pain that she could willingly give herself frostbite in the name of recovery! She thought "no pain, no gain" meant "more pain, more gain."

Another picture sticks in my mind exemplifying success through total commitment. During exam time at Harvard I remember walking into the dining hall in my building and seeing a premed student named Michael (not his real name) camped in a corner of the room. In addition to several stacks of books, he had brought the pillows off his bed and his own lamp. Its bright light emphasized the pasty complexion of his emaciated arms as he sat hunched over the books. Since the dining hall was open for twenty-four hours during exams, Michael could stay there round the clock, moving only a few feet for food or coffee. Yes, this kind of total commitment can get you top grades, entry to the best jobs, and perhaps a Nobel Prize. That is, if it doesn't lead to a nervous breakdown, emotional burnout, or physical illness first.

Seeing people suffering for success on Wall Street came as little surprise to me after what I had seen at Harvard. I was prepared to pay my dues and make my millions until the following incident made me stop and think. One weekend I had a special opportunity to assist a small group of executives working to finalize a bid to buy ConRail on behalf of an investor syndicate. Though only fetching coffee, sandwiches, and faxes, I listened, read, and observed the process. I learned one thing that I didn't expect.

One of the executives, Meredith (not her real name), asked me to retrieve a file from her desk. I looked up to her as a role model since she was one of the few women executives in the firm. Thinking someday I'd be just like her, I happily raced down the plush hallway into her corner office with giant windows and a panoramic view of Manhattan. As I picked up the file I noticed something attached to the wall near her desk. It was a crude crayon drawing, which looked very out of place in the grown-up world of Wall Street. I felt a chill on my skin as I realized what it was. There were two stick figures, a big one and a small one, separated by a heavy line. Under the big figure was written, "Mom at work." Under the little figure, which was shedding a giant tear, was written, "Me at home." I recoiled from the wall wondering how she could torture herself by seeing the picture day after day.

I was shaken as I walked back to the conference room. I realized that the novelty of working all night, seven days a week, might wear off eventually, even with tons of money to comfort me. I might prefer having a family to go home to on weekends rather than just another empty hotel room with more files to read and another plane to catch.

People like Katrina, Michael, and Meredith succeed at what they do, but at a very high personal cost. You probably know similar people. Maybe you are one.

The ethos of total commitment pervades American culture, where people regularly rise from rags to riches. Perhaps the main reason we believe in total commitment is because it works. Yes, sometimes you need to suffer a little in a workout to get physically stronger. Sometimes you need to work when your friends go to the pub if you want to be among the best. Sure, driving yourself and suffering will make you very good at what you do—at least until you have a nervous breakdown or midlife crisis.

It Doesn't Have to Be that Way!

BLENDING: THE ROAD LESS TRAVELED

The most exciting thing I have learned from working with the world's best in sports, business, and politics is that more success doesn't necessarily have to lead to more suffering.

I have met many competitive people who manage great public achievement and retain a sense of joy in life at the same time. When they "give it their all" it isn't the kind of total commitment described above. They don't eliminate or sacrifice parts of themselves to favor a limited set of specialized skills. Instead they cultivate all their resources and apply a diverse set of skills to their goal. This is the approach I call blending.

People who subscribe to blending as a philosophy say things like:

Do what you love and the money will follow.
Live by your values.
Don't sweat the small stuff.
Enjoy the contest, win or lose.
Focus more on getting the best from yourself than on beating the competition.
If you want to get value, give value.

Blending as an approach to success at the highest levels is far less familiar than traditional total commitment. In fact many people simply do not believe that you can become rich or famous without either suffering a great deal, having natural talent, or inheriting a fortune. But people do.

Total commitment, the win-at-any-cost attitude, is draining. If you continually give up what you stand for, who you are, and how you feel, after a while there isn't much left to throw at the target.

In contrast, blending is energizing. People who are blending have a glow of relaxed excitement that is fun to be around. They work hard, enjoy life, and seem to have limitless resources of energy and enthusiasm. Their joy and enthusiasm send out a ripple effect causing others to grow, succeed, and find more personal fulfillment, too. They achieve great things and do it in a way that is a positive force in the world. These are the people I look up to.

- Laura Tyson, the first woman to head the White House Council of Economic Advisers since its creation in 1946, impressed me by the way she stands her ground in closed-door meetings over the budget as well as on national television. She does her job with style, intelligence, and humor. "Humor is important. I choose my team to include people with a good sense of humor—my chief of staff, my deputies, and the senior economists. I also stay in touch with my sense of awe and wonder about being in the White House. It's a magical opportunity. I try to enjoy it." Laura has outlasted many other appointees and moved up to head the National Economic Council.

- Lebron Morgan, who sells advertising for Black Entertainment Television, has taken his daughters on many sales calls with him. "I want them to see how their Daddy earns a living," he explains. "I show them where the idea starts, the preparation, the meetings, and finally the finished ad." It can be a challenge, though. At Disney World his daughter told the client, "Give my Daddy the business so we can go to the park!"

- Bob Chappelle, son of a preacher, was considered an odd duck among car dealership owners because of his honest approach to car sales. Then he heard of a new car company called Saturn with a philosophy that matched his to a T. In five years Bob helped Saturn build a $50 million sales volume in San Diego alone based on honesty, low pressure, and educated customers. After twenty-five years in the car business he has proven definitively that good guys can finish first. "Truth isn't what you say you're going to do," says Bob, "truth is what you did."

- Susan Taylor, editor-in-chief of *Essence* magazine, is also totally engaged in her job and totally successful. She joined the magazine at age twenty-four because, "It was the only one on the shelf with pictures of women like me." With no college degree or previous experience in publishing, she left behind a business selling beauty products for a job as fashion and beauty editor. "I just wanted to be part of it," says Susan, eyes glowing twenty-five years later.

Today, her elegant profile and striking braids are recognized by all the magazine's 7.3 million readers. Susan doesn't ride around in limos and get mobbed by crowds of fans because of hard work and ambition alone, but also because of her love for *Essence,* her sense of mission and her devotion to its readers over the years. Her heart and soul guide the magazine that inspires men and women of all colors.

These athletes, politicians, bankers, and executives seem to win with an infuriating ease and actually enjoy the challenges they face. They move from success to success, or even from failure to success with a relaxed confidence. They create lives where success and personal sanity go hand in hand. To achieve at the highest levels they blend together their brain power, their sweat, and the passion of their convictions.

Throughout this book, you will hear stories, principles, and daily habits from the twenty or so role models I was able to interview. These people were selected by me based on a feeling or a hunch I had about them. Some I knew and had worked with; others I met in the interviewing process. I would have liked to interview so many more well-known people like George Foreman, Mary Kay Ash, Jenny and Sid Craig, Whitney Houston, Amy Grant, Heather Whitestone, Dolly Parton, Ray McGuire, Edwin Moses, and Oprah Winfrey. There were also many less well-known, really special people who I think are good examples, but who could not be included due to time and space constraints.

The more people with whom I spoke, the more I realized that there are a lot of people out there succeeding sane, blending joy and success. They are quietly working to build meaningful and achieving lives without the fanfare and publicity of those who succeed in a crazy or destructive way.

Lessons from their lives help all of us—from working mothers to harried waiters—to perform better while enjoying life more. The techniques that allow them to laugh under the pressures of national security, million-dollar budgets, or international media coverage can allow others to relax more under the stress of day-to-day living.

This contrast between total commitment and blending should give you that "aha!" feeling. It puts a name to something you already know to be true. You've met people who are joyfully successful. They love it, work hard, and make sacrifices but do it without gritting their teeth and complaining about it.

You, too, probably have felt this way about something in your life, whether it's your children, a job you had, or a hobby you love. When you are totally engaged time passes quickly, and you feel a good tired rather than a bad tired at the end of the day.

Having this image of joyful success in your head isn't enough, however, to show you how to turn that feeling into consistent achievement. Why can't we just do it? If it was easy to see how to do it, more people would already be doing it. In the rest of this chapter I will break it down into steps, and then in later chapters I'll explain how to apply the principles of blending in your life.

How Does Blending Differ from Total Commitment?

○

Total commitment:

Pick either your mind, body, or spirit and develop it for maximum achievement.

Blending:

Whether your goals are physical, mental, or spiritual, use all three resources.

You can compete and win either way. The side effect of blending is developing as a whole person, and you are more likely to win without losing yourself.

○

Michael, the premed student I mentioned above, for example, was trying to achieve in a primarily mental arena (college) using primarily the power of his mind. His pale skin, weakened muscles, and encamped position told the story clearly. Exercise, sunshine, and friends were all eliminated to make more time for studying. Although he attained a 4.0 GPA, entry to the leading medical schools, and prestigious fellowships to launch his career in medicine, he could have done it a different way. He could have gotten the grades and the accolades without losing himself.

He could have reduced his total study time by rejuvenating his mind with body and spirit activities. Studies show that after twenty minutes of concentrated cerebral work our attention and productivity start to drop off. By the end of two hours or more without a break, the brain moves along sluggishly at best. If Michael had periodically taken a walk outside or met a friend for a coffee break, he may well have boosted the overall productivity of his study time.

In particular, vigorous physical exercise would have boosted his brain power. "As you become aerobically trained, the body becomes more efficient at transporting oxygen," says Dr. Robert Dustman of the Veterans Affairs Medical Center in Salt Lake City. Other researchers think that links demonstrated between vigorous exercise and increased creativity are the result of a hormonal response or an increase in right brain stimulation. Exercise isn't just a feel-good activity; it actually makes you smarter.

However, blending goes further than just using body and spirit to augment the mind. Blending also means applying body and spirit resources directly toward a mental goal.

I knew another medical student, for example, who found funding to spend a summer in a rural African village with a team of doctors immunizing children against a rare disease spreading through a local community. The experience proved valuable academically in terms of seeing the cutting edge of immunology. But it also moved him deeply to be able to make a difference for villages full of children he met firsthand.

It challenged him physically, too. If Jeff hadn't been running three miles a day all year he wouldn't have been up to the hiking, camping, and physical labor involved in being part of the village in which the team was based. Jeff escaped a mental rut and got his body and his heart involved in medicine. That's blending.

Many people would see Michael studying day after day and say, "He's giving it all he's got." But compared to Jeff, who really throws his mind, body, and heart into medicine, Michael's "all" seems a minor contribution.

Is there a difference in succeeding one way or the other? I expect they will both win prizes, promotions, and recognition. Both of them will be great medical minds. However, the deeper commitment of

mind, body, and soul is likely to make Jeff a better doctor in a way that isn't always measured by awards.

Ultimately, the real difference between these two paths to the pinnacle is that Jeff is less likely to end up with burnout, poor physical health, and shallow human relationships. By giving more of himself, he becomes more and gets more in return. In addition to performing at high levels, he'll have more sanity, more joy, and more love. Which path would you take?

To summarize, you have got three bags of tricks with which to accomplish anything in this lifetime. You have a mind, a body, and a soul. Giving it all you've got, from what I have seen, means tapping into your unique strengths in each bag of tricks. Not everyone has the same tricks in each bag, but we all have three bags from which to draw.

In chapters 7, 8, and 9 you'll get a chance to think in more detail about what mind, body, and spirit mean; how to develop them; and how to use them. Before getting into any more detail about mind power, body power, and spirit power, stop for a moment and take the following twelve-question quiz to assess whether you are giving it all you've got. When you grade it and get the results, you'll find out more about where you stand. Which bag of tricks do you tend to ignore? Do you overuse a particular resource?

Quiz: Are You Giving It All You've Got?

Go ahead, take this short quiz to find out!

Please check *all* the answers that apply.

1. Do you do any physical activity on a regular basis?
   ____ Frankly, no. I am a couch potato.
   ____ Yes, but not regularly.
   ____ Yes, I do regular, low-impact exercise (walking, gardening, etc.).
   ____ Yes, lots! (gym, tennis, basketball two or three times per week)
   ____ Yes, and every year I set an increasingly challenging goal.

2. How do you feel about your physical activity?
   ____ I hate it: It is boring, sweaty, and sometimes even embarrassing.
   ____ I have fun doing what I do (running or lifting weights), but it's not what I would call intellectually or spiritually challenging.
   ____ I feel intellectually challenged (by classes, learning new aerobics routines, etc.).
   ____ I feel spiritually involved (as in karate, mountain climbing, or gardening).

3. Do you like your appearance?
   ____ I don't like the way I look.
   ____ Other people don't like the way I look.
   ____ My clothes and hair support my professional goals.
   ____ I strive to meet other people's standards of beauty rather than finding my own style.
   ____ I like the way I look.
   ____ I really enjoy the way I look!

4. Do you feel drained, tired, and exhausted?
   ____ Never
   ____ Rarely

_____ Frequently mentally exhausted
_____ Frequently physically exhausted
_____ Frequently emotionally exhausted

5. How often do you read books (not just newspapers, magazines, or TV!) that challenge you with new ideas?
_____ Daily   _____ Weekly
_____ Monthly   _____ Twice a year
_____ Once a year, whether I need it or not (or less)

6. Do you use any subconscious mind techniques? (You can count prayer if you want to.)
_____ Visualization
_____ Affirmations
_____ Self-hypnosis or meditation
_____ Positive thinking
_____ No, I don't use subconscious mind techniques
_____ Other_____

7. Do you use subconscious mind techniques to improve
_____ Positive attitude
_____ Self-motivation, professional goal setting
_____ Performance under pressure
_____ Exercise motivation
_____ Personal relationships
_____ None
_____ Other_____

8. How would you rate your abilities in terms of time management?
_____ Help! This is my weakest link.
_____ I'm good, but I could improve.
_____ I have a great organization system, but I still never seem to have time for me!
_____ Time management allows me to enjoy life more!

9. Do you live by your values?
_____ I'm not sure. I don't really know what my values are.
_____ I don't live by any code of ethics. Like Nietzsche, I have no regrets.

_____ I know what my values are, but I *often* fail to meet my own ethical standards.

_____ I know what my values are, and I *sometimes* fail to meet my own standards.

_____ Yes, I know my values and follow them rigorously.

_____ Yes, I have a written personal mission statement and/or a code of ethics, which I live by and update regularly.

10. Do you like your job? (Try to pick the most accurate statement.)

_____ I hate my job. I dread Monday mornings.

_____ It pays the bills.

_____ I have learned to love it.

_____ I'ts a good job, nice people. I am lucky to have a good job.

_____ I haven't figured out yet what I want to do when I grow up.

_____ This is one step in my plan to have the job of my dreams.

_____ If I won the lottery, I'd still do the same job!

11. Are you generous to strangers? When and what do you give to whom?

(Omit this question if you are not comfortable with it.)

Every: week—month—year (circle one)

I give $_____ money

I give _____ hours of time

To: charity groups—religious groups—political groups (circle one or more)

Other notes_____

12. Do you renew your spiritual strength through (circle one or more):

Nature—art—religion—family—service to others—Other_____

_____ Hardly ever.

_____ Some, but not as much as I would like.

_____ Regularly, but still not as much as I would like.

_____ Enough to keep me going strong.

_____ Enough to inspire me to do great things!

(Grade the quiz using the key in appendix C.)

Quiz Scores: What Do They Mean?

Your highest score shows you which area is your *comfort zone*. Your comfort zone is the set of skills you tend to fall back on when the going gets tough. Whether it is mind, body, or spirit, you like using this part of yourself more than the others. You feel good at it. When you think about personal development, you are more likely to develop this side of yourself because you feel it's worth developing. Your skills in this area may or may not be highly developed, but you enjoy using them. Your comfort zone is where you feel most comfortable.

Your second highest score may be close or even equal to your high score. In other words, you may have two comfort zones. It's up to you to decide whether or not you have one or two dominant zones for relating to the world.

Although it is natural to have a comfort zone, relying too heavily on one zone can cause poor performance, stress, and eventually burnout. If your high and low score are more than seven or eight points apart, you may be relying too heavily on one aspect and not giving it all you've got!

Your lowest score shows you where your hidden resources lie. Depending on how low your score was, your feelings about this part of yourself may range from mild discomfort to intense dislike. Chances are, you avoid getting into this zone whenever possible.

Most of us, somewhere along the line, have disowned a piece of ourselves because we think we have no talent or skill in that area. We have a discomfort zone.

"I can't do sports," my mother says.

"I'm just not a sensitivity kind of guy," a colleague of mine told me.

"I'm not smart. I'm not a thinker," I hear from far too many women.

The truth is that you do have resources in all areas. You need to use them if you intend to get to the top, become fulfilled, or both. The discomfort zone may actually be your truest, most meaningful set of skills though you are afraid to use them. The annoyance you experience in your discomfort zone is just a symptom of shying away from your greatness as you would look away from the sun.

The purpose of this book is to show you how to embrace not only your comfort zone but also to recapture your lost strengths. You will learn how to tap into your unused resources from your discomfort zone while staying in your comfort zone. In this way you can create a bridge back to wholeness.

A few caveats about the quiz scores:

- The numbers are only relative for you. Don't try to compare your scores with anyone else's. If you have a low mind score, for example, it doesn't mean you are less smart or less curious. What it may mean is that you tend to rely on your body and spirit resources more often than your mental ones. Only compare your own three scores with one another to see which is the highest.
- The scores reflect your subjective point of view, not "reality." If your body score is lowest, it doesn't necessarily mean you are actually in terrible shape. The scores tend to reflect how you feel about mind, body, and spirit rather than what you actually do. When I grade quizzes for my friends I have found that often they don't give themselves enough credit for reading books or for giving to charity or something else. People tend to give themselves the benefit of the doubt in the area where they feel most comfortable.
- It's only a twelve-question quiz; don't take it too seriously. If you end up with a diagnosis that you think is way out of whack, you're probably right. Read through what it means and ultimately judge for yourself. You know you better than I do.

To better understand your scores, read the descriptions of mind, body, and spirit power in the following chapters. You may want to read these sections in the order of your scores. For instance, if your highest score was spirit, read the spirit section first. Mind starts on page 86, body on page 96, and spirit on page 105. At the end of each chapter there is a special section that explains the significance of that particular comfort zone to those who scored highest in that area.

Before deciding whether you're giving it all you've got, consider the question "what have I got to give?" The better you understand what I mean by mind skills, body skills, and spirit skills, the better you can assess your own skill bank, invest it wisely, and expand it. Since everyone has different weaknesses and strengths, what improves one person's life makes another person's worse. The more thoroughly you read these sections, the better you will be able to understand and apply all the methods in this book to your own life.

As you read the following sections on mind, body, and spirit, think about your scores on the quiz and your answers to the questions. Ask yourself to what extent you have or use the skills described.

CHAPTER 7

Mind Power

When I asked Dottie Walters, one of the nation's leading motivational speakers, what keeps her sane, she said without hesitation, "Reading. What a gift it has been in my life."

As a high school student her hopes of attending college were destroyed. Abandoned by her father, Dottie took jobs in a bakery and a department store to help support the family.

"When I saw friends going off to college and I couldn't go, it broke my heart," said Dottie. "But I found this quote from Amelia Earhart that kept me going." Here it is:

> *Some of us have great runways already built for us.*
> *If you have one, take off.*
> *If you don't have one, then understand*
> *it is your responsibility to build one for yourself*
> *and for those who would follow you.*
>
> —*Amelia Earhart*

Says Dottie, "I carried that idea in my purse every day. It told me who I was."

"In my mind I talk to people from all ages, places, and times. Ben Franklin calls me 'honey.' Marriott, Lindbergh, and Emerson are all my teachers and tutors. I have a very vivid imagination."

Dottie indeed has a vivid imagination. She fostered teamwork in the fiercely competitive speaking industry by founding the International Group of Agents and Bureaus with the motto, "Not Competitors, Colleagues."

Dottie has indeed built runways for herself and others. Her determination and her ability to shape her reality exemplify the strength of mind power.

What Is Mind Power?

Mind power lies in the ability to choose. No other animal can remember the past, imagine the future, and change the present like a human being. For good or ill humans have redefined our role on the planet and taken control of our environment more than any other animal. The phenomenal power of the human mind allows us to flex our free will. A highly developed ability to choose relies on two things: seeing many perspectives and having the will to act when faced with options.

What Can Mind Power Do for Me?

Mind power, as I define it, is a critical skill for the twenty-first-century workplace. Actively seeking out new paradigms and new viewpoints gives you more power to identify creative solutions, more ability to negotiate between opposing parties, more potential to understand and help your customers, and more skills for communicating with your family.

As you get better at grasping and adding new paradigms, your ability to learn quickly increases, too. "A mind expanded can never contract to its previous size," wrote Emerson.

Creative thinking is often associated with the spirit or the right brain rather than the mind. However, I know many "outside the nine dots" thinkers and creative problem solvers who are not at all in touch with their emotions or their values. At Harvard, at Oxford, and in the

White House I was frustrated by those economists who played with the numbers, the policies, and the scenarios with no sensitivity for the people behind the numbers. From my experience I consider flexible-options thinking to be a sign of mind power, not necessarily spirit power.

A second dimension of mind power lies in developing will power. The power to decide quickly is increasingly crucial in rapidly changing markets and companies. There is no longer time for information to filter up to management, decisions to be made at the top, and implementation plans to be handed down layer by layer. In most industries and occupations employees and managers are getting more and more decision-making authority to handle situations as they arise. The power to decide separates the highly skilled from the peak performers.

Anyone in a leadership role, such as an executive, project manager, or even a house-spouse, can benefit from developing more mind power to improve their problem solving, team building, imagination, and other skills. Effective leadership demands superlative decision-making skill, which is enhanced by seeing lots of options and having the will to move.

In addition to being an essential professional skill, being able to see the world from many angles is personally very freeing. I notice that I have a sense of confidence and uninhibitedness that many others don't have. So many people worry about fitting in and obeying the rules—of the corporation, of high society, of the local gang. Having lived among lords and ladies in England, as well as lumberjacks in Oregon and surfer dudes in San Diego, I'm familiar with a wide variety of rules. Sometimes I choose to obey them, and sometimes I choose to make my own. I can always console myself with the knowledge that whatever I choose to do would be considered appropriate somewhere in the world. Like I told a woman who had recently become an amputee, "When people stare, pretend you're Miss America: Wave a little and smile a lot."

If you never see beyond where you were born and how you were raised you can only meet or fail other people's expectations. Seeing more and more new ways of life gives you the opportunity to set your own expectations.

For those of you to whom making more choices sounds scary—and I know there are many who feel that way—don't worry. Mind power is my comfort zone. But if it isn't yours, don't worry. You'll learn how to leverage your strengths and use more mind power even if it doesn't come naturally. It's very exciting to see that you aren't trapped when you thought you were. However, it can be scary at the same time, too. When you get used to it, being able to call your own shots, design your own life, and create the relationships you want makes it very worthwhile!

How Do I Develop More Mind Power?

The muscles of free choice grow stronger in two ways. First, one must see that choices exist. Second, one must have the courage to act.

In some ways our minds naturally prevent us from seeing choices. Psychologists say that the mind acts as a filter to screen out the complexity of the real world and offer each of us a view we can comprehend. Millions of sounds, sights, and feelings are available to us at all times, yet our brains reduce this to a few perceptions on which we decide to focus.

At this very moment your brain is screening out distractions. Listen, for example, to all the background noise you automatically filtered out while reading this page. Or feel the position of your tongue in your mouth. Take a quick look around you and then try to remember all the objects in the room while your eyes are closed. Each day, our minds work to sift through the barrage of input and keep only what we think we need to know.

"The function of the brain is to protect us from being overwhelmed and confused by this mass of largely useless and irrelevant knowledge by selectively shutting out most of it," says Aldous Huxley in *The Doors of Perception*. However, "once funneled through the reducing valve of the brain what comes out the other end is a measly trickle of consciousness."

The filters in our minds are not reality, but they serve as road maps for the real world. Good maps have certain features. They cover a limited range of territory such as one town or one state. To avoid confusion, they don't include every detail of the geography. Finally, they emphasize certain features like highways or tourist attractions depending on who publishes the map and what its purpose is.

The maps in our mind work in the same way. While everyone is dealing with the same reality, our mental maps or filters select which facts and ideas we notice. For example, two siblings may look back on their childhood and see it differently. One remembers good times, laughter, and camaraderie while the other remembers poverty, tension, and hunger. We all selectively remember the past depending on the road maps in our head.

Just as we change road maps depending on what town we are in or what we are looking for, most of us rely on more than one mental map. We may have one guide for how to behave at home and another guide for work. Sadly, many people have different filters for dealing with people based on race, religion, or gender. Our stereotypes and prejudices are simply a set of guidelines we believe to be helpful in sorting out a complex reality.

"Each of us is at once beneficiary and victim of our reduced consciousness," concludes Huxley. "We benefit insofar as it keeps us from going crazy. But we are the victim of our own mind if we believe that this reduced awareness is reality."

Hobbled and empowered by our conscious minds, what can we do to become more mentally powerful? If you accept that we can never consciously take in reality as a whole, the best we can do is take slices and examine them in turn. Becoming aware of your unquestioned assumptions, your personal biases, and your other unconscious maps frees you to move on to seeing other slices of the world. We can expand our perceived range of choices by continually seeking out new mind maps, new perspectives, and new frames of reference. The more facets of the world we take in, the closer we get to an understanding of the whole.

By this definition, having more credentials and degrees doesn't necessarily indicate more mind power. For some people, schooling provides almost none of what I mean by mind power. Studying one subject for many years teaches a lot of mental discipline but tends to offer fewer and fewer new perspectives as you progress. For example, my husband Grant earned three degrees in physics but learned very little about economics, literature, or foreign culture. Studying for many years in a specialty is like taking a single mental map and touring more and more of the territory. Formal education increases mind power if and only if you are challenging yourself with new ideas, seeing new perspectives, and continually developing new mind maps.

Thus, you can't jump to the conclusion that my husband Grant's eighteen years of schooling means his comfort zone is mind power. In fact, he's more spirit-centered than mind-centered. He's found his calling, loves his work, and builds strong relationships all around himself.

Schooling isn't the only way to develop mind power. Some people build their mind power through travel. As long as you're mixing with other cultures, suspending judgment, and seeing the world through other eyes, you don't even have to travel very far. Travel within the United States or even to the other side of the tracks in your town can be even more mind expanding than traveling across the globe, staying at a Hilton Hotel, and ordering room service. Increasing your understanding of another race, the opposite sex, or a different generation gives you new maps of reality as someone else experiences it.

Book learning, world travel, and mixing across racial and economic lines have all nourished my mind power. My brother, my sister, and I grew up in a house with bookshelves in every room and the expectation that we would each work our way through college. Although we lived on the wrong side of town—fifteen minutes from the Mexican border and near a navy base—my mother borrowed and begged for scholarships for us to attend private school on the wealthier side of town in La Jolla. We were exposed to rich and poor; black and white; and books, books, books.

In addition to book learning and travel, positive thinking techniques can provide new and improved mind maps. For instance, a person with very negative parents may inherit a map dictating their own worthlessness and showing dead ends in relationships, jobs, and finances. As long as a person believes himself to be a failure, he most certainly will be. However, with affirmations, visualizations, or self-hypnosis, a person can build new mental maps and see pathways to opportunities for jobs, education, love, and excitement. A new mind map, in this case, could completely change their reality.

Recently I was asked to visit a woman about my age who had her leg amputated two weeks prior. She had never met an amputee before. When I asked her what she thought amputees were like she said bluntly, "People who sit around the house." I described to her the amputees I know who climb mountains, ski, dance, and play basketball. Amputees run for public office, practice law, play golf, model, act and do just about everything "normies" do. In the course of a few hours of talking and seeing my baby daughter, her outlook had completely changed. She could see a new road into her future.

Meeting disabled athletes changed my image of myself as an amputee, too. Growing up I was always the crippled kid. Although I tried to
cover up my disability and mix with other kids, I still got picked last
for teams in PE. When I began meeting strong, independent, and funny
amputees on the ski racing circuit, it taught me to demand more from
myself. I lifted weights, ran, and cycled until I no longer felt physically
inferior. I had been an amputee for a decade before I realized I could
be an athlete, too.

Besides book learning, travel, and meeting new people, another
important source of new mind maps is our imagination. Fantasy, fairy
tales, and science fiction are rich sources of new perspectives. Without
imagination could man have invented flying machines? Moving pictures? Spaceships? Our ability to imagine the impossible allows us to
shape our reality and direct our future. Dreams are just goals that seem
unrealistic.

As a very young child I used to escape problems like my divorced
parents and my long hospital stays with fiction books. I read whatever
I found, including Nancy Drew, Ellery Queen, and Greek mythology.
After everyone went to bed I would lie on the bathroom floor reading
myself to sleep. I read on fishing trips with my neighbor, on school
buses, and in front of TV. Living in these magnificent imaginary worlds
equipped me, in part, with the skills to invent my own fantastic stories
like competing in the Olympics with only one leg. I became the hero-
ine in my own book.

As I've already said, seeing more choices is only half the power of
the mind. Finding the courage and self-discipline to select a choice is
the other crucial part.

Consider my daughter, Darcy, who is almost one year old. The parent experts tell me she won't develop her full "impulse control" until
the age of three. In the meantime, she knows she shouldn't grab the
toilet paper roll and pull, but she can't resist the impulse. As she
approaches near I tell her sternly, "No!" She looks at me, sees she has
a choice, but is incapable of acting on it. Whirrrrr. Darcy smiles proudly
surrounded by fluffy, white paper.

The parent experts are wrong about one thing: There is no guarantee
that she will develop impulse control by age three. Haven't you met
adults who can't control their impulses? My hand completely loses
impulse control near chocolate. Most of the time, however, my will
power or self-discipline is unusually high.

Practice is the key.

Try making decisions faster. Napoleon Hill, author of *Think and Grow Rich* says successful people make decisions quickly. I know I can agonize over decisions and put them off till the last possible moment in the hope that new information will make my decision easier or clearer. Just do it.

Many of us are effective decision makers at work but not at home. Clutter, poor financial management, and poor time management represent a lack of decision making. An unwillingness to make choices buries us deeper into stress, clutter, and things.

Less stuff = more time and more money

If you make active choices you can dramatically simplify your life. Throw things out more often. Decide what you will and won't buy. Schedule appointments with yourself as well as other people so that you decide how to use your time rather than letting others do it.

Without the discipline to act, collecting mind maps doesn't make you free. At the same time, self-discipline doesn't make you free if you can't see options. Whereas many gurus of high achievement tout self-discipline skills like time management and goal setting as the critical success factor, mind power requires both seeing the choices and the ability to act.

Free will = options + self-discipline

Having mind power affects your ability to develop in other areas as well. For example, more self-discipline allows you to stick to a physical regimen that increases your body power. Similarly, being able to see the world from many perspectives when combined with the strong emotions of spirit power results in a heightened sense of empathy.

As you develop the strengths of your mind, body, and spirit to higher levels, they become increasingly interdependent. While it is not my purpose to discuss at length the regions of overlap, there are some excellent books out there that do. Deepak Chopra, for example, covers extensively the effects of the mind on the body and vice versa in numerous books. Daniel Goleman, author of *Emotional Intelligence*, extensively studies the need in today's economy for skills that cross the boundaries of spirit and mind. These books show you how to leverage your mind power to develop more body power and more interpersonal skills.

While I don't want to pretend that mind, body, and spirit are separate, I want to show the differences in order to help people reclaim their missing parts. Embracing your comfort zone and using it as a launching pad makes it easier to venture out into your anti-zone.

If Your Highest Score Was Mind Power

You're like me. There's nothing better than a good intellectual argument or a good book. I love travel, particularly to live in other places and experience them instead of touring. When I live there, I really slip into their reality instead of mine. I am always curious about new places, new people, and new ideas. If you haven't had a chance to let loose your curiosity through travel, reading, schooling, or something, you have a lot of latent potential for creativity to tap into.

When facing a problem, mind-based people rely on their minds to find an innovative solution. Mind power is what they trust. I survive tough times by submerging my emotions and using sheer willpower to carry me through anything.

Carefully balancing new ideas with personal discipline is the hallmark of highly developed mind power. Those who have lots of curiosity but no self-control, or control without curiosity, have an underdeveloped ability to make decisions.

My self-discipline, for example, isn't perfect. I seem to be always revamping my time management systems after they fall apart. However, my self-discipline has seen me through the Olympics, college graduation, and working twelve- to fourteen-hour days on Wall Street and in the White House. I have a lot of willpower, but I could be a lot more organized.

Hidden resources, for a mind-motivated person, include the bustling physical energy of body power, as well as the spiritual energy from passion, fun, anger, and love. However, mind-motivated people feel bored unless they're learning, making decisions, or finding creative solutions. Thus, to tap our hidden resources we need to combine physical action or emotional activity with the exercise of our free will.

Use this information about yourself to help you expand your resources. Enjoy your physical activity more by signing up for classes and challenging your mind. You can learn new things about tennis or aerobics instead of doing the same old calisthenics over and over.

You can also incorporate more spiritual, nurturing elements into your mental life. Decide that it's okay to have a nice environment in which to work. Write out your values or code of ethics at least once a year. Do something indulgent for yourself and someone else at least once a week.

In Part III of this book, we'll talk about how mind-centered people can tap into spirit and body power in order to move ahead of the pack. In Part IV, you can learn how to infuse your life with more spirit and body activity to expand your resources.

I get a fair bit of mileage out of body power, which contributes to my ability to work long hours. My body power also means I am prone to take action on new ideas if I like them. I'm a doer and a thinker. Feelings, however, elude me.

The spiritual side is my discomfort zone. I'm not so good at nurturing either myself or others. Just as spirit people find exercise more tiring than energizing, I found relationships more tiring than energizing. I never was good at letter writing or staying in touch with old friends. I was always curious to meet new people and go to new places. Now that I am married and have a family I am learning to draw strength from my spiritual side, but it isn't easy.

If spirit power was your secondary score, you have a keen sense of mission and purpose. You combine the ability to feel strongly and choose decisively to direct the course of your life to what you believe is important. You're probably more in touch with your own needs and feelings, as well as those of others. As I mentioned above, mind-spirit people make fantastic, visionary leaders.

CHAPTER 8

Body Power

Less than two weeks after starting my job as a director on the National Economic Council in the White House, the Secretary of Labor was on a first-name basis with me. Let me tell you how it happened.

I'd had a great conversation with a member of his senior staff and faxed a follow-up memo to confirm and flesh out our ideas to revamp an interagency project. My fax, however, must have been intercepted by someone else and taken out of context. Someone was offended. They in turn bent the Secretary of Labor's ear about it. Within 24 hours after the memo went out, the secretary called my boss and asked, "Who is this Bonnie Deane?" In almost no time at all I managed to stand out among all the hundreds of new White House staffers and get noticed at the cabinet level!

I had arrived in Washington, like anyone young and naive, full of hopes to do my bit well. My face grew hot and red as my boss described the irate call from the labor department chief. How would I be able to continue my job coordinating labor and training policy if the administration's leading labor policy expert distrusted me? I wanted to fold my tail between my legs and slink away past the security checkpoints, full dress marines, tall white columns, and black wrought iron gates. My inexperience and ineptitude was so great, I couldn't even get a simple thing like a memo right!

That night I headed straight for the gym and pounded out my frustrations on a stair machine. Hour after hour I sweated, cursed, and pounded the machine. I hated myself for thinking I would make a difference and then being shown what an inexperienced idiot I was. I hated myself for being afraid of the secretary. Pushing my body to exhaustion gave me a way to punish myself for hubris, bad judgment, and being in Washington.

The workout helped to purge my bad feelings. Too often in modern society we get worked up about something and then sit and stew in our juices. Designed for a fight or flight response under pressure, our bodies shoot adrenaline into our muscles to get them going. If our muscles don't get used the adrenaline has a corrosive effect, breaking down the muscle tissue. Anger, fear, and other intense emotions can literally eat us up if we don't use that energy to do something.

Ironically, the physical workout had a positive effect beyond catharsis. Next morning, I looked strong, walked tall and straight, and had that healthy, relaxed glow of someone who is confident even though I still felt about two feet tall inside. By going through the motions of a person with confidence I eventually regained my own.

By the end of my time in Washington, I had built up a relationship with Secretary Reich that was so much better, he invited me to a personal lunch in his office on my last day. He really did know me on a first-name basis!

What Is Body Power?

Body power is strength, stamina, posture, grace, and agility. Body power is the ability to do things, to be active in the world. Most of all body power is comfort with and confidence in your physical abilities.

I heard a joke the other day that sums up the difference between mind power and body power: Three frogs were sitting on a log and one decided to jump off. How many were left? The answer is three. Although the frog decided to jump, he took several hours to actually move.

If you have mind power you can see new choices and decide to act on them. Without body power, however, you may not get from here to there very quickly no matter how good you are at making up your mind. Successful people use energy, enthusiasm, and stamina for hard work. That's where more body power makes a difference.

Let me be quite clear that I am not arguing for a particular physical ideal. As an amputee myself, I know what it's like not to fit into the accepted archetype. Fat or thin, one or two legs, big or small breasts don't matter. These things have little to do with what I mean by body power. You may look outwardly attractive and not have any of the following: energy, strength, stamina, posture, grace, or agility. On the other hand, I have seen people who may be called fat with odd-looking features who have a magnetic body power. Meeting an external standard of physical beauty is less important than feeling strong, coordinated, and comfortable with your body.

What Does Body Power Do for Me?

Body power helps you to take action, to work long and hard, and to approach life with the enthusiasm of someone who knows they have enough energy to deal with whatever fate dishes out.

Raw physical energy is magnetic. Anyone who needs to attract people and gain their confidence—managers, sales reps, speakers, realtors, insurance agents, social workers, car salesmen, suitors—can benefit from the power of physical strength. Leaders with body power enjoy a certain presence that instills confidence and attracts followers when they enter a room. Strong, hard-working people tend to make other people want to roll up their sleeves and get going.

As the first female attorney general, Janet Reno relies in part on her immense physical strength to give her an air of authority and toughness. When I lived in her building in Washington I saw her swimming laps at 6 A.M. every morning and walking to work. Were she frail and weak, she wouldn't have that "kickass" image that makes her autograph more sought after than Clinton's.

Johnetta Cole, former president of Spelman College and a magnetic, inspirational leader, sums up the importance of physical exercise to her job: "There is simply no way I will make it without that." Her grueling schedule includes getting on a plane at least one hundred times per year to make a presentation and request financial support for Spelman. With her stamina and determination this African-American women's college has raised $107 million in a campaign whose goal was $81 million. Her body power creates momentum.

On its own, however, physical magnetism is not enough to create leadership. Without knowledge, empathy, character, and other important qualities body power can appear shallow and pathetic. Body power is only one tool for a great leader.

In the example opening this chapter, I mentioned the positive effect that using my body had on my mental attitude. I could have used positive thinking or self-hypnosis to change my outlook, but exercise is just as, or more, effective. Having an arsenal of responses makes you most resilient.

While most of us have body power to some degree, some people rely primarily on body power as a way of getting things done. Not only sports nuts and outdoors types, but "body-motivated" people can also be found as housewives, sales reps, and other walks of life. Among housewives you can recognize the body-motivated person as the one who never sits down. She's always dusting, fixing, sewing, chasing children, or running errands. Sitting and watching the soaps or chatting on the phone all day would be intolerable.

Similarly, body-motivated sales reps, managers, or technicians are seldom found sitting at their desks. They are always on the move catching up with other people in their office building or driving off to meet with clients. If possible, they will find projects involving physical work with various things, places, and people. They want face-to-face meetings, physical results of their labor, and lots of change in scenery.

Body-motivated people want to solve problems by doing something about them. "Talking, meetings, planning, and thinking seem like a waste of time when we could be doing something!" says the body-motivated person. Body-motivated people won't last long in a job that involves sitting at one desk, in one office, day after day. Just as lack of mental activity would bore a mind-motivated person, lack of physical activity bores body-motivated people to tears.

How Do I Develop More Body Power?

You can develop a baseline of physical fitness just by being active. Susan Powter, author of *Stop the Insanity*, tries to debunk the health mysteries created by the culture of exercise and diet priests. She keeps the message simple. "You have to eat, breathe and move," she says. It doesn't matter whether you follow all the complicated steps in a routine. Just move—walk, dance, or wave your arms—for 30 minutes or whatever you can stand.

Any physical activity—sports, gardening, or dancing—contributes to body power. Whether you have a regular routine or you just pick up the activity you're in the mood for doesn't matter. What matters is getting off the couch, out of the chair, and out of the car.

There are two paths you can take, however, to further intensify your body power. The first option is to train your body specifically for the work you do. Hah! You may be thinking, "I'm an executive. I don't need any physical training to read financial reports and dictate memos!"

But that's where you're wrong. Today's executives need more physical stamina to cope with the demands of responding to crises in several time zones, world travel, and seventy-hour work weeks. "Executives are the real endurance athletes," says sports psychologist James Loehr, who has trained Olympic speed skater Dan Jansen and tennis star Arantxa Sánchez Vicario. "An average tennis star lasts five to seven years. You have to go on for thirty to forty years working fifteen or sixteen hours a day."

For leadership Loehr puts abdominal muscle exercise at the highest priority. "The abdominal muscles support the body's internal architecture," he says, "your posture and respiratory system." Strong abs make executives stride with confidence, stand tall, and hold their heads up and shoulders back. These physical cues provoke a physiological response to activate confidence in themselves and in others.

Just as you can get physical training for leadership, you can train for whatever your main line of work is. Pam Alexander, who heads her own PR agency and lists clients in the United States, Britain, France, and Germany, jogs three or four miles a day to give her the stamina and high energy her clients admire. Comedians like Jim Carrey and Steve Martin rely on agility and flexibility to pull off their personality changes and sight gags. What kind of physical training do you need?

Part of my preparation for a workshop is fitting in extra aerobics sessions with good music and a fun instructor. A day-to-day workout with weights and a stair machine doesn't give me the explosive energy and physical enthusiasm I want to give to others in my workshops.

By training appropriately for the activities you do, you'll develop an ease of motion or body confidence that you just can't get any other way. Being comfortable in your skin is so sexy!

Besides training your body for the work you do, the other way to increase your body power is to set a goal for your body, which is an end in itself. You can decide that this year you will run a marathon (or half a marathon) or play a round of golf or learn line dancing. Pick something you can achieve with your body.

After you achieve even a simple goal you get a feeling of pride and respect for your body's ability. Whether or not you stick with that activity, having done it once gives you an internal source of strength and belief in yourself. I don't ski much anymore, but I always know that I was once the second-fastest woman in the world on one ski. No one can take it away from me.

In addition to the big goals, the smaller goals I worked for along the way meant a lot to me, too. Like the time I trained all summer to meet the Burke Mountain Academy physical standards, including skipping a rope 300 times in ninety seconds. I felt so good passing that test on one leg! Just as facing up to mental and spiritual challenges stimulates your growth in those areas, tackling new physical challenges boosts your body power.

Although simple, this is a pretty important point. In the hundreds of self-improvement books I've read, almost all of them pay lip service to physical development as integral to mental and spiritual development. But they don't give body power equal importance in their philosophy.

Most self-help authors spend hundreds of pages discussing techniques for mental and/or spiritual growth and then cover physical growth in an "oh by the way" manner. Generally, less than 5 percent of the pages are devoted to the importance of physical energy. In the framework of blending, however, body power gets an equal billing alongside mind and spirit power. You'll get more pages on it, more ideas about how it can increase your effectiveness in a short period, and more reasons to get off your bum.

I want you to see body power in my philosophy not only as quantitatively different, but qualitatively different. Most personal development authors advise a good physical maintenance schedule. For example, thirty minutes every other day is considered sufficient. Such a maintenance program, however, will only give you a baseline of body power. True body power is fueled by more than a maintenance schedule. If you want your body power to grow, you occasionally have to let your body do something for its own primary reason. Let your body have the spotlight from time to time.

You don't have to set goals that are impossible, dangerous, or time consuming. Small things like being able to stretch to touch your toes are enough. I just got a new Flex-foot that allows me to run with a bounce in my step. If I can work up to running a mile, I'll be pretty proud of that. I know my goal is no big deal because I've met amputees who've run marathons and roller bladed across the United States. But for me, one mile is enough.

Take a lesson, try a new sport, or set a small goal. When you extend yourself a little, you build body power. You work a little harder at the extra physical training and/or healthier eating habits required to reach your goal. When your body proves it can rise to the challenge, you'll feel proud of it. One day you will come to like your body, faults and all. That's body power.

The crossover effects of body power in the areas of mind and spirit are enormously important. The energy, vitality, and action orientation of body power can be combined with either mind or spirit to attain new heights. Spirit-oriented people who can put hard work and high energy into those purposes they deem meaningful will find more satisfaction than those who dream big with little follow-through. Similarly, mind-motivated people will have a wider range of choices and options if they have body confidence and muscle power.

Realistically, bodily health and self-image are intimately bound up with attitudes, feelings, and self-esteem. The medical profession is only beginning to accept how much nutrition and fitness can affect intelligence, mental health, and one's emotional state. Whether body power is your comfort zone or your weak link, developing it to its fullest will have spillover effects on your mind and spirit resources.

If Your Highest Score Was Body Power

Body power is your comfort zone. Physical activity and stamina tend to be what you fall back on when the going gets tough. When faced with a crisis you want to take action while others are still thinking or mulling over their feelings. You pride yourself on being able to work long and hard.

You find lack of activity totally boring. You are probably the kind of person who is always planning to read this or that book, but you never really get around to it. You'll always choose to run an errand, take a walk, or do something with your hands rather than sit still. Thinking about abstract ideas or working on relationships doesn't feel like real work to you. You need to see the tangible results of your work.

If mind power was your second-highest score, you probably have disciplined routines to maintain the physical skills you value whether they are strength, agility, or stamina. You're probably in excellent health. Setting physical goals may well come naturally to you, too. Keep up the good work! Use the chapters that follow to help expand your spiritual activities and put more passion into them.

If you aren't disciplining your physical energies, you may be frustrated by erosion of the natural strength and abilities you had when younger. You probably find that relying on your ability to work hard and long hours eventually burns you out if you don't maintain muscles and cardiovascular capacity. Try to develop the self-discipline (mental) or internal desire (spiritual) that would fuel your commitment to restocking the tanks.

Use this knowledge about yourself to help expand your mind and your spiritual strengths. For example, accept that you probably won't sit around reading books. Find a way to get audio books that challenge you so you can listen while exercising, driving, gardening, or whatever. You need to get mentally challenged while on the move.

Likewise, if you find family get-togethers dull and sedentary, try to plan a family game or sports event. My cousin Donny instituted the

"Annual Father-Daughter Croquet Challenge" for our Father's Day barbecue. The game is not strenuous enough to exclude either the older or the younger generation, but at least it gets us out of our chairs and walking around the lawn. As a body-motivated person, you need to build relationships and nurture your own spiritual side while being physically active.

CHAPTER 9

Spirit Power

"You are more than what you have become.
You *must* take your place in the circle of life."
"How?"
"Remember who you are!"

—*The Lion King*

S pirit power comes from wrestling with your destiny. I knew a wealthy young man at Harvard who was always agonizing, praying, consulting gurus, and paying psychiatrists in his effort to find out "the Meaning of Life."

I imagine that God is shaking his head as he looks down and thinks "I made such a magnificent creature! I put him into a world so full of mystery and beauty that he could spend his lifetime studying water and never run out of things to learn, playing the violin and never stop improving, or raising children and never stop caring.

"Yet he is asking me to tell him what the meaning of life is! I gave each of you the entire world as your canvas because I was curious to see what each of you, as unique individuals, as my penultimate creation, would do with it. Don't ask me! Don't look outside yourself for God. I gave you a mind to think, a body to act, and a heart to feel. Do something meaningful to you! That is the purpose!"

What Is Spirit Power?

Imagine a giant, glowing circle in which energy flows at high speeds from person to person. Once you find your unique place in this circle of life, you give and receive energy, value, and creativity in fantastic, unimaginable quantities. Spirit power comes from being connected to the circuit board of life.

Spirit power is also the resource that helps you to navigate toward your place in the circle where you maximize what you contribute to the world *and* what you receive in return. Spirit power comes from listening to your inner feelings and figuring out how to live a meaningful life.

Elton John's song "Circle of Life," written for Disney's film *The Lion King*, paints a visual image for me. Whenever I hear the words I see the lush Savanna of Africa with herds of zebras, prides of lions, and flocks of birds flying overhead.

Just as the animals have a finely balanced ecosystem, humans have a finely balanced system of spiritual give and take. Elton John sings, "In the circle of life, you should never take more than you give." I feel the flow of life force when I hear the song.

Most of us spend our lives searching for our place in the circle of life, the place in which we give our best and which is highly valued by others. A lucky few find their talent early on, like Marcus Allen the gifted football player, or Mozart the genius composer. But others find their places in time as business leaders, educators, parents, or scientists.

Whether you believe in God, science, or both, you have to believe every human being is a miraculous and unique creation with something special to offer. In our modern, global economy we are freer than ever before to seek our fortunes by making our talents useful to others. Those who develop their best talents, give from the heart, and address the unique needs of others can reap tremendous rewards financially, spiritually, or both.

You know when you have really found your spot in the circle when you love what you do so much it hardly seems like work. You can't believe people pay you to do it. Giving and receiving become one and the same.

If you feel talented but overworked and underappreciated, you probably haven't found your place in the circle yet. You obviously don't enjoy what you are doing enough. You may also be putting in lots of work without sufficiently understanding the needs of others. Keep looking, keep bettering your best, and find ways to increase its value to others.

What Does Spirit Power Do for Me?

Aside from helping you to find your purpose in life, spirit power helps you to perform at peak levels. It gives you a grand plan with which to guide your actions and choices. Having a sense of purpose usually keeps you healthier and happier. Even if your purpose makes you angry, it will probably make you live longer.

When your life work is personally meaningful you feel energized and pay closer attention to detail. You can work longer without tiring. Your passion and enthusiasm infects others.

Thus, if you want to be the best, you must do something you can love. If you don't love what you do, someone else will. And it's pretty hard to compete with somebody who loves their work.

Having a strong sense of purpose not only helps you achieve, but can literally save your life. Viktor Frankl in *Man's Search for Meaning* talks about the connection he saw between a sense of purpose and staying alive in the German concentration camps of World War II:

Any attempt to restore a man's inner strength in the camp had first to succeed in showing him some future goal. Whenever there was an opportunity for it, one had to give them a why—an aim—for their lives in order to strengthen them to live with the terrible how of their existence. Woe to him who saw no more sense in his life, no aim, no purpose, no point in carrying on! He was soon lost. The typical reply with which a man rejected all encouraging arguments was "I have nothing to expect from life any more." What can one say to that? We had to learn ourselves and, furthermore, to teach the despairing men, that it did not matter what we expected from life, but rather what life expects from us.

How Do I Develop More Spirit Power?

The two main activities involved in wielding spirit power are exploring your values and giving to others.

Exploring your values involves more than developing a code of ethics. I use the word "values" literally to mean everything that is important to you or special about you. Do you love music? Nature? Being with family? Do you love closing business deals? Cooking? The laughter of children? Being in touch with what you love is what helps steer you toward your place in the circle of life.

Your values as I define them not only tell you what is right and wrong, but also tell you the quirky things that are special about you. I enjoy watching old black-and-white movies, playing squash, and eating chocolate desserts. I believe in helping others, monogamy, and disciplined children. I love gypsy-style clothes, antique clocks, Persian rugs, solitude with my thoughts, and a good intellectual argument. Those are my values.

No one is born knowing everything about themselves. Your values, your personality, and your gifts are revealed by living, striving, and loving. Your emotions—fear, hate, anger, love, excitement—are unique to you and will guide you in knowing who you are. You develop more spirit power by making time and space in your life for the things that are important to you. In this way you allow your unique purpose to be revealed.

Sarah Ban Breathnach tells us about a woman searching to understand her own values:

> In 1926 a young Englishwoman, Joanna Field, began to feel that she was not living a truly authentic life, that she did not know what made her truly happy. To remedy this she kept a journal in order to discover what specifically triggered the feeling of delight in her daily life. The journal, A Life of One's Own, was published in 1934. It was written, she confided, in the spirit of a detective who searches through the minutiae of the mundane in hopes of finding clues for what was missing in her life.
>
> —Simple Abundance: A Daybook of Comfort and Joy

Joanna Field decided that she found rapture in simple things like red shoes, sudden bursts of laughter, reading in French, answering letters, loitering in a crowd at a fair, and "a new idea when first it is grasped." The little things you love make you who you are, special and different from anyone else. Discover and treasure these clues.

When I asked Gloria Steinem about spirituality, she said, "I sense spirituality from those times in my life when I feel unity and happiness in inconsequential moments." As she spoke you could see the joy radiating at the thought of it. "Walking in the sunshine, drinking orange juice in the morning, or playing music." She got excited then, like a child. "Do you know Phoebe Snow? After I met her I went out and bought all her CDs. I spent the whole weekend listening to her CDs and dancing around my apartment. It was great! I was completely happy."

Gloria went on to describe the opposite of enjoying such simple abandon. "When I see people who are successful but obsessed and out of balance, it's not just because of something they are doing in the present. I think it tends to go deeper. It does have to do with an absence of a sense of self, which becomes like a vacuum or an empty hole inside. It sucks in everything until you become a workaholic or a foodaholic. . . ."

Developing and encouraging this authentic self requires a devotion to the task. "Put your ear down next to your soul and listen hard," the poet Anne Sexton advises. Many people say, "God didn't make no trash." It is up to us to find out exactly what God did make.

Seeking what you value, however, is not necessarily enough to help you find your place in the circle of life. You also need to listen with your heart to the needs of others. Building relationships creates the fabric for the circle of life. That's why it is called a circle—there is give and take.

"At the core of life is the joy that comes from giving," says Johnetta Cole, president of Spelman College. "My mission in life is to know joy." Under the glass on her desktop is a quote from James Baldwin that she looks at each day. "You ought to earn your death by confronting with passion the riddle of life."

Ideally, when you find your calling and enjoy your work, giving and receiving become one. Until then, however, you must give in ways that may not be so easy. Chalk it up to practicing like compulsories in ice skating. Donating money to charities is a good start, but giving your time (yourself) is better. Face-to-face giving creates an energy surge that writing a check can't replace. For those of you who still have trouble with this generosity concept, get started in the right direction by doing it for the wrong reasons. Spirit power is about maximizing what you give and receive, so don't be afraid to give to others in a way that pays you back.

Consider the following six totally selfish reasons to give to others:

1. It's a good idea to have a few people in your corner. If you really plan to succeed in your profession and be among the elite you can be assured that you will eventually be attacked and criticized by others. Either your competitors or others who are destructive by nature will try to drag you down as soon as you begin to get a lot of attention. In politics, business, sports, or entertainment, those in the limelight are a lightning rod for vicious character assassination. When that happens, it helps to have people who will vouch for your character. Better yet, people who will fight to defend your good name.

2. The simplest way to feel like a good person is to be one. It's hard to be terribly successful if you don't like yourself very much. It's hard to like yourself without being a good person. The simplest way to convince yourself that you are a good person is to act like one. Good people help other people.

3. It looks good on your résumé.

4. Working for charities is a great way to network. Often you can meet wealthy and powerful people with whom you would not have a chance to socialize any other way. Don't be ashamed to choose your charitable activity carefully to include the kind of people you would emulate.

5. You can learn and test out new skills. Charities need skills in computers, leadership, public relations, and all the other professional skills that corporate organizations need, too. By volunteering you can often get opportunities that your employer won't give you to take on leadership or forge into new areas.

6. Volunteer while job hunting. If you are job hunting you could offer your skills for one day a week in exchange for a desk and phone. Job hunting from a professional organization will boost your attitude and image while giving them your professional help at the same time. Heck, they may realize they can't live without you and hire you anyway.

The great thing about giving in person is that even if you do it for the wrong reasons, it is bound to help you grow. You'll become a better person, even if you didn't mean to.

In addition to charitable giving, spirit power involves giving more and receiving more at work and at home. Try to think about giving more value to your employer, to your customers, and to your family. What can you do that is important to them? Do you really know what is important to them? Are there small changes you can make that are easy for you, but mean a great deal to them?

Healthy relationships are conduits for the energy in the circle of life. Connections between people that support their unique feelings and individual personalities increase the energy flow.

Just as you are trying to find out more about yourself, your talents, and your unique purpose, you must question others and listen to find out more about them. Rather than giving them what you think you should or what you want, try to give to others what they value most. By finding ways to use your potential and provide more value to your customers, your employer, and your family, you begin to move closer to your place in the circle of life.

If you're the kind of person who gives too much, you need to spend more time exploring your own values. Get more practice receiving joy as well as giving it. Constantly giving is not a sustainable, growing position. To maintain the circle, energy has to flow in as well as out.

Instinctively I obey a personal ethic that dictates: "When the opportunity arises to give something that means little time, effort, or money to me, but means a great deal to someone else, it is almost criminal not to do so." Giving doesn't always have to be a sacrifice.

When I visit a person who has lost a limb, or give old clothes to charity, or give a free inspirational speech for a youth group, I know I give a lot without giving up much.

If Your Highest Score Was Spirit Power

Spirit power is your comfort zone. You have strong feelings and tend to rely on them. In a crisis, anger, love, hate, or other emotions pull you through.

When I interviewed Les Brown, the nationally recognized motivational speaker and author of *Live Your Dreams*, it quickly became obvious that the spirit is his comfort zone. Although I never gave him my
personal definition of spirit power—giving and receiving from your
unique personality and values—he talked to me in those terms about
everything.

"I train and develop young speakers," he said. "I help people find
their individual voice. What is it you showed up to give? Why are you
here? What is it of value that you are bringing that can help to create
a shift in the lives of the people who hear you?" Although his comments were related to the speaking profession, he could have been
talking about the spiritual journey all of us must walk sooner or later.

"Most speakers speak to impress," Les said. "When it comes from
the heart you connect, you give people a special experience. I teach
speakers to craft their message so the audience can find value in it for
themselves."

"Why do you do it?" I asked. "You spend more time than many other
speakers helping others."

"I believe it is my reason for being. As much as I have chosen it, it
has chosen me."

Through speaking and training other speakers, Les Brown has certainly tapped into his unique personality, passion, and values to provide
a service that meets a pressing need in today's society for hope, belief,
and inspiration. Yet, he gets as much out of it as he gives both personally and professionally.

"I feel totally at home on a stage. I love being out there constantly."
At the same time he has become fabulously wealthy from best-selling
books and tapes, TV appearances, and speaking fees. Les Brown's
speaking ability, his generosity, and his financial success are fueled by
large quantities of his spirit power.

Though you naturally rely on spirit power, your abilities in this area
may or may not be highly developed. If your spirit power is highly
developed you know what you value and surround yourself with it. You
stay connected with nature, family, music, art, or whatever moves you.
Giving to others happens naturally as part of what you love to do. You
build solid connections with friends and family through which you give
and receive energy, help, and love.

If your spirit power is not highly developed, you may not have learned how to balance emotional give-and-take. You may be the type who gives too much without taking the time to tune into your own values and restore your own spirit. Alternatively, you may be too selfishly involved in developing your own talents without really tuning in to the needs of others. Either way, building solid relationships proves difficult without a balance of give-and-take.

The hidden resources for the spirit-motivated person are the physical energy of body power and the creative, but disciplined, energy of mind power. In later chapters, we'll develop a plan for accessing these hidden energy resources. You will probably enjoy reading Part IV before Part III because it deals with quality of life first and goals as a second priority.

Tempering a spirit-dominated personality with mind and body power increases the spirit power tremendously. If mind power was your second-highest score, you are probably the sort of person who talks in terms of bedrock principles or a code of ethics. You have used the discipline of your conscious mind to clarify and make explicit your deeply held beliefs. Spirit/mind people or mind/spirit people make effective, visionary leaders.

As you will read below, mind power will help you to build more genuine empathy for others rather than giving in a martyred or patronizing way. The self-discipline aspect of mind power also tempers the impulsive, shoot-from-the-hip tendencies of spirit power and allows it to be channeled into a long-term goal or mission.

If body power was your second-highest score, you tend to be highly active as well as emotional. Physical activity can often smooth out the ups and downs inherent in having a sensitive emotional nature. You also have lots of energy to work on the relationships and activities that you love.

Both body and mind power enhance your spirit power. However, spirit power is what you tend to rely on or fall back on. You trust your feelings or beliefs more than you trust rational arguments or logical sleight of hand. If you love things like gardening, art, music, or decorating you feel you have a talent for them that is stronger than your mental or physical talents. You feel comfortable exercising those talents.

Just as physical inactivity bores body-oriented people and mental inactivity bores mind-oriented people, spiritual inactivity bores spirit-oriented people. Spirit-based people find it difficult to tolerate meaningless or insignificant activities in their lives, ugly environments, or activities that don't involve relationships with other people. "What else matters?" they think to themselves.

You can use all this information about yourself to help you develop a plan for giving it all you've got. For example, if you tend not to develop your body, you might want to find a body activity that is more spiritually involved. Rather than forcing yourself to stick with a dull or meaningless exercise routine, do something with friends, or do something beautiful or inspiring. Exercise outdoors. Walk precincts for your church or political representative. Take ballet lessons. Take T'ai Chi, the martial art that the Chinese do in groups at sunrise in the public parks. Get an exercise buddy. Join a team. Above all, do something you think is fun, friendly, or meaningful.

I know so many spirit-based people who say, "I know I should go to the gym, but I just hate it there. It's sweaty, smelly, and ugly." That person never will get into a regular gym routine, and why should they? Accept yourself and your emotional sensitivity. Find some other way to develop your body power.

Conclusion

We've covered a lot of background, and it's time to get down to the nitty-gritty. We've talked about why using mind, body, and spirit helps you to succeed with less burnout and personal sacrifice. Together, we've looked at your habits and assessed your strengths and weaknesses. We've talked in detail about what constitutes mind power, body power, and spirit power.

Here's what we discovered. Most people don't give it all they've got. Not really. They may work long hours, struggle, and sacrifice, or even give up everything to pursue a dream. When they still can't compete with others who seem to do it easily, gracefully, and painlessly, they wave their hands and say, "Well, he's a *gifted* athlete, or a *natural* salesman, or an *inspired* leader, or a *born* speaker." Dismissing "star quality" as merely talent or genius is to limit one's own potential. It lets you off the hook so you don't have to learn how to give it all you've got. But you now know how to avoid this trap.

Your mission, should you choose to accept it, is to finish this book and learn to really give it all you've got. You'll develop the resources you 're uncomfortable with as well as the ones you're comfortable with. By embracing the potential of your mind, your body, and your spirit all at once, you will not only enjoy life more, but find the star-quality performance inside you.

You can start by learning the strategies and doing the exercises in either Part III or Part IV. Which part you complete first is up to you. Part III is oriented toward finding paths to success that draw on all your strengths. If you have clear goals or ambitions you may enjoy looking up the chapters that pertain to your interests. You'll learn how to blend your comfort zone with your discomfort zone and pull ahead of the pack.

If you are a less goal-oriented person, you may want to read Part IV after Part II because it focuses on how to live a satisfying life that happens to support your successfulness. The ideas and exercises focus on day-to-day living rather than how to get ahead.

The following table summarizes the definitions of mind, body, and spirit and how to develop them.

Reference Page: Mind, Body, and Spirit Summary
(Photocopy and post this page)

What is Mind Power?	**What is Body Power?**	**What is Spirit Power?**
Free will	*Doing*	*Loving*
Choosing with your mind	Enjoying your body	Living by your values
Requires seeing as many "realities" as possible and choosing your own way.	Not just maintenance, but new physical activities and new skills.	Connecting to others. Knowing what you value; giving and receiving with love.
Whatever challenges you with new ideas and builds self-discipline.	Whatever makes you more able and more comfortable in your body.	Whatever evokes a strong emotional response in you.
Includes:	Includes:	Includes:
• Book learning (with new ideas)	• Aerobic capacity	• Love of art, music, poetry, nature
• Discussion, argument	• Strength	• Your religion
• Travel to different cultures	• Stamina	• Your politics
• Exposure to different classes, races, etc.	• Coordination	• Your values, ethics, principles
• Use of subconscious mind	• Flexibility	• Vision, mission, purpose in life
• Mastery over emotions	• Ease of motion	• Your talents, hobbies
• Positive thinking (as long as it brings you closer to reality)	• Grace	• Family, friends
• Psychological therapy (as long as it brings you closer to reality)	• Posture	• Self-esteem
	• Abdominal muscle	• Giving to others
	• Nutrition	• Beauty (clothes, makeup, furniture, decor)
	• Vitamins	
	• Water	
	• Breathing	

PART III

How to Hit Your Targets with Three Times the Punch!

Imagine an eight-year-old girl in brown ponytails playing dodgeball with a pack of kids on the blacktop of a school playground.

Looking closer you see that she has a funny sort of skip-run because her leg is a clunky, wooden artificial limb. Her jet-black eyes are riveted on the game with the life-and-death focus of an air traffic controller. When the ball comes her way, she pounces on it and twists her body to throw it before the kids nearest to her can run away. Bonk! Having hit another kid with the ball, she wins the right to enter the circle painted on the playground. The grin on her face shows the triumph she feels as she steps into the fray. Hobbling with her funny skip-run, she moves to dodge the ball. She hustles after the pack of kids, sticking her tongue out the side of her mouth with the effort, but gets left behind anyway. Exposed and slow moving, she is an easy target. Bonk! The little girl is back outside the circle after only two throws.

That little girl was me. The desire to keep up with the other kids in that dodgeball game is branded into my memory forever. More than I remember my parents' divorce, the surgeries to amputate my leg, or the first day another kid called me nigger, I remember wanting to play dodgeball and be like the other kids. More than anything, I wanted to be "normal."

With my entire eight-year-old being focused on dodgeball I thought to myself one day, "If I can't run as fast as the other kids, I have to use my brain to keep up." I watched and looked for a way. Most kids tended to run around the edges of the circle as the ball traveled back and forth through the middle. "If I ran through the center of the circle," I observed, "the running distance would be shorter, and maybe I'd keep up with the others." Although I didn't know any geometry yet, I chose to run the diameter instead of the circumference because it was shorter. I have to admit that my brilliant plan yielded only moderate success. I tended to get left behind the others less, but as a slow-moving object, other kids still found me a relatively easy target.

The real victory that day, however, was learning how to make mind and body work toward the same goal. My brain power had to compensate for my slow legs just to keep up with "normal" kids. I was forced to make mind, body, and spirit work together at an early age.

The benefits of having mind, body, and spirit working together followed me into adulthood. Later when training as a ski racer, brain power lifted me head and shoulders above my competition. I set a new standard for women in U.S. disabled skiing by training year round, training with two-legged skiers, raising my own money, and hiring my own coaches. Because I had more self-discipline and more new ideas than other women on the circuit I got more time on the snow and enough coaching to bring my physical abilities up to a world-class level.

As a ski racer I tapped into the power of the human spirit, too. Sponsoring my racing expenses was only a small part of the support given to me by the National Brotherhood of Skiers, a predominantly African-American ski association. Meeting thousands of African Americans who were educated, independent, wealthy, family-oriented skiers gave me what a lifetime of negative images on TV and the news had nearly destroyed: a sense of pride and identity as an African American. When my teammates saw thirty African Americans cheering for me at the Olympics they said, "You have an awfully large family."

"Yes, I do," I smiled.

My skiing drew on not only physical abilities, but also my mind and spirit resources, too. At eight years old I started using mind, body, and spirit just to keep up. A decade later, my philosophy of blending landed me on the winner's podium at the Olympics.

Packing mind, body, and spirit power into my punch created an unstoppable force. You will learn in chapter 10 the universal principles for unleashing your mind, body, and spirit power all at once. The chapters that follow focus on how to apply these principles to specific areas like sales, goal setting, and sports. Most of the chapters have exercises to help you immediately improve your performance. You'll probably want to read chapter 10 and then skip ahead to whichever chapters in Part III interest you most.

Facing Challenges with Mind, Body, *and* Spirit

When Jon Secada stepped out onto the stage crooning with his smooth, passionate voice I could hardly stay in my seat. I was in the live audience for the television production of the *Essence* awards in Madison Square Garden. Sinbad and Natalie Cole hosted the show with talent that included Brandy, Stevie Wonder, and Oprah Winfrey. Awards went to Janet Jackson, Colin Powell, and other less famous but equally heroic individuals. The entire show dazzled my senses. I particularly liked Jon Secada because my husband and I played Secada's "Just Another Day" over and over. A few moments into the song, however, Secada seemed to be going adrift and hesitating. Then the sound cut off entirely. Sinbad came out on stage and took Jon off to one side. Jon turned back to us and smiled. "No backup!" he explained, pointing at the empty mikes off to one side of the stage. The singers came out, the number started over, and the television audience at home would never see the goof when the show aired in several weeks.

As he sang the second time through Jon paid special attention to his backup singers. He smiled at them and at us. He seemed to be laughing at his own mistake of starting without the backup singers. Even a great voice like Secada's sounds better with backup.

Facing Challenges in Your Comfort Zone

Similarly, we tend to rely on the skills in our comfort zone as the "lead singer" in the band. Whether it's your ideas, your feelings, or your ability to take action, you probably tend to lead with certain skills when you face a challenge.

The important thing to remember, however, is that no matter how good you are at thinking, doing, or feeling, you'd perform better if you let your weaker zones sing backup. Even Jon Secada needs backup. How can your weaker zones lend extra support? Short bursts of activity outside your comfort zone can provide rest for an overworked mind, body, or spirit.

Robert Fulghum, best-selling author of *All I Really Need to Know I Learned in Kindergarten*, rests his mind by doing something physical. He says, "Productivity seems to drop rapidly after the first forty-five minutes of writing. I take frequent breaks outside to walk, chop wood, or hike. I get some of my best ideas that way."

What Fulghum learned by trial and error, scientists have confirmed through research. "For some people, the creative thinking that occurs during and after exercise is quite pronounced," says Kenneth Callen, M.D., an associate professor of psychiatry at the Oregon Health Sciences University in Portland. For example, students who participated in aerobics classes could think of more uses for an ordinary object, like a pen, than those who didn't take aerobics, according to a study by Dr. Joan Gondola of the City University of New York. Exercise actually boosts the brain's creative power.

Not only writers, but anyone who works intensively with his mind would benefit from frequent breaks. "No matter how much pressure you feel at work," says Dr. Joyce Brothers, "if you could find ways to relax for at least five minutes every hour you'd be more productive."

A highly spiritual person like Les Brown, the famous motivational speaker, needs to take a break from the crowds who want to draw on his spiritual strength. Exercise and reading offer respite from his vocation of giving his stories and himself to millions of others. It also gives him more physical and mental vitality to draw on when he returns to the stage.

Mark Allen, six-time winner of the Ironman championship triathlon

in Hawaii, remarked on the importance of taking two months off training to read books and hang out with family and friends. "Most athletes
are afraid to stop training. After two weeks, they panic because they feel
fat and out of shape. So they start training again." Most of us feel scared
and unsure outside our comfort zone so we jump right back into it.

Another reason why we find it so difficult to take breaks outside our
comfort zone is that we find it hard to believe it will help us reach our
goal. At a very primitive, subconscious level I connect more work with
more success. Intellectually I know that taking breaks is good for my
health and sanity, but I find it hard to accept—at a gut level—that
taking breaks gets me closer to my goal. A crucial element of my
philosophy is to understand that these techniques not only make you
saner but also more successful at the same time.

"In my sport," says Mark, "which requires a 2.5-mile swim, a 112-
mile bike ride, and a marathon, all of the top athletes abuse their body
in order to win." Mark Allen stayed at the top of one the most grueling
sports for so long because he allows his body to recover from the abuse
of training and competing while at the same time he restocks his
spiritual and mental tanks. He uses his spirit and mind to give his body
a much-needed rest.

Whether you lead with mind, body, or spirit, you have to pay attention to the backup roles, too. In the examples above you'll notice that
the writer took breaks on an hourly basis while the speaker took longer
breaks on a weekly or monthly basis, and the athlete rested up for two
months on an annual basis.

How you blend your breaks from your comfort zone is up to you.
Probably most superachievers find a personal rhythm of both shorter
daily breaks and longer annual breaks. The important thing is to stop
pretending you can stay in your comfort zone slugging away at your
challenges nonstop. Let your weaker zones help your stronger zone.

In his book *The Tom Peters Seminar*, Tom Peters, my favorite management consultant, puts it in perspective for the business world:

> *Insist that everyone take vacations.* When you're blessed with phenom-
> enal growth or extraordinary problems, people, especially in key posi-
> tions, tend to work thirteen-hour days six or seven days a week. They
> think they're strong, tough, invincible—and fresh as ever. They may
> be strong as oxen, but fresh? That's a bunch of baloney.

I had a good friend at McKinsey, one of the cleverest folks I know who each summer took a month's vacation. We were a macho, type-A organization. I couldn't imagine why he did it. At any rate I knew that I didn't need a month off, I of boundless energy. Then one year I spent August at a cabin on the Northern California coast. When I got back, I was immediately aware of what a burned-out shell I'd been. Let me say it—to toughen up, lighten up.

Tom Peters goes on to say that eventually you need a longer sabbatical to rekindle the creative mental energy that hits mega-home runs in the new, bonkers economy. "Been on the job for five years without a three-month (six-month) break?" asks Peters. "You're flat. Trust me."

Don't try to use the lead singer for the entire song. Even Jon Secada sounds better with backup singers. Bring in your backup talents from time to time. Your best strengths will only get better.

Facing Challenges Outside Your Comfort Zone

What happens when a body person has to get outside her comfort zone?

Diane Buchta, featured on CBS and NBC sports as the personal trainer for two triathletes who have won world championships seven times, has an unusual approach. "I needed to plan a three-hour lecture on very short notice, so I went running," she explained to me in her living room as though it made perfect sense.

"You mean, you were trying to avoid getting started?" I asked.

"Not at all! I stretch and warm up my body while focusing my mind on the class I have to teach. Then when I run, I just let the ideas flow. My mind works better that way." Research shows that exercise stimulates creative ideas in many subjects.

"Hmm," I said. "I'm not sure I could run and think at the same time."

"It takes practice," she smiled. "For any new runner it takes about three or four months to program the muscles until you don't have to think about the running. All of a sudden you get this freeing feeling."

She not only uses her body to augment her thinking skills, but incorporates physical elements into spiritual activities as well. Diane socializes with friends and business associates while walking or running together, or meandering along the beach. "Exercise is a way of communicating with my soul or with other people." Diane is in tune with her body-motivated personality and tries to keep herself moving while learning, building relationships, and even doing chores around the house: "I stretch while folding my laundry," she proclaimed. She uses her physical orientation to tackle big and small challenges outside her comfort zone.

Of course not all activities could or should be blended. Some things require total focus. Others you may simply enjoy better unblended. Blending should only be used when it reduces your overall tension, improves your performance, or both.

I asked Diane for other blending examples from her life.

"I'm very big on audiotapes. I listen to educational programs in my car. I know that isn't terribly original, but it works well for me." For body-motivated personalities, audiotapes can be a winning strategy because they allow you to keep moving—in your car, running, or in the house—while learning new ideas or enjoying fiction. Body-motivated people need to acknowledge that sitting still is not their forte.

When you have a task that is truly outside your comfort zone, you have to use skills that don't come so easily. Let your stronger skills assist your weaker ones. Diane used her body skills to make mental and social tasks more pleasant and invigorating.

Conversely, if you are a mind-motivated or a spirit-motivated person, you need to rely on your particular strengths when facing challenges outside your comfort zone. A mind-motivated person may tackle a problem using books and classes while trying to keep the time commitment to a minimum. A spirit-motivated person may need to embrace a challenge in a way that expresses his unique personality, benefits others, or involves his relationships with others.

When you are outside your comfort zone, be careful of advice from experts. Experts in any subject are usually well within their comfort zone and don't understand your problems. What excites them probably bores you to tears. You should approach the problem differently than someone who is in their comfort zone. Find an expert who sympathizes with your point of view.

For example, a body-motivated person may enjoy aerobics videos designed by the number-one aerobics instructor in the country. Conversely, a spirit-centered person may find those steps too difficult and the perfect bodies of the instructors intimidating. A spirit-centered person will probably relate more to Susan Powter who has been over-weight, hates complicated exercises, and shares her personal story. Another good bet would be Richard Simmons, who focuses more on fun than bodies in his *Sweating with the Oldies* tape. Find experts who share your comfort zone.

For more ideas on how to create activities that bridge out from your comfort zone into another arena consult the inventory in chapter 18. You can look up activities that bridge across mind/spirit, or body/spirit, or mind/body. Look up the two sections that include your comfort zone to identify activities that are enjoyable yet challenging. More discussion on this subject is also included in Part IV where we work on blending more mind, body, and spirit activities into your daily life.

Facing a Challenge with the Power of Synergy

You may recall the story about Michael, the premed student from chapter 6. Taking breaks could have reduced his total study time by rejuvenating his mind power with body and spirit activities. The power of synergy, however, goes further than just using body and spirit to help the mind. For a mental goal, synergy means applying body and spirit resources directly to the problem in addition to the mind.

In one of my workshops, a woman immediately grasped this concept of synergy and packing all your resources into your punch. Furrowing her brow she asked, "I'm a schoolteacher. I can't do that all the time. I'd be too tired."

Of course she's right. You can't punch at everything with the full power of your mind, body, and spirit. I can't. I target that force only at goals that are important to me. It could be something you are struggling to achieve now using only one or two resources.

Developing your resources differs from *using* your resources. Developing your mind, body, and spirit resources on a day-to-day basis is a good idea. Chapter 20 shows you how to expand your resources continuously as part of your daily life.

The techniques we are discussing in this chapter, giving it all you've got here and now, are meant to be used judiciously to go after what you want out of life. Burning up your resources willy-nilly, spending them before you can restore them, won't work.

As corporations demand more and more from people, the need for a balance between pushing hard and restoring energy becomes more apparent. Says management consultant Peter Senge, "Ironically conflicts between work and family may be one of the primary ways through which traditional organizations limit their effectiveness and ability to learn. One cannot build a learning organization on a foundation of broken homes and strained personal relationships."

The process of synergy, of using everything inside you, can be exhausting. It should be reserved for the greatest challenges you want to tackle in life. My question for the schoolteacher who didn't want to put mind, body, and spirit into her teaching day in and day out is: What do you want to give your all to doing? If you can't find something worth giving your all for, it's hard to be successful or sane.

I'll close this chapter with one of the best stories I heard about the synergy of mind, body, and spirit. Mark Allen told me "more than I thought I would," about his experience of using mind and spirit in competition. "I've been in triathlon for fourteen years," he explained. "It wasn't long after I started that I realized I wasn't as physically talented as the other guys. It's a plain fact. If you stuck me on a treadmill and did the VL2 max, I wouldn't be the best. I asked myself, how am I going to make up for that?

"The biggest race in our sport is the Ironman in Hawaii every October. It's a long day: 2.4 miles swimming, 112 miles biking, and then a marathon. No lunch breaks, no taking naps, nothing. It takes over eight hours to finish.

"Dave Scott was the king of that race. At other races he was nothing spectacular, but he would get off the plane in Hawaii and his strength just came out." Mark spread his arms wide and shrugged his shoulders.

"Whenever I arrived in Hawaii, it was more intimidating than any other place. So I adopted this mental mantra, 'Be like Dave. Be like Dave.' Each year I went, I tried to imitate his strength and tap into the same things that motivated him.

"I went six times and performed anywhere from mediocre to disastrous. I even ended up in the hospital. But there was still this shred inside me that believed I could put together a good race. Even if it wasn't enough to win, I wanted to do it.

"In the winter of 1989 I took a hard look at myself and saw three things. First, I wasn't matching the desire to win with the reality of what it took in terms of physical training. Secondly, I realized that every thought I was feeding myself was negative, like 'I'm too tired today, I can't get the workout done.' Thirdly, this 'Be like Dave' thing wasn't working. I needed to figure out how to be like Mark and figure out what my own strength is.

"For a couple of days I tried to feed all positive thoughts into my brain. When I would start to say something negative to myself, I would say something positive even if I didn't believe it.

"Even after a couple of days there was a big shift. In training things got easier to do. I didn't feel overwhelmed by the whole task. I kept up the positive thoughts for the whole year." Working on his mental attitude toward training helped Mark to attain the level of physical training necessary to be at the top. But the problem of finding his unique spiritual strengths remained.

"I was less sure of how to remind myself of my own strengths," Mark told me while sitting on my patio in San Diego. "Then, on one of my last practice runs I found it. There's this stretch along the lagoon in Cardiff where I always feel at peace with myself. When I am feeling good, it makes me feel better. If I am feeling lousy, it becomes okay to feel lousy on that stretch.

"I stopped and grabbed a handful of the marsh grasses saying, 'I can look at these in Hawaii to remind myself of this feeling of peace.' I didn't even tell my wife I was doing this. She would have thought I was crazy.

"Once I was in Hawaii, I went to a small church near the ocean along the course. I'm not really a church guy, but this place seemed special. It's right next to a sacred place where the Hawaiians do a lot of ceremonies. The energy there was strong.

"I went there at sunset, when the light comes through this little window, and walked up to the altar with my little reeds. Placing them there I said, 'Let it be okay that I come with my strength this year.'

"I sat down on the benches and closed my eyes. Then suddenly I felt like the island was talking to me: 'You can have what you came here for.' Immediately I start thinking: 'great! I'm going to win this thing.'

"But the voice continued, saying, 'It's going to take courage.' I didn't know what that meant, but I figured I would find out soon enough.

"The race began. Dave and I were together coming out of the water.

We were together getting off the bikes. We were together step for step on the run. Initially it was fast, too fast. Then it slowed down. It was cat and mouse. We hit the turnaround with only ten miles to go. One of us was going to win. Each mile we went faster and faster.

"I noticed that Dave was getting tired because he was slowing down on the uphills. Whenever he slowed, I slowed just a bit more. I felt good, and I didn't want him to know.

"At one point I thought, 'I can win this!' But at the exact same moment my legs started to hurt so badly that I didn't know if I could keep going. I was struggling within myself thinking: 'I know I can win, but I don't know if I can keep going.'

"Then the image in the church came back to me, and I understood what it meant to have courage. I had to have the courage to take it all the way to the finish line. On the last long uphill I pulled away from Dave and won by a little less than a minute. What a tiny, tiny fraction over the course of eight hours! I won my first Ironman competition at last.

"For me it was a process that took seven years to get right. Any time you ask for greatness you are going to be challenged. For me there is always one point in the race that I don't know if I can finish. That's like the last and ultimate challenge I have to resolve.

"My drive to win gets me right up to that final challenge. At that final stumbling block you feel as though you're bouncing off it, pushing and persisting. However, getting through that doorway always requires taking a deep breath and letting go. Letting the greatness that is inside come out.

"Letting go means doing it without worrying whether you'll win. It means not doing it for anyone but yourself. Then you can let the greatness out for the simple reason that it's in you to give. That's what it took me seven years to understand."

Exercise One: Taking Short Breaks

IDEAS FOR SHORT BURSTS OF BODY ACTIVITY
ESPECIALLY FOR MIND AND SPIRIT PEOPLE

- Get a timer, a quiet one, to put on your desk to remind you to walk around the building every ninety minutes.
- Keep a large glass of water on your desk. Not only is drinking it good for you, but it will also give you a natural rhythm of exercise breaks through trips to the rest room.
- Keep a list of exercises you can do at your desk. Magazines often run articles with a list of ten or so exercises. I have included my own list of ideas, called Desk-ercise, in appendix B. Or make up your own.

IDEAS FOR SHORT BURSTS OF SPIRIT POWER
ESPECIALLY FOR MIND AND BODY PEOPLE

- Think of ways to pamper yourself a little more while you work. Can you bring in designer coffee? Get a new footrest? If you are the boss can you hire a masseuse to give everyone a five-minute back rub?
- Take your work to your favorite coffee shop or restaurant for a couple of hours.
- Stop and think about whatever you love most about your job. Or focus on what you love about your long-term career goals.
- Spend five minutes counting your blessings. Your family, friends, food, health, education, free country, etc.
- Mind-centered people who excel in self-discipline have a tendency to drive themselves with "shoulds" and "ought tos." Better to stop once a day and try to think about why you really do the work. Put a sign over your desk that says: WHY AM I HERE? Or better yet, put up a picture or phrase that answers the question.
- Pin up a picture or find an object that symbolizes your mission or the meaning of your vocation. Looking at it during the day will give you small spiritual jolts throughout the day.

- If you have a very private office, get a candle and light it once a day. Staring into the flame can be very soothing to the mind. In addition it can be a meditative tool for counting your blessings or looking into your own soul.

IDEAS FOR MOMENTS OF MIND POWER
ESPECIALLY FOR BODY OR SPIRIT PEOPLE

- Think about what you have learned today or what you could learn today.
- Spend five minutes assessing your priorities. Are you working on first things first?
- Take a five-minute break to sit down and think about whether there is a better way to approach your project or your work.
- Look up the name of someone who knows more than you do about something you are interested in. Call that person and ask permission to interview them for fifteen minutes.
- Buy a book or check one out at the library. Browse it.
- Ask several people what is the most interesting book they've read in the last year. Let them tell you about it. Then you can talk about it and you don't have to read it. You won't be the only one using this short cut, trust me.

Exercise Two: How to Remind Yourself to Take Breaks

When you get focused on working in your comfort zone, stopping and doing something outside your comfort zone doesn't come naturally. You need something to remind yourself periodically throughout the day. Remembering to take breaks is more than half the battle.

I've created a special reference page for you to hang near your desk or wherever you work to remind you to tune into your less-used zones from time to time. When you see it, let it be a reminder to stop and get out of your comfort zone for a moment or two (or into your comfort zone for a break).

What have you done for you . . . lately?

FOR YOUR BODY

Get up and move a little bit!
Drink water.

FOR YOUR SOUL

Ask yourself:
Why are you here?
Count your blessings.

FOR YOUR MIND

Put first things first.
Ask: What have you learned
today?

Or, create your own reminder sheet highlighting your discomfort zones and displaying the break ideas *you* like most. (I suppose you spirit people will make your own, whereas the mind people will enjoy saving time by just photocopying the page provided!)

Exercise Three: Using the Power of Synergy

To get help in finding ways to apply mind, body, and spirit synergy to a particular goal, turn to the exercises in chapter 12.

CHAPTER 11

Reduce Stress, Produce More!

A s I walked into my first exam at Oxford University my palms were sweating, my head ached, and my muscles felt weak and shaky. Although I had graduated magna cum laude from Harvard, the pressure of being examined on two entire years of studying at once was new to me.

To make matters worse, I didn't feel at all sure that I would be able to pass the exam. Oxford professors had been telling me how dumb I was from the day I arrived. Many Dons, as Oxford professors are called, aren't very comfortable with women or blacks at their university. But they reserve a deeper dislike for "rich American Rhodes scholars" or "Rhodents." They consider us to be jocks or playboys rather than serious students.

As a disabled black woman from modest means it was new to me to be discriminated against for being wealthy, athletic, and American. It would have been funny if I hadn't gotten so near to despair. For the first time in my life my usual sunshine attitude was wearing down in the face of open hostility.

"I remember you," a professor told me while pointing a finger in my face. I had already been rejected by the economics department once and was reapplying. I stayed after his class to ask him whether I could attend while my application was pending.

"You can come to class," he said with a smile that looked more like a sneer. "But you'll never get into the department anyway." I almost expected him to add, "I'll get you my pretty! And your little dog, too!"

With my usual bullheadedness, however, I stuck in the classes, found a few faculty members to support me, and gained admittance to the program for a master's degree in economics. I researched my thesis and tried to stay out of trouble. I unlearned the writing style I developed at Harvard and learned a new, English way of analyzing facts and figures.

Finally after two years in Oxford I had won the right to sit in a qualifying exam covering the entire subjects of macroeconomics and labor economics. I had never taken an exam in England before. If I didn't pass this one, I would have to leave without a degree. I had been fighting to study graduate economics at Oxford for two years, and it all came down to two three-hour tests.

Dressed in the required black cap and gown with a white shirt and a black bow at my neck, I cycled down the narrow alleys between the fifteenth-century stone buildings. Gargoyles on the rooftops looked down jeering, taunting, and laughing at my predicament. I parked my cycle in front of the "Exam Schools," a cavernous old building that seemed to block out the sun. Though I had taken almost a hundred exams in my life, never had I experienced the terror I felt as I walked into that building, found my room, and took a seat.

My eyes blurred as the proctor explained the time allotment and the general procedures. I felt my bowels shift and wondered whether I could wait until the tests were handed out before asking permission to use the bathroom. When I finally did get permission, my legs felt wobbly and weak.

Never before had I felt so much stress while in a high-pressure situation. At the Olympics I channeled my nervous energy into excitement. I danced and sang a Patti LaBelle song in the gondola on the way up. "I'm so excited, I just can't hide it." I hummed the tune and flung my arms wide to soak up the crisp air and the panoramic view of the Alps. Using my LaserWalk technique (appendix A), I focused my mental and physical energies into a peak performance while staying calm.

I also stayed calm before the notorious Rhodes scholarship interviews. I did what I always did facing competitive pressure: relaxed my body with stretching exercises and used the LaserWalk technique to focus my mind. Being able to switch on my peak alertness, peak personality, and peak intellect helped me to sail through the cocktail parties, the state interviews, and the regional interviews with relative ease.

Although I had honed my techniques for staying cool under pressure, the Oxford exams put me through the wringer as never before. In the past, three-hour exams had flown by. This time, however, was like running a marathon. Still feeling sick, I visited the bathroom three more times, which cut into my exam time significantly. Somehow I managed to finish the exam before the time ran out.

In preparation for the exam I used my LaserWalk mind-focusing technique as I had before in job interviews, exams, and at the Olympics. If nothing else, it helped me hold it together enough to finish the exam and then finish the next exam despite the fact that my body was falling apart. As weak as my peak performance was, I gave it.

A week later I was notified of the result: pass! I had survived the ordeal. Not only did I pass the qualifying exam, but I continued on to finish my research and earn an M.Litt. degree despite the professor's predictions to the contrary.

This story raises a lot of questions in my mind: Why did I experience more stress in the Oxford exams than I did competing in the Olympics? Why did I experience so much more stress in the Oxford exams compared to exams at Harvard? Why did the stress attack my body, weakening my muscles and giving me the runs?

And the most important question: Can you avoid stress and its physical symptoms in your life without dropping out of your profession? In other words, can you train yourself to respond to stress like I did at the Olympics instead of the way I responded to Oxford University? And the answer is: Yes! Yes! Yes! If only I had known then what you are going to learn in this chapter!

I have fantastic news about stress: Developing your mind, body, and spirit power according to the Succeeding Sane model will allow you to handle more challenges with less stress and wear and tear on your body! This chapter, the art of handling stress, goes to the heart of the issues for succeeding sane. If I get no other idea across in this book, I want to convince you of one thing: You can't be very successful in sports, business, academia, or politics without facing potentially stress-ful situations on a daily basis. You have to fight battles if you want to win wars.

○

Super-achievement can cause stress and burnout . . . or be rejuvenating . . . it's your choice. Really.

○

Applying the ideas and following the exercises in this book will not only make you more successful at whatever you do, it will also help you to cope with the accompanying stress much better. Thus, you don't even have to read this chapter in order to blunt the impact of stress in your life. It's a package deal. It comes with the philosophy of blending.

However, if you want to understand *why* and *how* it works, read on! A better understanding of your stress reactions will help you to apply my philosophy in a way that more effectively combats burnout.

Furthermore, cultivating an understanding of the facts will convince you once and for all of the importance of developing your blending habits. You'll do it better when you believe it. So read on. As Tod Barnhart, author of *Rituals of Wealth*, says, "A ritual is a habit backed by belief."

What Is Stress?

Stressful situations—robbery at gunpoint, exams, or negotiating a multimillion-dollar deal—trigger our deeply rooted fight-or-flight in-stinct. Your body releases hormones to kick off a chain reaction affect-ing blood flow, blood sugar, breathing, heart rate, and even sweat glands. This ancient physical reflex provides us with the energy to meet a crisis.

Our bodies release signals that divert energy from the immune sys-tem and other regenerative processes to prepare us to face our foes. It is almost as if Captain Kirk from *Star Trek* ordered the power diverted from life-support systems to the shields or photon torpedoes during a crisis.

In some ways this stress reaction is healthy. We need to mobilize our energies to tackle challenges, to stretch ourselves and grow. Too much stress, however, can literally kill you. When the effectiveness of your immune system is reduced for prolonged periods, it's like open season on your body.

Imagining problems before they actually happen, as I did at Oxford, increases stress beyond necessary levels. Whenever we feel anxiety about something that may happen in the future like getting laid off or breaking up with a lover, our stress reaction can be just as intense as if the situation had already occurred.

Over a prolonged period, this state of readiness causes physical wear and tear as well as leaving us more vulnerable to relatively minor accidents and illnesses from pneumonia to heart attack. The state of total exhaustion caused by long periods of stress is often called burnout.

When I felt my body falling apart during my Oxford exams, it was the result of too much stress. Living in a state of fight or flight readiness for two years left my body weakened and sickly. It was as though I had been physically beaten by my fear of failing the qualifying exam as well as my anxiety about being a black, female, American Rhodes scholar in an ancient, ivory-tower world. The energy required to study and pass my classes was minor compared to the energy I was wasting by living in fear of the Oxford Dons. Excess stress weakened my muscles, my health, and my performance.

Excess stress and burnout block the path toward succeeding sane for many people. Some never strive for greatness because deep down they fear that achieving more must be accompanied by more stress. It's as if each of us is climbing a ladder toward personal or professional success. When we start to feel each step becoming more tiring and more stressful, a little voice in our head says, "Gosh that was hard! If the last two steps were that hard, what will the next two steps be like? I sure don't want to climb all the way up if it is this hard already!" So we slow down or get off the ladder and try to be content.

Avoiding stress, however, doesn't work. I know, I tried that strategy, too. The only way to avoid stress is to avoid growth. But without growth, it's hard for anyone to be content.

The key to succeeding sane is managing stress rather than trying to avoid it. Many of us think of stress as a chain reaction that is outside our control as shown in the first chart on page 139. (1) Stressful things happen; (2) The fight or flight hormones are triggered; and (3) the body

Overview of the Stress Chain Reaction

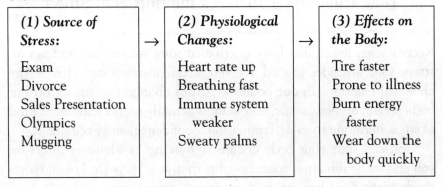

(1) Source of Stress:		(2) Physiological Changes:		(3) Effects on the Body:
Exam Divorce Sales Presentation Olympics Mugging	→	Heart rate up Breathing fast Immune system 　weaker Sweaty palms	→	Tire faster Prone to illness Burn energy 　faster Wear down the 　body quickly

becomes worn down, sick, and exhausted. Like rats trapped on a wheel we run as fast as we can, but the stress just keeps hitting us.

However, this chain reaction and the damage it causes is not inevitable. You can minimize the damage of stress by using your mind, body, and spirit to break the chain at each point. Developing body power helps your body to resist the physical ravages of stress. Using mind power you can actually change the hormonal reactions that are triggered so that they are more helpful and less harmful. Spirit power, or tuning in to your unique temperament, values, and mission, can eliminate several major stresses at the source.

I can hardly wait to share with you the research that explains how mind, body, and spirit power reduces or eliminates the impact of stress, freeing you to achieve peak performance with joy and laughter.

Use Your Mind, Body, and Spirit to Break the Chain Reaction

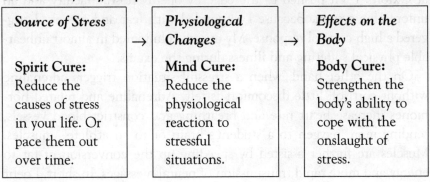

Source of Stress		Physiological Changes		Effects on the Body
Spirit Cure: Reduce the causes of stress in your life. Or pace them out over time.	→	**Mind Cure:** Reduce the physiological reaction to stressful situations.	→	**Body Cure:** Strengthen the body's ability to cope with the onslaught of stress.

How Mind Power Reduces the Impact of Stress

Recent scientific studies have uncovered some astounding findings on stress: Our attitudes toward a given stress situation can change the chemical reactions in our bodies and thus change the impact on our bodies. Fear, anxiety, anger, and sadness actually trigger a different kind of stress hormone than determination, confidence, and excitement.

"You can start your body chemistry moving in whatever direction you choose by directing your thoughts that way," says Dr. Loehr, sports psychologist for Olympic gold medalists, tennis stars, and golf pros. "Equally important, the more you practice this skill, the better you become at it."

Isn't that amazing? Dr. Loehr has analyzed the literature on the hormones released by people under pressure from groups as diverse as Norwegian army paratroopers, U.S. Navy recruits, and college students during exams. All the studies found high levels of adrenaline (epinephrine) associated with those who performed well. Poor performance, on the other hand, tended to be linked with high levels of a different hormone called cortisol.

As cortisol increases we tend to feel irritation, discomfort, and misery. High cortisol levels are a signal that we are reaching the edge of our coping ability. It means that the stress is becoming excessive. Chronically high cortisol levels are associated with depression, neurosis, and even anorexia. Since cortisol is one of the principal hormones responsible for suppressing the immune system, triggering it also makes people more susceptible to colds, infection, and other ailments.

For me this explains perfectly why I was so miserable in my exams at Oxford. I felt pushed to the edge by openly hostile faculty and an unforgiving system. Because I responded with fear and anxiety I triggered a high cortisol response. My misery culminated in almost unbearable physical suffering and illness during the exams.

On the other hand, when a stressful situation triggers adrenaline without cortisol, little discomfort is felt. Adrenaline and related hormones increase heart rate and breathing and constrict blood vessels, sending more oxygen to a student's brain or to an athlete's muscles. Muscles are further assisted by speeding up the conversion of fat to energy and more rapid transmission of neural messages. In short, Loehr tells us that adrenaline can help a person under pressure to function at a heightened intensity.

This correlates perfectly with how I normally react to stress. At the Olympics I felt excitement, comfort, and anticipation in the face of competition. I can remember wrestling with my anxiety and using the LaserWalk to put it aside. In the end I skied better than my best, provoking one of my teammates to confess years later, "I was really surprised you beat me in Austria. I didn't think you had it in you."

Since we can, to some extent, control whether we respond to stress with a sense of challenge and anticipation rather than fear and anxiety, we can influence whether our hormones alleviate or intensify our suffering. Learning positive thinking skills like writing affirmations, visualizing success, and seeking out role models can actually transform your body chemistry and therefore your experience of performing under pressure. In addition to changing the direction of your stress chemistry, your mind can help by limiting the intensity of the physiological reaction.

Just because something stressful happens doesn't mean your heart rate has to increase or that your blood pressure has to rise. Back when we wore buffalo skins and wielded clubs, summoning our physical energy in a crisis made sense. Our primitive reaction to any threat was going to be physical: Run away or stand and fight.

In today's world, however, many crisis situations require a less physical response like making a decision, gathering more information, or simply waiting for the right opportunity to act. In these situations, being able to stay calm, breathe normally, and keep your immune system functioning to avoid illness would be more help than a primitive stress reaction.

I asked Dr. Pat Daily, the renowned heart surgeon, how he handled the stress of life-and-death operations day after day.

"I'm very low key," he said. "You could take my pulse from beginning to end of a surgery and it wouldn't change." What is his secret? "We have a good team. Everybody knows exactly what to do because we've done it so many times before." Dr. Daily focuses on the routine rather than emphasizing the life-and-death aspects. "Playing classical music during surgery helps. Also, we talk about other things besides the surgery. Sometimes we even joke around. We stay very relaxed.

"I've seen other surgeons come out soaking wet," Dr. Daily told me.

"The hat, the gown, everything." He shrugged. "They just have a different style."

Call it a different style if you want. Personally, I'd rather have my heart cut open by someone who is relaxed.

I also have experienced a sense of limiting the intensity of my stress. At the Olympics I remember repeating to myself over and over "it's just another race." In many ways I missed the excitement of the flags, the event, and the crowds until it was all over because I tried not to think about that. I focused on the routine, the snow, and my skis in order to stay as relaxed as possible.

Dr. Loehr, however, cautions that eliminating all negative emotions can sometimes backfire. In an experiment where some hospital patients were given relaxation therapy before an operation, they experienced more anxiety upon entering surgery than those who had not been relaxed. Perhaps it is better to work through anxieties and redirect our fears to create positive energy instead of trying to eradicate them. Many athletes and movie stars claim to need a certain amount of nervousness to perform at their best.

"Feeling pressure is good," Bruce Jenner, Olympic gold medal decathlon winner, told me. "It means you care."

With practice you may be able to limit the intensity of your stress response. However, no stress at all probably won't work.

In addition to redirecting your stress or limiting its intensity, you can use your mind to limit the duration of your stress. Imagining terrible things beforehand and stewing in your juices afterward uses up physical energy you can't spare. My aunt Pearl had a needlepoint picture in her bathroom that sums it up: "Worrying is just praying for something you don't want."

It is quite clear that the mind has a tremendous effect on how we handle stress. But can we learn new thought reflexes? Dr. Loehr's research and his experience in personal practice makes him passionate: "Control the direction and content of your thoughts, and you will exert considerable control over how you feel."

Dr. Loehr cites numerous studies that show such responses can be learned. Animals exposed to manageable levels of stress at intervals that allowed them to recover actually developed larger adrenal glands. Other studies demonstrated that too much stress, too little stress, or prolonged stress were not effective in promoting a better chemical response, i.e., high adrenaline with low cortisol levels.

"From all the available research, the ideal toughening process is intermittent exposure to stress followed by well-defined, regular periods of recovery," concludes Dr. Loehr. For recovery from stress he recommends anything that makes you laugh, fosters positive thoughts, or strengthens your body such as yoga, funny movies, walking, swimming, or positive visualization.

Using Your Mind to Reduce Stress

"If my reaction is a reflex," you may well ask, "how can I stop it? It happens before I even think about it." Reflexes can be trained. You can train your self-defense reflexes against muggers by going to a class in which you go through the moves. You begin to imagine yourself in a situation of attack reacting with strength, confidence, and the right moves. By practicing and imagining your defense reflexes, you retrain them. Your physiological defense reflex can be retrained in the same way.

RETRAINING YOUR REFLEXES

Step one: First observe yourself reacting and look honestly at what you do. Imagine yourself in a situation recently that caused you stress such as public speaking, a first date, or a job interview. Did you have sweaty palms, faster heart rate, or other stress symptoms? Think about what you did that contributed to your stress reaction. What were you thinking about?

Step two: Now imagine yourself in that same situation relaxed and breathing normally, with only the energy you need—nothing extra. Imagine yourself from beginning to end staying calm, confident, and in control. Taking time to relive your stress reaction and practice a more positive, relaxed, or humorous reaction to a difficult situation will eventually change how you respond.

What are you thinking about that is different? Sometimes I try making myself laugh to relieve the tension. Other times I mentally thank my body for trying to give me extra energy, but tell it that I don't need the adrenaline rush.

What can you do differently? You may want to go to the restroom and stretch or do push-ups to get rid of the extra energy your body is giving you with the adrenaline. Try standing straighter and looking more confident, even if you don't feel it.

STOPPING THE STRESS-CALATION

Retraining your reflexes is a good start, but what can you do when you feel your stress reaction already kicking in and you want to stop it?

Visualization can provide first aid. When you feel your fight-or-flight reaction kicking in, pick up a simple object like an apple or a paper clip. Look at it for a moment or two, then close your eyes and imagine the object. Studies show that this simple trick has a calming influence on the brain and body.

Next, give yourself a cheer for noticing. Seeing what is happening and expressing the desire to stop it is nine-tenths of the battle. Take a few moments to assess what you are thinking about, what you are doing, and what is causing your stress. Of what are you afraid? Are you angry? Try sitting down, closing your eyes, and acknowledging the legitimacy of your feelings. You have a right to feel the way you do.

Then tell your body that you want to have normal breathing, normal blood flow, and normal blood sugar levels anyway. Tell your body that you are no longer a caveman or cavewoman so you can rise to all your challenges without so much adrenaline. You can feel angry without having steam pouring out of your ears, your heart pounding, and blood vessels throbbing.

My own method for performance under pressure, the LaserWalk, contains many of the elements that help break the stress chain: visualization, positive self-suggestion, and self-hypnosis. Look it up in the appendix of the book and begin to use it on a regular basis to combat your stress reflex.

Now that I understand the physiology of stress I also take time to meditate on strengthening my immune system when I am in a prolonged period of stress. When I am on the road speaking, for example, my body redirects energy out of normal regenerative processes to increase the physical and emotional energy I have to give on stage. To avoid getting sick, I have to regularly remind my body to return my life-support systems to full power. Instead of feeling hyperalert, I relax a little more and leave some energy for my immune system.

I have meditated on this so many times now that I have a shorthand for it. In my mind's eye there is a stairway to the basement and a series of circuit-breaker switches on the wall. When I sense that my immune system is off, I go down and flip the switch back on. Sometimes under heavy stress, I blow my fuse three or four times a day. I know my meditation is working when my body relaxes a little bit, my heart rate calms down, and my body lets the energy flow back into maintenance. I can feel the difference.

How Body Power Reduces the Effects of Stress

The mind, however, is not the only factor that determines how well our body chemistry responds to stress.

Physical fitness (or body power in my lingo) also plays a key role in determining whether we have stress with or without suffering. As we described above, cortisol hormones are associated with emotional and physical misery whereas adrenaline hormones are not. Dr. Loehr's research shows that physically fit individuals are more able to:

- Sustain adrenaline-induced, high metabolic rates for longer periods.
- Delay cortisol responses longer.
- Reduce cortisol levels rapidly after it has been released.

In plain English that means greater fitness makes stress easier to take. Even though you may not be doing physical work, stressful situations take a toll on your body just the same. As the body releases adrenaline and other hormones, your heart rate goes up, your blood sugar rises, and a host of other reactions are triggered. It's hard work.

Your hormones don't care whether your heart, lungs, and muscles are used to working hard or not. If you are out of shape, they push you anyway. Although you may not be doing anything more than sitting at home worrying about how to find a job, your body gets run down as though you had been out running marathons.

When your body can't take the workout any more it starts releasing cortisol, which makes you feel depressed, achy, and miserable. This increasing feeling of discomfort is your body's way of telling you to stop: The stress has become excessive. Out of shape people get that "give up" feeling too soon, probably before they have found options, help, and answers.

Body power allows you to take more stress—be it mental, physical, or emotional—without hurting yourself. The stronger your heart, lungs, and muscles are, the longer you can stand pushing them harder with adrenaline to give you heightened levels of alertness, intensity, or energy without distress. You can stand being keyed up long enough to solve your problem.

Furthermore, Dr. Loehr says that building physical fitness helps to shorten your recovery time. Your body can disperse the stress-related hormones more quickly and be ready for the next battle. Whether you are a corporate executive dealing with rapidly changing global markets, a basketball player in the third quarter, or a working mother at 5 P.M., a faster recovery time allows you to move on quickly to the next challenge.

You can also use your body movements to direct your hormonal reaction to stress. When you stand up straight, act confident, or smile you may begin to convince your body to produce less cortisol and more adrenaline, thereby accessing more energy with less pain.

Just as your emotions lead to actions like sagging shoulders, lowered eyes, or tense facial muscles, your actions can affect your emotions. It goes both ways. Whether or not you feel confident, going through the motions can start a positive cycle of stronger emotions, good hormonal response, and less pain. Training your body to respond positively to stress is just as important as training your mental reflexes to respond to stress.

Whereas old-fashioned workaholics impressed the boss with dark circles under their eyes from late nights at work; endless nights out with clients; and a hard-drinking, heavy-smoking, tough image, today's high achievers do only what is necessary to win. If they carve out some free time, they will spend it playing tennis, reading nineteenth-century French literature, or spending time with family rather than putting in unnecessary work hours. They give themselves a chance to recover from periods of stress.

Above all, real superachievers are good at building the physical robustness that helps heal the damage caused by stress. They exercise, keep their weight down, and get seven or eight hours of sleep on average.

Safi Qureshey, chief executive of AST Research, relies on sheer physical stamina. As a model of today's Superexec he leaps over hemispheres in a single bound; makes more powerful decisions than the mainframe computers he builds; and fields faxes from time zones around the world.

After a ten-day trade mission to Beijing with Commerce Secretary Ron Brown, Qureshey told *Fortune* magazine several years ago, he immediately hopped a flight to Europe where he spent a week with customers and sales reps in six countries from Spain to Sweden, plus an AST factory in Ireland. Catnaps in rigid airport seats are perhaps one secret to his seemingly limitless energy and drive. By 7 A.M. the day after he returned to California, he was at his desk. Well, near it; he doesn't sit much. He likens competition with IBM to riding a tiger: "To get off one of those cats is to be eaten alive."

Executives like Queresy don't view exercise or rest as "personal" activities, but rather as essential to maintaining the high-performance levels to which they are committed. They know that a human being cannot work at their best in crisis situations, meet deadlines around the world, and hand out decisions on which millions of dollars ride without taking care of the body. The more stress you want to put on it, the more crucial it is to have an equal and opposite force of physical healing, rest, and recovery.

ARE YOU STRONG ENOUGH FOR YOUR STRESS?

- Think about how often you encounter stressful situations that get your heart going, breathing rate up, and tense muscles.
- Are your heart, lungs, and circulation strong enough to sustain it?
- Write down a plan to exercise your cardio-vascular system at least as often as you stress it.

More Spirit Power Means Less Stress

Many articles treat stress as merely the result of too much mental, physical, or emotional work. *Newsweek,* for example, ran a cover story called "Burnout" with this lead in:

> We're fried by work. Frazzled by lack of time. Technology hasn't made our lives better, just busier. No wonder a quarter of us say that we're exhausted. We need to chill out before we hit the BREAKING POINT.

With interviews, *Newsweek* paints a picture of techno-stress: mobile phones, faxes, and E-mail demanding ever faster responses; plus downsizing-stress: too few to do the work of many. The cure seems obvious: Reduce work hours, take a vacation, or disconnect the modem.

Yet, this approach to stress ignores the fact that some entrepreneurs, farmers, or philanthropists quite happily work sixteen-hour days for long periods. I did it for months at a time while on the economic team in the White House. When a Ralph Nader or a Donald Trump is pursuing their vision they seem to have almost limitless energy. Why can some people work so hard and stay enthusiastic while others crumble under far less strain?

According to Suzanne Ouellette, a psychologist at the City University of New York, "Stressful jobs are not equally stressful to all people." A balance of feeling committed, challenged, and in control in the workplace allows people to work hard and perform at their peak much longer and with less risk of burnout.

Developing and using spirit power can eliminate two major sources of stress that bog down the vast majority of people.

- *Feelings of purposelessness or meaninglessness in your work.* It's not just the invasion of faxes, cellular phones, beepers, and computers that makes us feel stressed—it is the pointlessness of it all!
- *Going against your grain, temperament, and values.* Working in an environment that is too hectic or too boring causes stress. Working in an organization that requires you to regularly bend or break your principles is even more damaging.

Let's talk about each of these spirit-based stressors in more detail.

A feeling of purposelessness or meaninglessness in your work is such a serious stress that it can kill you. According to Deepak Chopra, a pioneer of mind-body medicine, "More people in the Western world die on Monday morning than at any other time." What a tremendous feat it is that the cells of your body can tell the time and the day of the week and schedule your demise accordingly. Can you imagine hating your job so much that the mere thought of it kills you one morning?

This insight provides a big clue as to why some people can work much harder than others with less stress. You can have a happier, healthier stress response when you love your work, make a difference, or experience a sense of purpose in life.

To its own surprise, the Association for the Advancement of Medicine found in a recent study that churchgoers experience far less disease and live longer than their secular counterparts. Although the study concluded that there was no obvious reason why this should be true, the answer seems clear to me. Having a sense of mission, a purpose, or more meaning in your life eliminates one of the leading causes of stress in modern life. With less stress and anxiety, your body can put its energy into the immune system and other regenerative processes. Leaning on the Lord can be scientifically linked to better physical health! You don't have to be religious, however, to put more meaning in your life.

HOW TO REDUCE THE STRESS OF MEANINGLESSNESS

What can you do to treat stress from feeling purposeless? Good news for succeeding sane aficionados: Pulling back on the throttle won't necessarily reduce stress. Getting an easier job, moving to the country, or otherwise opting out of the fast track won't help *unless you find a way to put more meaning into your life at the same time.*

For many years I was one of the world's greatest achievement junkies. Olympic medals, degrees from Harvard and Oxford, a Rhodes scholarship—if there was a prize to be won I was there. After getting married and living in Europe for a while, I thought I could return to America with a slower-paced lifestyle and smell the roses a bit more. Instead of applying to work on Wall Street again, I signed up for a sales job at IBM.

"It will be a saner lifestyle," I thought. "Nine to five with great maternity benefits. And I can still work with big business, learn sales and management, and stretch myself professionally." But within a year or two, I grew restless for more challenge, more creativity, and more growth. Although I didn't know it at the time, what I needed was not less work or more work, but more purpose to my work. As an inspirational speaker and writer, I get a great deal of satisfaction out of touching the lives of so many people. I also put more meaning into my life by using my job flexibility to spend more time with my daughter Darcy in the first years of her life.

EXERCISE #1: ASK THE RIGHT QUESTIONS

At a recent conference in Dallas, a woman was asking me about how to find her sense of purpose, her place in the circle of life.

"There may not be a quick and easy answer," I told her. "But if you are asking the question, that is the first step. For so many years, I never asked that question in earnest." Once you start asking, looking for answers, trying out things and listening to your heart, you will eventually find the answer. Be patient with yourself. Have faith that the answer is coming. And in the meantime, keep your day job!

EXERCISE #2: REFILL YOUR SPIRITUAL TANKS

As you look for your mission, try to include things in your life that refill your spiritual tanks. I love to be outdoors so when I am responsible for watching my daughter, I take her outside.

For a simple, time-efficient boost to the spirit, "I just look up at the sky," says Blair Saddler, the CEO of Children's Hospital in San Diego. Can you put more moments of pure happiness into your life?

EXERCISE #3: TAKE SMALL STEPS TOWARD
MAJOR TRANSFORMATIONS

Think about your long-term goals for family, work, and self. Where do you want to be five or ten years from now? What small changes can you make today to steer you in that direction?

EXERCISE #4: PUT LOVE INTO YOUR WORK

If you don't love your work, you can't work hard enough to compete with someone who does. People who love their work pay closer attention, come up with better ideas, and add an element of poetry, which is humbling to behold. As senior executives for *The People's Network*, Lisa and Eric Worre have a mission. They work in the same company and share a passion for what TPN represents: positive, empowering television programming available in your living room. Together they pursue careers, raise their kids, and change thousands of lives for the better.

HOW TO REDUCE STRESS ON YOUR PERSONALITY

Purposelessness or meaninglessness isn't the only spirit-based source of stress. Another cause of spiritual stress is *going against your grain, your temperament, or your values.* "Some of us approach life more like a rabbit darting here and there, nibbling this and that, and shooting off in all directions," wrote Hans Seyle, author of the psychology classic *The Story of the Adaptation Syndrome.* "Others are like turtles moving forward slowly, with careful attention to detail."

Both extremes are healthy. What is unhealthy is when the rabbit boss repeatedly reprimands the turtle sales rep, "You're too slow. Take chances, be adventurous." The longer the turtle is forced to act like a rabbit, the more stress builds up. Rabbits and turtles may well be able to excel in sales, albeit with vastly different techniques.

Do you spend too much time trying to be someone you are not? Do you realize the toll it takes on your body? Living life at someone else's pace or according to someone else's values can be causing you to work twice as hard as you need to. Ultimately the stress may interfere with your immune system and provoke more frequent illnesses.

Rudyard Kipling wrote, "There are nine and sixty ways of constructing village lays, and every-single-one-of-them is right." In the competitive worlds where I have traveled—Olympics, Wall Street, Oxford University—many people will try to tell you that there is a "best way" to do something. In the world of personal development many experts on sales, nutrition, or relationships will tell you that they have found "The *best* way." Forget it. There are at least nine and sixty ways to reach any goal.

EXERCISE #5: DO IT YOUR WAY!

Listen to all the experts and then choose a path that feels right to you. Experts can be the worst advisers when they are in their comfort zone and you aren't. Exercise and diet experts, for example, who are really into body stuff, may expect you to do all kinds of things you may hate like going to gyms, weighing your food, or counting calories. If you can find an expert who has the same comfort zone as you do, they will recommend strategies that you find more palatable. The best way is the way in which you have the most fun, feel the most comfortable, and enjoy the trip. It can't be the best way if you hate every step of the way!

EXERCISE #6: PUT FUN INTO YOUR WORK

Putting more fun into everything you do is a good way to cut stress and find the path of least resistance. A few major corporations, like Saturn and Southwest Airlines, are starting to figure out the value of fun in dollars and cents.

I recently attended the training for car sales reps at Saturn because I think their company exemplifies the concept of putting mind, body, and spirit into what you do. One of the secrets of their success is having lots of fun. Whenever they sell a car in National City, they play loud music, all the sales reps rush out to the front, and they dance the hokeypokey. Then they give a cheer for the new car owner that comes from a traditional Indian rite of passage ritual. Why not?

My idea of enjoying work is taking my laptop to a Del Mar cafe overlooking the ocean and typing away while soft strains of classical music waft by. Sometimes my husband comes along and we work together. Everyone has a different idea of what makes work fun. Find yours and go with it whenever possible.

EXERCISE #7: LET OTHERS GO WITH THEIR GRAIN

If you are a manager, don't insist that your employees do it the "best way," a.k.a. *your* way. If anything, insist that they do it their way, with their skills, their personality, their style. "Fun helps remove the barriers that allow people to motivate themselves," says Herman Cain, CEO of Godfather Pizza.

Although empowerment policies have proliferated throughout corporate America, the newfound freedom is seldom linked to having more fun. Most people are told that empowerment enables them to find a "better way" or to be more responsive to the customer's needs. Few employees, however, are told to use their empowerment to have more fun and to work in their own style. Empowerment should, in part, allow employees to be more responsive to their own needs and thus reduce stress.

Tuning into your spiritual resources—your purpose, your values, and your personality—can profoundly reduce your stress and let you achieve more in whatever job you take on.

Conclusion

We've looked at how to reduce stress by tapping into what you think, what you do, and what you care about. Although your environment will present you with a stimulus that could stress you, your reaction is in your hands. You can stop the chain reaction of stress that we described at the beginning of this chapter.

Where you break the chain depends on what is best for you. You can use your mind, your body, and your spirit. A mixture of all three strategies is best. The better you are at healing your body with rest, exercise, nutrition, and periods of nonstress recovery time, the more sources of stress you can allow into your life without causing long-term damage. Similarly, the better you are at using your mind to stop your body from triggering unnecessary physiological reactions, the more stress you can stand without needing extra recovery time. Finally, you can eliminate unnecessary causes of stress altogether. With these three strategies you can manage the level of stress necessary for growth, challenge, and improvement in your life.

You can use your comfort zone as a guide for determining which kinds of stress reduction will make the most difference. We often feel the most acute stress when threatened in our comfort zone.

For example, an injury or hospitalization causes more stress for a body-motivated person. This is not surprising since a body-centered person is accustomed to solving problems with action, relaxing with activity, and drawing on his raw energy in a crisis. Being bedridden robs him of all his habitual coping strategies. A mind- or spirit-centered person may enjoy reading or writing to friends while laid up, but a body-centered person is more likely to get depressed.

Conversely, a spirit-centered person will feel most stress when deprived of meaning in their life. For example, a social worker who took the job to make a difference will feel intense stress if the program is underfunded or poorly designed, or if he is otherwise unable to help people. Whereas a mind- or body-centered person can survive longer with little or no deep meaning in their work, a spirit-focused person cannot.

As a mind-centered person, I am highly susceptible to negative imagery, ideas, and attitudes. It is crucial for me to surround myself with positive mental food and new ideas. A repetitive job or being surrounded by negative people would cause more stress for me than anything else.

We all feel trapped and frustrated when cut off from using the resources and coping mechanisms with which we are most comfortable. Thus, dealing with the stressors in your comfort zone should be a high priority to get you functioning at even an average level.

To reach and exceed your peak performance levels, however, you are going to have to use stress management techniques outside your comfort zone as well. The better your approach to handling mind, body, and spirit stress, the fewer obstacles you experience on the road to success. You start to feel propelled forward by higher levels of energy, joy, and enthusiasm instead of fighting your way forward every inch of the way.

For Further Reading

Books on mental and physical training for stress:

Ageless Body, Timeless Mind, Deepak Chopra
The Owner's Manual for the Brain, Pierce J. Howard, Ph.D.
Toughness Training for Life, Dr. James Loehr

Books on tuning into your spirit, your values, and your sense of purpose:

What Color Is Your Parachute?, Richard Nelson Bolles
Do What You Love, The Money Will Follow, Martha Sinetar
Wish Craft, Barbara Sher
Your Sacred Self, Wayne Dyer
Simple Abundance: A Daybook of Comfort and Joy, Sarah
    Ban Breathnach
What Really Matters, Tony Schwartz

CHAPTER 12

Synergistic Goal Setting with Mind, Body, and Spirit

If you consider yourself a goal-oriented person good at achieving results, you may enjoy these new perspectives on the old system of goal setting. The following exercises will help you to reach your goals in a more fun and enriching way.

Exercise One: Totally Engaged Goal Setting

Write down five major goals in your life now. Next to the five goals, write down the main thing you feel you have to do to reach them. Designate each of your goals as mind goals, body goals, or spirit goals. Put an M, B, or S in front of each one. (If you aren't sure about the definitions of M, B, and S, check the summary definitions chart on page 116.)

- If a goal is primarily outside your comfort zone, can you modify it to be more in your comfort zone? For example, if you have a project that requires a great deal of research and writing, can you incorporate a number of interviews to make it a more interpersonal, face-to-face project?

You can change the means of getting there or change the goal itself slightly to be more in your comfort zone. Find a way to achieve your goal that builds on your strengths.

- Is there an area—mind, body, or spirit—where you have no goals? Can you set some goals? Tack them onto the other goals if possible (see goal blending in the exercise below).

Exercise Two: Expanding Your Goals

If hearing the words "aim higher" makes you feel stressed, try my secret weapon: *Goal blending and "two-fers."*

Goal blending is finding creative ways to modify a goal so it fits in with your other goals. One woman who came to my workshop managed a restaurant and was not happy with her long hours of hard work. She enjoyed meeting with other women in community groups and reading, but felt stretched too thin for time. After attending my workshop, she decided to start a book club that would meet in her restaurant!

Try to combine goals of different types for maximum motivation. In the example above, the woman was able to bring more personal satisfaction into her work hours. If you have a long-term goal like learning a new skill, add short-term payoffs like new clothes or tickets to a play to reward yourself for accomplishing small steps.

Alternatively, blend self-centered goals with community-oriented goals. For example, if you need exercise and believe strongly in a political cause, join a group that walks the precincts for a candidate or interest group. Alternatively, if you feel torn between spending time for community service versus professional networking, volunteer to work with a charity group that will give you more exposure to people who are more powerful or wealthier than you. Combine your goals.

Doesn't everyone need to be learning new skills and serving the community in some way? Almost any charity, political organization, or association would appreciate help leading committees or promoting fund-raisers. Or teach a course in time management for your church or synagogue. Help disadvantaged kids learn to use a computer program you need to learn. Help others as a means of helping yourself.

Review your master list of goals and find other creative ways to combine them. Want to get more exercise? Sign up for a walk or run sponsored by a charity. Create a business, religious, or vocational networking group that meets at a gym.

In addition to blending your goals together, you can find two-fers, or ways to reach two different goals with one piece of work. For example, I literally get paid twice for the same idea when I develop it for a workshop and then write about it in a book or an article. Being just a speaker or just a writer is more than half of the work of being both.

In a similar vein Gordon Burgett, author of more than 1,500 magazine articles, taught me to research an article thoroughly and then write it from five different slants for five different magazines. Once again, you get paid five times after one big research session.

By the way, don't worry if goal blending and two-fers sound like pretty much the same thing. It's two ways to look at the same thing. Just pick whichever makes more sense to you! Either way, goal blending and two-fers let you reach higher and achieve more without needing nine lives to do it. Bigger, expanded goals make life more worth living.

Paradoxically, downsizing your goals does not make them easier to achieve. Smaller goals are less exciting and therefore less motivating. When a struggling person lowers his sights he finds it even harder to get out of bed in the morning and get through the day. Lowering your targets becomes a vicious cycle of smaller goals and less motivation. "Ask life for great gifts and you encourage life to give them to you," writes Napoleon Hill.

Get out a list of your goals and ask yourself:

- Can you combine two or three of your goals to create one blended goal?
- Can you think of some activities that will get you closer to more than one goal?

Exercise Three: Goal Checkup: Are You Giving It All You've Got?

Pick any goal that is important to you and ask yourself the following questions about it:

- In what ways do you already use new perspectives, paradigm shifts, or creative thinking? Could you use more?
- In what ways do you exercise self-discipline and time management? Could you use more?
- In what ways do your physical health, strength, and appearance help?
- What changes in your physical routine would help?
- In what ways do you use your unique perspective and values?
- Would emphasizing your values and interests more be constructive?
- In what ways do you respond to others' unique individuality and interests as you strive to meet your goal? Would being more responsive to others' needs make you more effective? What do you have to give?

CHAPTER 13

Win in Your Favorite Sport

"As a professional, it became so clear to me that great mechanics, speed, talent, and even fitness were not enough to achieve enduring competitive success," says tennis champion Chris Evert in *Mental Toughness Training for Sports* by Jim Loehr. "Although I felt my ground strokes were the best in the game for many years, I didn't possess a killer forehand or knifing volleys. I was certainly blessed with exceptional athletic ability, but I was neither the fastest nor the strongest in the game at the time.

"So how could I become the number-one player in the world, win 21 Grand Slam titles and remain ranked in the top of women's tennis for so many years? My weapons were concentration, competitive spirit, confidence, fitness, and poise under pressure." This goddess of tennis sums it up this way, "I won because I could compete better."

Let's assume that you know training your body is important. If you haven't tried getting physically stronger, taking lessons, or practicing regularly, I would suggest you start there. Even if you have natural talent, you still have to train, work, and sweat to fully exploit that talent.

On the other hand, if you are training your body and want an extra edge against the competition, let's talk. Among athletes, everybody trains their muscles and moves. Your mind and your spirit, however, can give you an extra weapon to compete and win. It only makes sense that it is much easier to stand out in the crowd if you harness your mental and spiritual resources in addition to your body.

When I was kicking these ideas around with Bruce Jenner over the phone, he summed it up simply. "You have to be able to use all your emotions and make them work for you, not against you."

I told Bruce about a woman who attended my seminar on peak performance. Afterward she told me how excited she was to meet me since she was training to qualify for the Olympic track team. "My coach told me this would be a waste of time. He said I don't need to train my spirit, just my body."

Bruce exploded. "That's what it is all about! Competition in sports is 80 percent mental and 20 percent physical. Get a new coach!"

Florence "Flo Jo" Griffith-Joyner, winner of three gold medals in the 1988 Olympics and a silver medal in 1984 for running, says, "Without the spirit, you don't have the gas pedal. It's like your body is the car and your mind is the steering wheel. But without your spirit, you don't have the gas pedal." If anyone knows where the gas pedal is, Flo Jo knows.

I also believe that athletes who have and use more mental and spiritual resources are less prone to injuries. Many injuries—not all—result from either lapses in concentration or a subconscious self-sabotage desire. By engaging spiritual resources and mental resources, athletes can increase their concentration and develop an undiluted personal desire for the sport, thereby reducing their likelihood of injury.

Using Spiritual Resources to Compete in Sports

How do you harness your spiritual resources for competition?

"You gotta be hungry!" says Les Brown. Or put another way, you have to feel excitement, desire, or even a sense of fun as you step forward to play ball, swim, or swing a club. As soon as you lose the thrill of the game, you've robbed yourself of a crucial weapon.

I don't necessarily mean the killer instinct, either. Lots of coaches and friends have tried to encourage me before races by shouting, "Are you going to win?"

The correct response was, "I am going to SHRED the competition!" But that wasn't my style. "I don't care," I would answer, to their dismay. "I'm focused on performing at my best, on looking at the snow, on the course. I'm too busy to worry about winning."

I used to wonder if there was something wrong with me because I didn't participate in the posturing and chest thumping so many men seemed to think necessary. At the Olympics in Austria I remember really hitting my stride when I started singing on the way up the mountain. I danced by myself and enjoyed the breathtaking view of the Alps. "I'm about to lose control and I think I like it!" I was having fun. Maybe shouting, "I'm going to WIN!" helps some people, but for me having a sense of fun unleashes the tension in my muscles and unleashes my secret source of strength.

Musicians have the same need to nurture their spirit to combat the drudgery of daily practice, travel, and exhausting performance schedules. Yo-Yo Ma, the famous cellist, played for many hours every day as a child. He began to hate the routine, the practice, the teachers, and the cello. His father, however, understood the concept of nurturing the spirit. He knew that his son loved to play Mozart.

"Before you go to sleep each night," he suggested, "play a little Mozart. Play whatever you like. Play it just for you." This evening ritual helped Yo-Yo Ma retain his love of the cello while continuing to maintain the work of developing his skill. What are you doing to nurture your love of the game?

An author and friend of mine who has interviewed hundreds of successful people commented to me that, "Greatness is just a statistical event.

"Great musicians, great athletes, great businessmen have merely tried over and over and over and over again until eventually they become great." Frankly, I think he has missed the point of succeeding sane. Sure, you can drive yourself like you can beat a horse, and you may even get where you are going. But in order to win the race without losing your mind, you must create the conditions in which you joyfully run toward success rather than forcing yourself to do what is required.

Simple repetition is not enough. Without nurturing their inner flame, many people cannot stand the endless statistical repetition of practice and training to win. Others maintain the regimen but find the victory hollow and unsustainable. Succeeding sane is not merely a statistical event, it is a different path.

Phil and Steve Mahre, twin brothers and reigning ski champions for many years, understood the importance of nurturing the spirit. They shocked the international ski circuit by announcing that they would forego the summer training on glaciers, which was de rigueur for serious racers. As the Mahres played soccer, swam, and fished, dire predictions were made about them losing their touch and falling behind those who trained on snow year round. However, when the next winter came, the Mahre brothers had a hunger for snow and an excitement for the sport that gave them new speed. The Mahres destroyed the competition by an even larger margin than before. Sure, physical training is good. But the Mahres decided restocking their spiritual energy was better.

Their dramatic results reverberated throughout the ski racing world. When the Mahres returned to snow faster than ever, experts decided less summer training was clearly the best training regimen. Like lemmings playing follow the leader, most serious competitors (including me) cut their summer glacier time down. Of course, not every athlete responded so favorably to less time on snow. Many athletes probably didn't understand that the point of getting off snow was to renew their energy by playing, laughing, and doing something fun.

In truth, there is not one best way. Nurturing your spirit is a personal process guided by feel, not by formula.

As a skier I faced many tough times when I wanted to give up. I ran out of money so many times I can't count. I moved away from my family and friends to follow the snow and the coaches winter and summer. There was that time I broke both my legs. So many times I wanted to give up.

Fortunately, I received quite a lot of spiritual nourishment from two groups of people. First, the ski organization for the disabled that sponsored the competitions and organized the U.S. Disabled Ski Team gave me an opportunity to meet so many confident and athletic amputees like Diana Golden, Martha Hill, Greg Manino, and Bill Demby. Through Disabled Sports/USA I changed my vision of myself from less-than-able to athlete. Now as an official spokesperson for the organization, I can help others to do the same.

The second organization that nourished my spirit was the National Brotherhood of Skiers, the club for African-American recreational skiers. Not only did the NBS help raise the funds that kept me in training up to the Olympics, but they gave me an extended family across the country as I traveled from Vermont to Colorado, and Oregon to Tahoe. I had places to stay, clothes to wear, and friends to talk to wherever I went.

Suddenly I had thousands of role models who were black like me: Educated, successful, generous, and athletic role models who were proud of their identity yet unafraid to compete in a white world on skis or in the board room. They told me about W.E.B. Du Bois, Angela Davis, and other historical figures who didn't get covered in the typical school curriculum. My NBS family lent me books by black authors like Gloria Naylor, Alice Walker, and Toni Morrison.

Without the love, support, and affirmation I received from the National Brotherhood of Skiers, I would never have made it to the Olympics. Thank goodness I needed money, because I don't think I would have been smart enough to seek out the spiritual help I really needed.

To reinforce the concept of nurturing your spirit, you can go to your local video store and rent *Searching for Bobby Fischer*. In this movie about a young chess champion, the parents have to fight with their six-year-old child's chess coach to let him play chess on the street with the hustlers, which is what he does for fun. When even this is not enough to prevent burnout, the dad says, "Let's go fishing and forget chess for a while." His parents are totally unlike the other supercompetitive parents who drive their kids mercilessly. As a result, the boy continues to compete and win long after most wunderkinds wear out.

Hoop Dreams, a true story, is another great film about the importance of nurturing the spirit. I rented *Hoop Dreams* because Mr. Siskel said it was one of the best films he'd ever seen as a film critic. For four years a documentary film team actually takes cameras and follows the lives of two talented young basketball players from one of the poorest neighborhoods in Chicago.

The young man with more natural talent gets a high school scholarship, a posh summer job, and a coach from hell. However, the constant badgering, pressure, and demeaning style of the coach slowly destroys any fun the kid ever felt in the game. Once the desire to play begins to crumble, he begins to sabotage his own success. He becomes more vulnerable to injuries, his grades drop, and he acts up socially with drugs and sex. His cry for help goes unheard.

Meanwhile, the kid with less talent gets less help and less pressure. He is left to struggle in worse schools combating pressure from gangs. He has to want to play or it isn't going to happen. Despite his father being jailed for drugs and his mother being on and off welfare, he works to stay in school, to stay on the team. Finally he wins a college scholarship and goes on to play ball better than ever. By the end of the story, it is clear that he is a happier, healthier person more likely to be successful with or without basketball. Are you?

You may think to yourself, "Sure, I enjoy my sport. That's why I do it." But do you really? Have you lost the sense of play in your quest to win? What do you do to kindle that fire that first brought you into the game in the first place? What do you do to forge your sense of identity, pride, and security apart from the game?

Using Mind Power to Gain an Edge in Sports

Although I am a medal-winning Olympic skier, body power is not my primary strength. Mind power is my comfort zone. And that's why I won.

As a disabled athlete I didn't have the benefit of an organized system for identifying and training talented kids. I had to find my own coaches, make my own travel arrangements, and find sponsors to pay for it. Like the less talented kid in the movie *Hoop Dreams*, I had to want it.

Because I could run circles around most of the other athletes when it came to writing proposals, booking flights, and coming up with new ideas for training, I got more time on snow, better coaching, and more dry land training than any of my American competitors. I became faster, stronger, and more skilled than those who might have had more so-called natural talent.

I also relied more on mental techniques to focus and to achieve a consistent peak performance in competition. Ski races last from as little as thirty seconds up to two or three minutes at most. Although a tennis player can have a lapse in concentration and recover the points later, a skier must have complete, undiluted, intense concentration for the entire race. Harnessing the power of my mind made my body far more effective.

Early on in my ski career a friend and coach gave me a copy of the *Inner Game of Tennis* by Tim Gallwey. Other coaches can tell you what you are supposed to be doing with your feet or hands, but Gallwey describes better than anyone else what is supposed to be going on in your head while you do any sport. I strongly recommend getting a copy of his book and doing his exercises for increasing concentration, changing a habit, or examining your motives for competition.

In addition to using Gallwey's mental techniques for competition I developed my own personal system for achieving a focused mind prior to competition. Using a combination of self-hypnosis, positive thinking, and visualization I created a system that I used while waiting in the snow for my turn. I also used the LaserWalk, as I call it, to create the right mind-set for training in the morning. After I stopped racing I continued to use the LaserWalk to perform under pressure in job interviews, sales presentations, and on camera. Step-by-step instructions for my LaserWalk are included in the appendix of this book or you can purchase an audiotape and learn it as a guided experience.

Any successful athlete has a way of focusing his mind, clearing out the negative emotions, and dismissing the flotsam and jetsam of errands and to-dos. After the boyfriend of ice skater Tonya Harding was arrested for bashing in Nancy Kerrigan's knees, reporters asked Tonya, "How can you continue to skate and practice for the Olympics when you are being threatened by the International Olympic Committee, questioned by police, and hounded by the press?"

"I tree it," she answered. "As I enter the rink I touch a piece of wood and leave all my problems there." When she finishes practice, she touches wood again and reenters the real world. Every great athlete, every great competitor has a way of getting mentally focused.

Putting It All Together: Winning the Gold with Mind, Body, and Spirit

The story of Dan Jansen's battle to harness his mental concentration and spiritual resources lasted over six years before he struck Olympic gold. His story underscores the importance of drawing on mind, body, and spirit.

On Valentine's Day 1988 everyone expected Dan Jansen to skate to glory at the Calgary Olympics. Stronger and healthier than ever before, he had recently won the World Sprint Skating championship. But when news reached him that his sister Jane's long battle against leukemia had ended in death, Dan's world was turned upside down.

"When I finally got on the ice for the 500-meter race," writes Dan in his autobiography, *Full Circle*, "I felt wobbly, as if I hadn't been on skates in six months." Thoughts of Jane spun in his head. "Jane is dead. Should I be here? Jane is dead. How can my parents cheer for me while facing the burial of a child? Jane is dead." Totally unable to concentrate, Jansen started slow, skated slow, and then tripped, knocking down Kuriowa, a Japanese competitor. Later in the week in the 1,000-meter race, Jansen's skate wavered again, sending him sliding across the ice and snatching away his hopes for an Olympic medal of any hue. Dan's devastating sense of loss was compounded by guilt. "You jerk," thought Dan, "your sister just died." He thought losing the race shouldn't matter in the circumstances, but of course it did.

Dan's experience at the 1988 Olympics was to haunt him for many years to come. At the 1992 Olympics, Dan's concentration betrayed him again. When he fell again at the Olympics despite his wins in other international competition, Dan was labeled as a "Choker." Dan's coach finally convinced him to contact a sports psychologist, Dr. James Loehr, to help him train his brain as well as his body.

But things did not go well for Dan in the 500-meter race. When Dan's brother back in America heard, "Daddy, Daddy! Uncle Dan slipped!" he was angry at his daughter for playing a joke. But it was no joke.

Three days later, Dan was scheduled to skate the 1,000-meter race, not his best event. Though he had never won it before, it was now his last chance to win a gold medal. Having spent the first twenty-five years of his life in competitive skating, Dan knew that his athletic career was coming to an end.

As part of his training, Dr. Loehr had asked him to write over and over, "I love the 1000m." His physical coach, Peter Mueller, had pushed him to build endurance to spare.

As he approached the starting line, he touched the ring around his neck containing an emerald, his eight-month-old daughter's birthstone. Dan and his wife Robin had named their daughter Jane after Dan's sister.

Although Dan slipped yet again, he kept going. When he crossed the finish line the noise was deafening. "I don't know what type, but that's a medal," Dan thought. It seemed like forever before he got the hood of his uniform off and focused on the clock. Dan's time was not only a personal best, but also a world record. He had finally won his gold medal.

After years of intense training, four trips to the Olympics, and five humiliating falls, Dan Jansen finally won his gold medal in the Olympics. He was not able to win until he had let go of the pain of his sister's death, grown into his own marriage and fatherhood, and worked through the guilt he associated with skating in the Olympics. Dan had to pull mind, body, and soul together before he could taste victory. Dan himself says that the real test didn't take place on the ice, in the world of skating in circles, but in his heart and mind.

I am not saying that you cannot win without developing and applying your mind and spirit resources. There are plenty of examples of successful athletes who compete using primarily physical talents. You know who I mean: football players who, when interviewed on TV, can hardly put together a complete sentence; athletes who chase women, do drugs, or don't care about their influence on the young kids who admire them. Sure, there are lots of great athletes running on body power alone. But no matter how good your game, applying mind and spirit resources will improve it.

It makes sense that one of the best resources on developing mind, body, and spirit for competitive sports would come from Dan Jansen's coach, Dr. James Loehr. His latest book, *The New Toughness Training for Sports*, shares many years of experience with golf pros, tennis stars, and other athletes. He knows what it takes to win and how to train for it. If you want to apply the concepts of *Succeeding Sane* with mind, body, and spirit to sports, you must get his book.

Loehr teaches you to cultivate the mental state and the emotional state needed to win consistently. Whereas Gallwey covers what you are thinking, Loehr goes far deeper into who you are. You start out by benchmarking your personal level of toughness. Were you coddled as a child? Do you have low self-esteem? Then, no matter where you start, he shows you how to increase your emotional, mental, and physical toughness.

Are you training your mind and your emotions as well as your body?

The best story I heard on putting mind, body, and spirit into one thing to pull off a superhuman performance was from Mark Allen, the six-time winner of the Ironman triathlon in Hawaii. He told me his story while sitting on my patio. His words make you feel his seven-year journey toward winning his first Ironman, including the moment of rising above what any normal human being can achieve. In fact I loved his story so much, I couldn't put it in the chapter on sports where some people might skip over it. I put it at the end of chapter 10, the main chapter on mind, body, and spirit synergy. So if you haven't read that chapter already and you are a sports enthusiast, please check it out. He explains better than anyone else ever has the feeling I get when I push beyond what I think I am capable of doing. Share the feeling of greatness. Turn to chapter 10, read it, and weep.

Exercises for Using Mind and Spirit to Win in Sports

Here are a few simple ideas to help you tap into more mind and spirit power for your game. Try one or two of these, or think of your own!

- Rent videos that illustrate the importance of nurturing the spirit of a champion: *Hoop Dreams, Searching for Bobby Fischer,* or *Little Man Tate*
- Buy books or tapes on using mind power to compete: *The Inner Game of Tennis,* Tim Gallwey (for sports enthusiasts of all levels, in all sports)

   The Winner's Mind: Unleashing Your Peak Performance, Bonnie St. John Deane (audiotape. For sports, business, or any situation where you must perform under pressure.)

   The New Toughness Training for Sports, Dr. James Loehr (Serious competitors will particularly benefit from this book.)
- Put more fun into your sport. Play with a friend, run for charity, or do something silly. Debi Thomas, the Olympic ice skater, used to enjoy doing a clown routine imitating a young girl in her first competition. Rather than showing off in exhibitions she made people laugh! What would be fun for you?

CHAPTER 14

Sell as the Top Performer
in Your Company

When Lebron Morgan tried to sell advertising space in *Essence* magazine to a major lipstick manufacturer back in the 80s, he was told by one executive: "We don't want our product associated with big, African-American lips."

He tried to laugh it off by saying, "Bigger lips mean more lipstick! Black women will buy more just to cover those big lips."

The lipstick executives were not amused. Lebron, however, didn't get angry. He didn't sue for discrimination. He didn't give up. Lebron decided to do whatever it took to convince the cosmetic company that African-American women were a valuable market. "I proved my point with numbers," he told me.

Lebron found reports and studies citing that black women spent over $400 million on health and beauty products in 1987. He took pictures of lipstick racks in black neighborhoods. He showed the executives pictures of black women buying their brand of lipstick. When that wasn't enough he went to malls for three weeks asking women to sign their name, address, and their lipstick brand. He gathered thousands of names of black women who were loyal customers.

Lebron finally broke through and convinced that cosmetic company to advertise in *Essence* magazine. "I went through the same process for hosiery, cars, and many other mainstream corporate advertisers. I had to educate Fortune 500 executives about the value of African-American customers before I could get them to advertise. But I did it time and time again. Even though I worked out of Atlanta, I beat the sales volume in New York and Chicago several times."

Although Lebron's goal was primarily a mind goal—changing the perspective of corporate executives—he put his mind, body, and spirit on the line. From his mental resources I would say he drew on self-discipline, perseverance, and new information about the purchasing power of African-American women. He also used body power, getting out into the community taking pictures, collecting signatures, and putting in long hours to get what he needed. His active, high-energy approach was crucial.

However, what really set Lebron apart from any other advertising salesman was his passion, his spirit. He was on a mission. He realized that the way African-American women see themselves, their self-esteem, and their ideal of beauty is often shaped by how they see themselves in magazines. It burned him up to see that cosmetics companies, department stores, and other manufacturers could take millions of dollars from black women and then refuse to support the one magazine that told them they were beautiful.

Such policies are not only immoral, but illogical. Rather than ignoring loyal customers, companies should be going after more of their business. By showing companies the value of African-American women as consumers, he convinced them to support the magazine that values them as people. Within seven years, Lebron brought the cosmetic company from its first ad to unveiling their own line of products for African-American women.

Lebron gets the highest possible marks from me in terms of succeeding sane and blending. His success as an advertising sales rep contributed to the growth of new markets for his clients and affirmed the value of African-American women in our society. This is "Win-win" thinking taken to new heights of meaning and significance.

At IBM one sales rep stands out in my memory as putting mind, body, and spirit into his job. When I joined the IBM sales force in 1991 people still puffed up their chests with pride and called themselves "White Shirts." White shirt, shiny wingtip shoes, navy suit, and a red power tie symbolize the archetypal IBM salesman. Mostly it was the white shirt. No stripes, no pastels allowed.

In the old days of double-digit growth at IBM, the white shirt promised affluence and prestige in the form of a BMW, a big house, and a flourishing career in management. But it also entailed duties like exceeding customer expectations and acting with integrity both personally and professionally. The white shirt stood for quality, respect for the individual, and customer service. Even the repair engineers wore starched, white shirts while they crawled around on the floor under big machines.

Imagine a sales rep, let's call him Tom, who stopped wearing a tie, bought a set of striped oxford shirts, and finished his ensemble with sockless Topsider shoes. To say he created a scandal in our office in no way captures the subtle forms of daily disrespect dished out by his peers, his manager, and the administrators.

Tom's orders were processed late, his performance ratings slipped, and whispers followed him around the office like a wake. Had Tom suffered a personal tragedy leaving him emotionally unbalanced? Why did he do it?

Assigned to the University of California territory, Tom noticed that the academics, technicians, and administrators were much more comfortable talking to him when he dressed more like they did. In his "Dress for Success" uniform, they viewed him with distrust. Wingtip shoes screamed "outsider" and "snake oil salesman" rather than quality, customer service, and respect for the individual. Unlike all previous IBMers assigned to the territory, Tom decided that "dress for customers" was better than "dress to impress." Tom chose to be a pariah in the branch office in order to get closer to the customer.

His gamble paid off. Tom gained access to the engineers, went head to head with Sun and HP, and won market share for IBM's Unix-based RISC machine. Better rapport with the administrators secured a key order for a mainframe upgrade. IBMers stopped snickering about his wardrobe when he left his sales quota far behind in the dust.

This seemingly simple change was a symptom of the way Tom used his physical, mental, and spiritual assets to become a star salesperson in our branch office. On a spiritual level, connecting with the customers was his constant focus. He used his physical appearance to underscore his attitude. Mentally, he chose his own idea of Dress for Success, weathered the stares and rudeness of coworkers, and ultimately changed their views on customer service.

Tom gave it his all. Do you?

Exercise: Totally Engaged in Sales

Write down the name of a client you worked with recently, whether it went well or badly.

Were you totally engaged with mind, body, and spirit?

- In what ways did you use your mind?
- In what ways did you use your physical energy?
- In what ways did you use your personal passion or beliefs? Your customer's?

In what ways could you have applied more mind, body, or spirit?

CHAPTER 15

Deepen Your Relationships with Lovers, Family, and Friends

There is so much I don't know about relationships, I'm not sure where to start! Perhaps a disclaimer is a good place.

Before applying anything in this chapter, consider this caveat: Some relationships will never work no matter how much work you put in, no matter how much you try to improve yourself.

I learned the hard way that a person is not a goal. I used to go after guys like I went after Olympic medals or job promotions. I trained, competed, and expected to win. You can probably imagine that being on the receiving end of such an awesome force was less than pleasant.

You can't just pick someone and go after them like a goal. People are not things. Sometimes the other person just doesn't want a relationship with you or isn't right for you. Having respect for the other person and his free will means that you have to acknowledge limits to your ability to "fix" everything.

All that said, your relationship is likely to benefit from putting your whole self into it and from seeing the other person in terms of his or her whole self: a mind, body, and spirit, which is developing into its own potential.

Try any of the following four exercises to help your relationship thrive on all levels.

Exercise One: Mind, Body, and Spirit Relationship

Think about an intimate relationship you are in now or envision the relationship you would like to have. Try to imagine your relationship spanning mental, physical, and spiritual dimensions. Write down what happens or could happen in your relationship on each level. You can do this exercise not only for a lover or spouse, but also for a close friend, a child, or a relative.

Exercise Two: Comfort Zones and Compatibility

Choose a relationship to work on in this exercise. For example, you may want to focus on an intimate partner, a friend, one or all of your children, or a colleague at work.

List the last few things you have done together. How do you spend time together?

Are these activities primarily mind, body, or spirit activities?

Is the person you are thinking about primarily a mind, body, or spirit person? Think carefully before you decide. Often obvious things can be misleading. For example, although my husband is a physicist he is more of a spirit-power person than a mind person. You may want to give them the twelve-question quiz on page 80 or answer the questions for them to the best of your ability.

Are the things you do together primarily in your comfort zone or theirs? Or neither?

Can you think of activities that would involve both of your comfort zones?

If you have the same comfort zone and spend most of your time together there, can you incorporate other aspects to stretch yourselves a little?

Exercise Three: Mission Possible

Do you help one another explore your unique values and purpose? Whether or not you are spirit-centered people, you may not have thought about helping one another find your potential as a central purpose of your relationship. Once again, this exercise can apply to any nurturing relationship whether it's with a significant other, your child, or a close friend.

Try this exercise together:

Each person takes out a piece of paper and divides it in half. Set a timer for five minutes and quickly write down the special things about *your partner*. Write down favorite foods, favorite colors, pastimes, clothes, movies, whatever. If you don't know, then guess. What talents do they have? What makes you proud of that person? Also write down their values in terms of ethics and principles, if you like. (Alternatively, for a more left-brain version of this exercise, write down what you think their mission statement would be.)

Set the timer again for five minutes. This time write down special things about yourself and your values on the other side of the paper. (Or write down your brief mission statement.) Do it quickly without agonizing over your answers. It's a game.

When the timer goes off compare lists. Did you find out anything new? About your partner or yourself? Do each of you get to express your unique values in the relationship?

Exercise Four: Getting to Know You

Put the following questions on small sheets of paper in an envelope. Pick one out at random to start interesting discussions. During dinner, a long car ride, or on a walk could be a good time. Listen to the answers the way you did when you first started dating.

- What one thing would you like to know more about?
- What kind of people would you like to know? Who in particular would you like to see more of and why?
- What kind of food would you like to eat more of?

- What kinds of things would you like to do more of? Active things like sports or travel? Cultural things like plays, music? Cocooning with music, books, wine, or videos? Spiritual things like worship and family?
- What will we be doing on this day five years from now?

CHAPTER 16

Increase Your Sexual Ability

"I am Don Juan DeMarco," says the masked youth in the recent movie by the same title. "I am the world's greatest lover. Women react to me the way that they do because they sense that I search out the beauty that is within them until it overwhelms everything else . . . and then they cannot avoid their desire to release that beauty and envelop me in it."

"You are a great lover like myself," Don Juan says to his psychiatrist, who is played by Marlon Brando. "Even though you may have lost your way . . . and your accent."

Sex is the ultimate mind/body/spirit activity; do you use it all?

"Professional lovers—prostitutes, hookers, call girls, hustlers, courtesans—make sex their business, and those who are successful and stay successful have trade secrets that keep business booming," writes Alexandra Penney, author of the best-selling book, *How to Make Love to a Man*. "Many of the great courtesans were not beautiful or even pretty, but they were extraordinarily and uniquely educated in their ability to heighten a man's pleasure, and thus they were paid extravagantly, not only with money, but with houses, jewels and servants." Wouldn't you like to know how the pros keep their clients begging for more at any price?

I dedicate this chapter to Alexandra, whose book is my favorite among the hundreds I have read on sex. Yes, being a mind person I tend to read a lot on anything that interests me. Sex interests me. I've read *Joy of Sex, More Joy of Sex, The Kama Sutra*, erotic literature, and even erotic trash like letters to *Playboy*. I like to be good at things I do. So I study.

But Alexandra told me what I really wanted to know: how to please a man out of his mind, the step-by-step instructions; not just physically, but also mentally and spiritually. I wanted to blow all the circuits.

For men the equivalent book is *How to Please a Woman Every Time (and have her begging for more)* by Naura Hayden. Again, you get no-nonsense, step-by-step instructions as well as logical explanations so you can understand the why as well as the how. If you want the exact physical instructions, you'll have to get one or both of these books. I'm too shy to repeat any of the details here.

What I can do in this chapter, however, is help you look at your sexual habits from the mind, body, and spirit perspective. It may help you to identify hidden sources of strength or ways to improve.

How Can I Use Mind Power to Improve Sex?

"Concentration is the key to being good in bed," emphasizes a New York professional (quoted by Ms. Penney in *How to Make Love to a Man*), who operates out of a champagne-colored apartment with soft lighting and rare antiques on Manhattan's elegant Sutton Place.

"I force myself to concentrate on what I am doing. For instance, if I am on top I become totally involved with the movements I am making. If I am doing something that he has specially requested, even though it's not something I'm crazy about, I don't let any other thought enter my brain except what my body is doing and the pleasure I'm giving. Maybe a man can't precisely tell if you're distracted or fantasizing, but I'm sure men know and feel it when you're totally and completely centered on giving them pleasure."

Can you remember the first few months of a passionate relationship? The way time seemed to stop while you made love? You were fascinated by every inch of your lover's skin. Everything he said was funny or insightful.

After a relationship goes on for a while, most of us tend to lose that feeling. While having sex your mind may wander to what you will be feeding the kids or a problem you have at work. I suppose a lot of infidelity happens because people want to recapture that feeling of being the center of someone's full attention.

Thus, something you can do to dramatically improve your sex life right now is try paying more attention to your partner. A simple way to keep yourself focused in the here and now is to use your senses more fully. Try listening with a curious ear and letting the sounds you hear arouse you. Or let your mind single out just looking, touching, smelling, or tasting. By concentrating on your senses one at a time, you may experience things you have never really noticed before. Then you can choose to focus on the sense that brings you the most pleasure.

○

"One night," explains Don Juan to his psychiatrist in the movie Don Juan DeMarco, "I watched Dona Inez at the window in her slip. I noticed for the first time how a woman's underclothing barely touches her skin . . . and I understood how a woman must be touched."

○

The principle of paying attention extends beyond the act of intercourse itself. Paying close attention to what is on your partner's mind, what mood he is in, and what he likes or dislikes is also highly erotic. A man who can truly listen with interest to a woman and learn little special things about her just by observing is always sought after by women. The same is true for a woman who can listen with interest to a man's problems and learn about him as an individual rather than stuffing him into a role as the provider or stud.

Penney concludes, "The biggest secret of the top-quality professional remains focus and undiluted attention to the man she's in bed with. One articulate call girl who is paid over one thousand dollars a night for her services by an international clientele said, 'I focus totally and completely on the man. I try to make him feel he's the only man in the world.'"

What do you do with the knowledge you gain by paying close attention in and out of bed? That creates a good transition to putting the spirit power into great sex.

How Do You Use Spirit Power to Improve Sex?

Earlier I defined spirit power with reference to the theme song from Disney's animated movie *The Lion King*. "In the Circle of Life," croons Elton John, "you should never take more than you give." Our individual spirit drives us to find a place in the circle of life where we give and receive simultaneously based on our unique talents, personality, and beliefs. We steer toward this ideal by means of our values in the broadest sense: everything we value about ourselves including our abilities and our idiosyncrasies as well as our ethics.

Sex—particularly in a committed, loving relationship—can be a perfect expression of the circle of life. We have been designed with this wonderful capacity to give and receive pleasure at the same time! We steer closer to this ideal of mutual pleasure by tapping into one another's unique personality.

Thus, if you used your concentration and focus to learn lots of special little things about your partner, you can use them to create a magical, transporting sexual experience.

Alexandra Penney suggests that we imitate the great French courtesans of the nineteenth century "who were the ultimate practitioners in pleasing a man's senses while making him feel completely at home."

One imaginative woman ordered truckloads of orchids strewn in the marble hallways for her lover to feel the sensation under bare feet. Another famous mistress always changed her silk sheets, towels, and tablecloths to reflect the colors and monogram of her current noble visitor. Once she even dyed her dog blue in honor of a favorite duke.

Another courtesan bathed her lovers in a solid silver tub with a lapis lazuli faucet using their favorite scents. Yet another played teasing games with slices of rare fruits or feathers on her lover's naked body. While you needn't rely on extravagant gestures, can you apply the same level of zeal in pleasing your lover's senses?

○

"*Have you ever met a woman,*" asks Don Juan DeMarco, "*who inspires you to love until your every sense is filled with her? You inhale her, you taste her, you see your unborn children in her eyes.*" Can you fill your lover's senses with pleasure?

○

Consider each of your lover's senses in turn and ask yourself, "What does he like?" or "What stimulates her gently, rather than putting her to sleep or making her rowdy?" Try different types of music, food, wines, and scents. Keep track of the results. Get Alexandra Penney's book and try out some of her ideas for testing your lover's senses. In addition you may want to take the straightforward approach and ask your partner for a list of the things that please him.

Later you can use this information to plan the perfect seduction. It may be that a meal of home-cooked food with Tammy Wynette on the stereo and afterward an old video like *Casablanca* in front of a roaring fire with popcorn would be just the right prelude to relaxed, sharing sex. Or if she likes more drama, perhaps a fancy restaurant with violins playing Puccini followed by a professional massage and sex in a Jacuzzi surrounded by a hundred small candles.

For another person, dancing to disco music might warm up the blood. The key is setting the scene, not according to what makes sense to you, but with every detail to please your lover.

Ladies, you may think this is something only men are supposed to do for women, but guess again. Take the advice of the professionals: Men love it as much as we do! Take the lead a few times and then ask him or her to return the favor. Or create a blending of your tastes and styles for the ultimate shared experience.

I realize some readers will be thinking that this is "fake" or "immoral." Some people (probably you spirit-centered types) will think that doing detective work on your lover and then using the information to seduce them is too cold and calculating. "Nice people don't take advantage that way," you may say. Or "I already know what she loves—the same things I do," or maybe "Real love is spontaneous, it should just happen."

Spontaneous sex can be great. And I hope you have as much of it as you want. But it can also be uncomfortable, too fast, or interrupted by strangers. If you have kids, it simply may *never* happen. Planning can achieve some spectacular results.

Besides, wouldn't *you* like it if your lover planned a special evening to please all of *your* senses? Even if your answer is no (which I doubt), don't dismiss the idea without asking. "Hey, would you like it if we cleared everything off the calendar next Friday, sent the kids to my mother's, and planned a special evening with your favorite food, drinks, and music, culminating in fantastic sex?" Unless your partner suspects ulterior motives, a surprised but enthusiastic "Yes!" will probably come rushing out. Try it.

One final warning is in order regarding the use of this technique. Use it with respect for your partner and yourself.

As I mentioned at the beginning of the chapter on relationships, I learned the hard way that people are not to be won through sheer hard work like medals and degrees. No matter how well you have done your detective work and planned your evening, the other person will not be seduced unless they want to be. You have to respect the other person's free will as an individual. You cannot force, trick, or trap anyone into true love.

Furthermore, you must have respect for yourself, too. You can't always be the one giving, listening, and planning perfect evenings. In a healthy relationship the effort goes both ways. Remember the "Circle of Life" is a circle. Too much giving is just as damaging to the spirit as too much taking.

Putting More Body Power into Your Lovemaking

I remember the day I realized what it meant to be sexy. I was waiting between planes at Kennedy airport at the age of sixteen or seventeen. Tired, I leaned across several seats on one elbow, letting my legs drape across a few more seats. After a few men started glancing sideways at me, I looked at myself in my mind's eye and saw myself languidly draped across the seats.

In that moment I realized being sexy wasn't necessarily about makeup, tight clothes, or a hairdo. The way a woman moves tells a man whether she is comfortable with her body in every little way. A woman who walks like she thoroughly enjoys the body she has with all its imperfections can also enjoy yours—with all its imperfections.

"How is a woman with one leg so comfortable with her body?" you may ask. A little bit of cellulite or a scar is no big deal, I guess, when one of your appendages is hacked off. Other people may worry about perfecting themselves, but I can never be perfect. Why should I worry?

A beautiful but uptight woman may get more marriage proposals because a woman like that looks good on your arm. For comfort, however, men instinctively sense and gravitate toward a woman who feels comfortable naked. It shows.

Likewise, for women there is nothing really attractive about a superbuilt man who isn't comfortable with his body. I think a woman can usually sense a man who "performs" in bed rather than making love because he has to continually prove himself. When a man is totally focused on his own body, he isn't thinking about her. The body communicates in so many little ways where the spirit and head are.

To sum up, a sexy body is one in which you are so comfortable, you are hardly conscious of it. To reach this ideal, you need some sort of exercise and vitamins or healthy food. You need to treat your body with friendliness and respect.

Holding this ideal in your mind should lead you to a different kind of food and exercise plan than the traditional idea of a sexy male or female body. Instead of asking yourself, "How can I beat up and starve my body enough to look like Patrick Swayze or Cindy Crawford?" you can ask yourself, "What can I do to make myself feel more comfortable and more sexy in my body? What can I do to have fun in my body?" The answer may be belly dancing lessons or karate rather than more weight lifting or running.

On Mind Power and Sex

You don't have to try everything or have lots of partners to get exposure to a wide variety of ideas. Read books on sex. (Not just magazines, guys. Books. With words.) Try to learn about sex in other cultures and countries. What are their attitudes and taboos? How have Christian attitudes toward sex changed over time and in different countries?

Seeing other perspectives helps you to clarify what does and doesn't feel right to you.

Make a conscious decision to set aside time for sex if it is important to you. In *More Time for Sex*, Harriet Schechter recommends simply making an appointment to meet in bed half an hour earlier than usual. For special occasions you'll need to plan time for preparing special treats as well as the time for enjoying them.

On Body Power and Sex

There are specific exercises for the abdominals and pelvic muscles that increase sexual drive and energy. Books on yoga often have exercises for sex. Ask any professional personal trainer for more ideas.

For very specific physical instructions to improve your sexual technique I recommend Alexandra Penney's book for women and Naura Hayden's for men. Each provides valuable insights that no one else will ever, ever tell you. I certainly won't repeat them here. I'd be too embarassed.

On Spirit Power and Sex

It's hard to pay close attention, learn all the little details about someone, and feel completely comfortable if you don't really care. In sum, your best chance to experience total mind, body, and spirit sex is going to be in a loving, respectful relationship.

If you need to do more work on your relationship before you can improve your sex life, you can try the exercises in the previous chapter. For further reading, I can recommend a couple of my favorite books: *Getting the Love You Want* by Harville Hendrix; and *Men Are from Mars, Women Are from Venus*, by John Gray.

One of the important reasons to write this chapter is to help married couples see a new perspective on looking for greater sexual thrills. Rather than trying kinkier, stranger activities, we can look for a more complete celebration of the unique personalities of two very special people.

Checklist of Mind, Body, and Spirit Ways
to Improve in Bed

- Decide to concentrate more.
- Start a detective's list—what pleases each of your lover's senses?
- Plan an evening of seduction (get permission first).
- Read a book on sex or relationships.
- Change your exercise routine to include exercises that increase your libido or make you more comfortable with your body.
- Ask your lover to plan an evening of seduction for you.

PART IV

Finding Fulfillment
on the Road
to Success

Fifteen years ago, a radio talk-show host asked a question that hit me like a fist in the gut. I was being interviewed on her show after returning with six medals from my first time at the National Handicap Ski Championships. When I told her of my desire to attend Harvard and ultimately earn an MBA, she asked, "Statistics show that successful women tend to have rotten personal lives: higher divorce rates, problems with their children, suicide, alcoholism—you name it. Are you willing to cut back your ambitions to seek a better life?"

Although I tried to laugh off her question and confidently state my intention to have it all—husband, kids, and a successful career as a corporate executive—I felt doubt and fear. Long after the interview ended, I turned over in my mind the issue she had thrust in my sixteen-year-old lap.

Could I succeed outwardly—with money, power, and position—

while still staying personally sane? Fifteen years later I can say "Yes!" with confidence. And I am not the only one who can say yes. The more people I interviewed for this book, the clearer it became to me that lots of wildly successful people are quietly going about the business of being a positive influence, raising children, and having quality of life. They are good people blending success and joy. Unfortunately, it is those who are destroyed by success who make headlines.

Whereas Part III focused on the *success* side of succeeding sane, Part IV emphasizes the *sanity* side. Because achievement comes from doing one thing exceptionally well, Part III looked at the way you do a particular thing like selling. Fulfillment, on the other hand, comes from the way you do all the little things every day and the way they come together to create the whole fabric of your existence. Thus, Part IV examines the way you live your daily life.

CHAPTER 17

Why Balance Doesn't Work

Leading a "balanced" life means allocating the right amount of time for each activity. Like an assembly line we do one thing at a time: go to the gym for body, go to church for the soul, and go to night school to learn. Each activity needs its own time slot. Everything is specialized and intensive. Experts tell us the "right" way to use our minds, bodies, and spirits.

My skin crawls when I think about balancing everything. I've been to workshops where you have to list all your goals around the spokes of a wheel to see if they are balanced across all the essential areas of life. My head begins to hurt just thinking about how to find time to do all the activities I would need to have a balanced life.

I used to think that everyone but me knew how to fit in time for everything from flossing to thank you notes to parenting to career. But I've found that I'm not the only one who has trouble.

No one can fit everything into their schedule. So what happens? If you want to be good at something, you drop all the extraneous activities. For example, as an athlete you may drop church, family, school, or anything else that gets in the way of workout time. Voila! the attitude of total commitment or win-at-any-cost is born. And it's all because people accept the notion of mind, body, and spirit being very separate. Unable to maintain all three, they begin letting go of certain responsibilities. I know the feeling myself. You say to yourself, "I'm so busy. I'll never be good at that! Why do it at all?"

As a result, most of us give up on something. Businessmen, as a gross stereotype, tend to settle for very few spiritually developing activities and specialize in mental activities like hunting down new customers, new markets, and new product developments. Physical development may continue as a second priority, or it may not happen at all.

Women who choose to work in the home end up heavily biased toward spiritual activities: rearing children, beautifying their home and themselves. Housekeeping or going to aerobics class may keep her fit, or she may give up on body power. Comparable to career men giving up spiritual activities, women in the home tend to settle for a less demanding schedule of mental development. Household chores tend to be repetitive and not mentally challenging.

When a couple splits up the work this way, each specializing in an area the other virtually gives up, it's no wonder they lose any sense of common ground for discussion. Obviously it doesn't have to be that way. Raising kids can be a chance to see new horizons every day. Business leadership can be spiritually challenging and rewarding. But our chopped up, specialized lifestyle has made blending the exception to the rule.

"There are so many forces whose purpose it is to convince us that some of our human qualities are shameful, wrong or not acceptable," Gloria Steinem, founder of Ms. magazine, told me. "Gender roles do it, race roles do it, class roles do it." These restrictions push us into overusing certain resources. "If I'm a little girl I have to be loving and nurturing," Gloria explained. "If I am a little boy, I can't be."

Dropping Mind, Body, or Spirit Causes Roadblocks

For really driven, totally committed people, giving up development of either body, mind, or spirit causes severe problems. At first it saves time and feels like you are getting ahead faster. But eventually you reach roadblocks.

The premed student at Harvard discussed in chapter 10, for example, used only his mind and let his body and spirit atrophy. Initially, he can spend more time studying because he doesn't waste time exercising, socializing, or helping others. Eventually, however, his research progress may be hampered by poor health, lack of enthusiasm, and general burnout.

Similarly, Meredith's performance as a Wall Street executive may eventually suffer when she realizes her children are losing their sanity. One Ann Arbor, Michigan, study found that 36 percent of the children of executives undergo psychiatric or drug abuse treatment each year, as opposed to 15 percent of children of nonexecutives in the same companies. Driven people may lose their drive when they reach their goals and see the price they have paid.

If one aspect of yourself is developed out of proportion to the others, you reach a point at which you can't move forward anymore. For athletes this bottleneck is very apparent. As an Olympic skier I saw it among my peers. We all trained hard and skied well. However, I rose head and shoulders above my competition because I learned to use self-hypnosis to achieve more consistent physical performance.

The more developed you become in any one area, the more the boundaries between mind, body, and spirit blur. There is a synergy in developing mind, body, and spirit all at once.

Tapping Unused Resources Is a Hidden Advantage

Athletes with body power are a dime a dozen. Using mind and spirit, however, is like having a secret weapon. No one expects it! Likewise using body and spirit power in business leadership gives you a tremendous edge over people who rely mainly on their brains.

In business most executives succeed through the use of their brains. As you move ahead, however, you may find that without certain social skills, without values and vision, your career hits a brick wall. Business requires you to inspire groups of people to work well together and produce results.

As you move even further ahead you'll find physical exhaustion could drag down your ability to perform at your best. Today many senior executives jealously guard their workout time knowing that they can't maintain their seventy-hour work weeks and global travel and meet other demands without basic physical stamina. All businesspeople have basic mental skills. Those who would become the great leaders must also develop their spiritual and physical skills. As in sports, it's like having a secret weapon.

Getting out of your comfort zone isn't easy though, or everyone would already be doing it. Gloria Steinem, founder of *Ms.* magazine, described her efforts to begin nurturing herself for the first time at the age of fifty. "It's hard to change because it feels like you're out there on the edge of the universe with the wind whistling past your ears. It's new."

Beyond the Roadblock: Burnout!

Trying to succeed while relying on pure mind power or pure body power or pure spirit power eventually leads to an impasse. Despite hitting these roadblocks, some people push on, trying continually to accomplish more. That's how they become the suffering successful.

The harder it gets, the more they feel, "I've always relied on my brain (or my heart, or my stamina) to get me through this, and gosh darn it I know I can do it now." Insanity in this case can be described as doing the same thing over and over and expecting the same results. When you overuse one side of your strengths, you exhaust that resource.

Thus, it's easy to see why total commitment leads to either physical, emotional, or spiritual burnout (or all three). The suffering successful are trying to accomplish everything with only a fraction of their human resources. Eventually, they must push and drive harder and work longer to get the same results.

Can you imagine a farmer trying to get a full crop out of one-third of his land? Of course the soil would be exhausted and drained. Planting the entire field or rotating crops would probably result in higher yields.

Can you imagine a banker refusing to invest two-thirds of his money? No matter how many long hours he puts in or how aggressively he invests the one-third of his fortune, he is unlikely to do better than someone else who invests a comparable fortune conservatively, but in its entirety. Total commitment of a limited resource is less effective than blending together the resources of a whole person.

It's About Time!

What is the point? We all have only twenty-four hours a day in which to pursue health, wealth, love, and happiness. Some people do it by dividing up the hours into shares: eight hours for work, two hours for family, and one hour for exercise. These people may never become superstars, but they get a little bit of everything. That is what I call *balancing*.

Others decide to give up on something like exercise or relationships in order to spend more time at work. They may become a Nobel Prize winner or a millionaire, but their health and happiness may suffer. This win-at-any-cost attitude is what many people call total commitment.

Succeeding sane requires that you organize your life and your time around the principle of blending rather than balancing or total commitment. Instead of pursuing idealized, intense, and separate activities, you can find ways to combine the things that are important to you.

I was explaining this concept in a seminar, and I saw the light go on in someone's mind. "I get it," he said. "Sometimes I need to do things that don't seem like the right way or the best way. Blending things together may make my life as a whole more efficient, but each individual task might take longer." That is exactly right. You might not get to do your first-choice thing every minute of the day, but the sum of the parts is better than trying to cram all your first-choice activities into twenty-four hours.

I have successfully applied this logic in my own life. I was having a difficult time fitting in exercise while finishing this manuscript, speaking around the country, and still spending time with my husband and daughter. I decided there was no alternative but letting my exercise routine lapse for a few weeks while I finished the last round of editing.

Then I started taking advantage of the exercise I can get while I look after Darcy in the afternoons when I am in town. I do water resistance exercises with one of her plastic buckets while we splash in the pool. In addition I join in with some of her kiddy exercise programs on TV like Bloopy-cise and Elmo-cise. It may feel a bit silly, but it's amazing how much exercise I can get, even when I have absolutely no time for it! Of course Elmo-cise isn't a permanent exercise program for me, but it can augment my routine.

As the man in my seminar commented, the best solution may not always be the ideal solution. I would prefer to exercise with my Cher workout video or at the gym. But rather than lose another hour with Darcy or another hour of writing time, *or lose my mind* trying to cram it all together, I settle for aerobics with Elmo and Darcy. Once my book is done, I can go back to my preferred routine augmented by being active with Darcy.

I benefit by getting more done in less time, and you know what? She'll grow up learning the value of exercise because she will see me doing it. This way it probably won't be long before she'll do Cher-aerobics with me, after all. Blending isn't always perfect. Sometimes, though, it is greater than the sum of the parts.

You, too, can apply the same principles. You can make the time you spend with your friends and family more active. Simple things like walking, splashing around in the pool, or playing croquet are important though they may not seem like exercise to the experts.

Substituting anything that requires movement in place of "doing lunch" or plopping in front of the TV together would make a tremendous difference over time to your health and fitness level. A sedentary life punctuated by trips to the gym is truly less ideal than a life with more movement in small doses from morning till night.

The philosophy of blending suggests that small changes like these in the way you live your daily life add up over time. This principle that small changes add up not only improves your body, but can be used to expand your mind and develop your spirit.

Those who achieve both professional excellence and personal happiness do so by finding creative ways to blend these elements of their unique lives. Like the rest of us, they have only twenty-four hours. By infusing more mind, body, and spirit into the hours available, the time in your life is worth more.

In the chapters that follow you'll get more ideas on how to create a blend that is unique to you. In chapter 19 you'll get an overview of some exemplary lives and a list of the principles my role models follow. In chapter 20 we'll break it down into steps you can follow to assess your daily life and find the little changes that have a big effect.

Keep in mind that blending is an ongoing process. It involves experimenting with the activities in your life and finding out how to make them fit together better. Since things change—you move, your job changes, your interests change—you have to keep finding new blends that work for you. It isn't a "do it once and it's over" thing. It is a new way of approaching living. You need to practice a new way of thinking, seeing, and doing.

Ideally you should reread this book many times to let the ideas become second nature to you. The exercises in chapter 20 are especially useful for quickly identifying more blending opportunities on a regular basis. This book will help steer you in the right direction toward instinctively creating a life where personal and professional goals are mutually reinforcing.

CHAPTER 18

An Inventory of
Blending Activities

U se this inventory to browse for ideas. You'll refer to this chapter as
you finish the book and complete exercises that make over your
week, change the way you tackle your goals, or blend activities for
couples. You'll get new ideas, reinforce old ones, and see how to extend
yourself into new activities without leaving your comfort zone.

These are not revolutionary concepts. In fact, you may see many
things that you already enjoy doing—great! Browsing through the
inventory may give you more insight into why certain activities bring
out the best in you and others don't.

These lists are by no means comprehensive, either. Use them as a
jumping off point, as examples. You may have better ideas that you
already use. I'd love to hear them. Please write 'em down and send
them in for my next book.

The items in the list are organized under the following headings:

MIND/SPIRIT (p. 197)
MIND/BODY (p. 208)
BODY/SPIRIT (p. 213)

You probably will want to start looking under the headings that include your comfort zone and your backup zone. For example, if you are a *spirit-motivated* person and you want to branch out into more physical activity, try looking under body/spirit. You'll find ideas that appeal to you more than pure athletic activities.

On the other hand, if you are a *body-motivated* person looking for spiritual growth opportunities, go to the same heading: body/spirit. The same bridging activities that help you move from spirit to body can help you get from body orientation to spiritual skills. Not every item works in both directions, so just pick up what appeals to you and forget the rest.

My dominant zone, for example, is mind power. Activities listed under body/spirit are not the kinds of activities I gravitate toward. Body/spirit activities feel more alien and uncomfortable to me. However, I don't need to throw myself completely outside my comfort zone to put mind, body, and spirit into my life. I can enrich my life while staying in my comfort zone by adding activities from mind/body and mind/spirit listings.

Mind/Spirit Blending Ideas

JOIN (OR START) A BOOK CLUB

Books can be more fun for those not mind-oriented if you can discuss it with others. Conversely, for mind-motivated people who need to get more into connecting with family, friends, or professional contacts, a book club will be more appealing to you than just sitting around eating together.

Start a group to read a book a month and meet to discuss it. Your group could include family or friends. Coworkers or friends from other companies could make your group good for networking as well as mind expanding. Don't worry that it has to be highbrow literature or a best-seller. Pick something you think you'll enjoy.

READ JUNK!

For many years I stopped reading fiction altogether because I took myself so seriously. I felt guilty when I didn't finish one book before starting another, or worse, if I bought a book and didn't read it at all. Since I bought a lot of pretentious nonfiction books, I felt guilty a lot.

All that changed in college. My friends at Harvard included a brilliant medical student who read trashy sci-fi and a French literature major who read Harlequin romances. They didn't seem to feel guilty about reading for fun or picking up and dropping books. After that I gave myself permission to read the stupid detective mysteries I've loved ever since Nancy Drew.

Give yourself permission to read what, when, and where you like!

DO IT WITH A FRIEND

Take anything mind-oriented and do it with a friend. My mother, for example, used to go to coffee shops late at night with her girlfriend and practice writing positive affirmations.

If you have to study, write a report, or redesign your monthly budget, gather up your stuff and plan a retreat with a friend who has a similarly unpalatable chore. Take your study buddy to Denny's for a few hours, to a fine hotel for the weekend, or anything in between. My husband and I went to a local bed and breakfast for an eight-hour day of working together in beautiful surroundings. How can you make it fun?

END YOUR DAY BY WRITING IN A GRATITUDE JOURNAL

Before bed try to write down at least three things from your day for which you can be grateful. This idea comes from Sarah Ban Breathnach, author of *Simple Abundance,* who says that sometimes all she has to be grateful for is that she survived the day, that it wasn't any longer, and that it is over!

Most of the time, however, there are special friends, magical events, or growing experiences to record. Many great motivational writers, high achievers, and profound thinkers have observed that what you focus on in your life multiplies whether you focus on the bad things or the good things. Keeping a gratitude journal helps keep you focused on the things in your life that you would like to expand.

TAKE A CLASS, GO TO A CONFERENCE
OR PROFESSIONAL WORKSHOP

You can learn mind-centered skills in a group. Spirit-oriented people benefit from learning subconscious-mind techniques, self-discipline skills, or other new perspectives without getting bored because there are people to meet. Mind-oriented people benefit from developing more people skills, making new connections in a context that doesn't bore them like cocktail parties and family gatherings.

DINNER CONVERSATION

Rather than just watching TV, arguing, or criticizing other people, use dinner conversation with friends and family as an opportunity to learn something. Try asking both adults and children, "Did you learn anything today?" Consciously focusing on the opportunity to learn will make you a better listener—you can't learn while talking!

DINNER GAMES

My family used to play "Top-Ten Dinner Club." A topic would be proposed such as sports, and each person would have to name a sport until somebody couldn't think of another one or repeated. Some topics were unusual like kinds of doctors (podiatrist, cardiologist, etc.) and others quite ordinary like musical instruments.

FIND YOUR BLISS

Knowing what you like and who you are can help you to blend more spirit power into your daily life. We lose track of our genuine selves when bombarded by the demands of work, children, TV commercials, social expectations, ad nauseum.

Spend ten minutes with a piece of paper writing down some of your values in the broadest sense. You can structure it by answering a few of the following questions if you like. Try to answer them quickly without thinking for a long time. You don't have to get it right the first time.

- What feeds your soul most? Pick two or three of the following: art, music, family, food, nature, religion, literature, movies, newspapers, solitude, laughter, giving to others, history, politics.
- If you had one free day this week with no responsibilities, what would you do?
- What do you like to eat most?
- What is interesting and unique about your personality?
- Which Ten Commandments do you live by (use the old testament or write your own)?
- Which causes or political parties are most important to you?
- If you were going to die in three days, with whom would you spend the time?
- Of which talents or skills are you most proud?
- Which talents or skills would you like to develop someday?

SEE YOUR IDEAL SELF IN YOUR MIND'S EYE

If you could wave a magic wand and be perfect in your own eyes, what would you be like? An important part of who you are is defined by this paragon to which you unconsciously compare yourself on a regular basis. Would you look better? How? Would you be stronger? How strong? Would you give more to charity? Which one? Does your religion dictate the ideal? How does that apply to you personally? Your idea of your perfection is unique.

Rather than beat yourself up in your mind for not being that person, realize that life is a process of striving toward your understanding of perfection to the best of your ability. By striving toward your ideal, it becomes part of you. Like a caterpillar in its cocoon or a moving cloud you are already perfect in the process of becoming. Revel in your unique image of what you are becoming.

READ A MIND-BASED BOOK WITH A SPIRITUAL MESSAGE

Here are titles of a few spirit power books that would appeal to more mind-oriented people. People who are already very spirit oriented will have their own, very different list:

Jesus, CEO: Using Ancient Wisdom for Visionary Leadership, Laurie Beth Jones
Man's Search for Meaning, Viktor Frankl
The Fifth Discipline: The Art of the Learning Organization, Peter Senge
The 7 Habits of Highly Effective People, Stephen R. Covey
Love, Leo Buscaglia
Revolution from Within, Gloria Steinem

TAKE A TRIP THAT HAS SPECIAL MEANING OR SIGNIFICANCE

Four brothers who emigrated from (the former) Czechoslovakia in their twenties ventured back in their sixties to visit their parents' farm in the Caspian mountains. As Marcel Proust said, "The real voyage of discovery consists not in seeking new landscapes, but in having new eyes."

Stephen Covey tells a story of a man who organized a trip with his son across the Unites States to attend one major league baseball game with every team. Upon hearing the price tag and the time involved, his friend asked, "Do you like baseball that much?"

"I love my son that much," he answered. "Actually, I hate baseball." For him the trip cemented their relationship with quality one-on-one time. The trip telegraphed the message "You are important to me" loud and clear.

Can you organize a trip with special significance?

READ ALOUD

You've probably heard me say more than once that I like coffee houses. I do. And my favorite ones have a bookstore built in. When I go with a group of friends we make an encampment at one of the tables with our coffee and muffins. Each of us wanders around pulling books off shelves, and alternately reading, sipping, and talking. You get snippets of each other's books read out whenever someone hits something funny, appalling, or informative.

Reading to your children definitely counts as a mind/spirit activity. What kind of books do you choose? Find out what interests them. What is the environment? Do you have a regular reading time?

POETRY EVENINGS

Poetry is meant to be heard, not read. One of my favorite mind/spirit things to do is read poetry with a group of friends around the fire with good wine or port and really expensive chocolate truffles. It isn't easy though. Even in the most educated crowds most people get embarrassed about reading poetry. But hey, it isn't nearly as bad as Japan's karaoke tradition where they make everyone sing!

What you have to do is serve lots of wine during dinner, wait until people are feeling relaxed, and then casually bring out a few poetry books. If you can get a few people to read the momentum builds. Having a few allies ahead of time helps. After they see it doesn't kill you, usually everyone finds a poem they like and reads it aloud.

I love hearing different voices and the kinds of poems my friends choose. But please don't force anyone to participate in my name!

Alternatively, you can pitch the event as a great family activity. I grew up in a house where poetry was recited. Why badger your kids to study English literature if you aren't willing to live it?

Shortcuts: Buy poetry on tape for the family to listen to together. Attend a poetry reading with family or friends at a local bookstore or coffee house.

Variation: Buy a Stephen King book on tape and listen to it outside by a big bonfire while toasting marshmallows.

ATTEND A WORSHIP SERVICE OF A DIFFERENT FAITH

Try a Vietnamese congregation, a synagogue, or a rollicking African-American service. Quaker services are very unusual and moving. Ask people you know if you can go with them one week. Get together with a friend or take your family to share the experience. You will remember this for the rest of your life!

TRY NEW THINGS YOU HAVE BEEN SECRETLY LONGING TO DO

Mind power is fed by trying new things while secret longings show you your values. Do you want to learn belly dancing? French? Wine tasting skills? Oil painting? Golf? Palm reading? Indulge yourself in just a taste of what you want without feeling like you have to take it seriously.

GET THE SCHEDULE OF EVENTS FROM LOCAL BOOKSTORES AND LIBRARIES

Often there are authors speaking to groups, panel discussions, poetry readings, storytime for children, and much more! These events bring new books and ideas to life for those of you who would rather fraternize than spend solitary time reading.

PERSONALIZE YOUR WORK

Do you have a job that thousands of other people in the world could do? Take steps to personalize the way you do your job. Put something of yourself into it. Tom Peters, coauthor of *In Search of Excellence*, observed that many entrepreneurs plan, save, and sweat to create a new restaurant, hardware store, or boutique only to create something that is totally normal, ordinary, and acceptable. Why, he wonders, don't they put more of themselves into such a personal creation?

What can you do to put more of your personality into your job? Start in simple ways. Put an etch-a-sketch and transformer toys on your desk in the sales department like my brother did. Or be the only policeman with Impressionist prints near your desk instead of pinup girls.

"We must overcome the notion that we must be regular," wrote Uta Hagen. "It robs you of the chance to be extraordinary and leads you to the mediocre." That's how I feel now about having one leg. It's part of what makes me interesting and unique, like Barbra Streisand's nose or Danny DeVito's height. Imagining myself with two legs I see someone too much like everyone else.

PERSONALIZE YOUR IMAGE AS A LEADER

People follow real people more than abstract ideas. Part of good leadership involves letting people see a little bit of the real you.

In one writing class, we created characters with three adjectives from a list of virtues, flaws, and deeply wicked traits. Surpassingly, the characters with all good (or all bad) traits tended to fall flat. You can't relate to someone too perfect. It doesn't seem real. The best characters had a lovable mix of virtues and flaws. Even a character who wrestles with his own streak of wickedness resonates with our humanness more than goody-goody types.

As a leader, you can think of yourself as a character, too. Do you try to present a perfect image? Letting a few parts of your unique personality—even your flaws—show in your leadership style gives your team a real person to rally around.

TAKE INTO ACCOUNT OTHER PEOPLE'S PERSONALITIES

Think about your employees, your customers, your spouse, and your children. Do they like their physical environment? Do they get to choose music? Food? How much are they able to influence the way they work? Studies show that going against the grain of someone's personality is a major source of stress.

In your job, do you really think about what other people want or do you give them what you want to give?

PLAY THIS MIND-SPIRIT GAME WITH FRIENDS

The object of the game is to guess how a person will answer a question. Whoever can guess the answers most frequently wins. This game teaches you to think about someone else's views and try to put yourself in their position.

Explain how the game is played to everyone. Once they understand, ask everyone to write questions on small pieces of paper and put them in a bowl. The first person selects a question, reads it aloud, and writes down the answer. Everyone else guesses how that person will answer the question. Ten points for each correct guess!

Ideal questions seek opinions on anything from personal tastes to political issues. "What is your favorite toy?" "What is your best physical feature?" "What would you do first if you were president?" The only restraint should be that someone may draw their own question . . . and have to answer it.

WRITE DOWN YOUR CREDO, THE SET OF BELIEFS THAT GUIDES YOUR BEHAVIOR

Robert Fulghum, author of *All I Really Need to Know I Learned in Kindergarten*, said that his best-selling book emerged out of doing this exercise once a year.

WRITE A MISSION STATEMENT

Spend five to ten minutes (with a friend, perhaps?) writing or talking about your personal mission or your purpose in life. It may be using a talent like creating music, leading others, or learning. One person in a workshop I attended said his purpose was simply to listen to others. For others a mission is accomplishing something very specific like Mother Teresa saving children. Still others see their mission as striving to live better and to be a better person, every day. What is your mission?

Don't worry if your mission isn't clear enough, yet. It changes over time. Just choose something now and rest assured that as you practice choosing a mission and exploring it for a while, you will get better at it. The choice is always yours!

Taking the time to structure your thoughts and put them into words encourages you to apply your conscious-mind skills and make choices in concert with applying your deepest feelings.

PAMPER YOURSELF MORE WHEN YOU
HAVE TO DO MIND THINGS

For example, how can you make paying the bills or budgeting a more positive experience? Good music? Ice cream? Can you promise yourself a certain reward every time you do it? Maybe it would help if you invested in good equipment like desk organizers, filing system holders, return address labels, etc. Make sure that the items you purchase are attractive rather than simply utilitarian. Is there anything you could do that would make you *love* to do a mind task you currently don't like? I would bet you have never asked yourself this question before!

When I study or write I often go to a coffee shop and plug in my computer. It's clean and pretty with no telephones to ring or dishes to do. I can get all the coffee I want, with snacks and nice music. Even when I don't feel like working, the appeal of the coffee shop pulls me over the threshold of getting started. Even when I worked in sales at IBM coffee shops helped me to focus on getting my reports done or planning a proposal. Just because mind power demands self-discipline doesn't mean you can't have fun, too!

Tony Robbins had a similar example about having fun while working hard. After a long trip he was greeted by a stack of over fifty phone calls to return. At first he thought about putting it off until later or just doing a few. "What I really wanted to do," he was thinking, "is just get in the Jacuzzi and forget about it." And that's when it hit him! Take the portable phone, get in the Jacuzzi with a cold drink and do the calls all at once! Instead of choosing between work and play, he blended the two together.

When I first heard this story, I thought, "Well, that's fine for a multimillionaire like Tony, but what about the rest of us nine to fivers?" But the truth is, most of us have enough control over our jobs and our lives to inject at least a little fun into the hard stuff. There is no law saying that hard work has to be unpleasant.

LEARN MIND-BASED SKILLS IN A SUPPORTIVE,
FRIENDLY ENVIRONMENT

If you are a very spirit-centered person, don't try to learn skills like time management and goal setting from a book. Go to workshops, classes, or seminars where you can meet interesting people and make a connection with others. If possible talk a friend into going with you. Don't beat yourself up for not getting it out of a book. That is not your style.

Don't be surprised if you have to try many different methods until you find one that fits your personality and lifestyle. Mind-centered people tend to act as if there is only one way to do something. That's bunk. There are hundreds of styles of exercising financial discipline, time discipline, or any other personal discipline. Try to find a teacher whose temperament resembles yours.

EXPLORE NEW HORIZONS IN A SUPPORTIVE, FRIENDLY ENVIRONMENT

All my life my mother talked about how much she wanted to travel. She said that her mother, a woman who ironed shirts for forty dollars per week and was proud to have graduated from being someone's maid, died with brand new suitcases in the closet.

But the only times my mother has gone abroad were to visit me in Oxford, to attend the Olympics, and to visit Niagara Falls on her honeymoon. Finally I realized that she likes to travel with someone and for something particularly meaningful involving family, or momentous like the Olympics. Whereas I will fly off at the drop of a hat by myself to Korea, Portugal, or France, she needs a travel buddy or a purpose to get her moving.

MEDITATE DAILY

This exercise uses the mind to nourish the soul. Spend five minutes in the morning or evening calming and focusing your energies. Close your eyes and relax. Imagine yourself in a beautiful place or a place with special meaning. Try to let yourself be there in all five senses. Hear the wind, music, or any other noise. Feel the air, sun, or sand. What do you smell? Look at the details of what you are wearing and doing.

TO DO LIST BEFORE BED

Write a list of things to do for the next day before bed. Over night your subconscious mind works on the problems and gets you fully prepared to tackle the list the next day. Take advantage of this secret store of energy and focus. Thank you to Jill Kelsey for this idea!

TRY A FEW NEW CULTURAL ACTIVITIES

Try chamber music, theater, ballet, opera, galleries. Try modern cultural activities: rock, jazz, modern dance, etc. Try non-Anglo cultural activities: Spanish dance, of African or Russian gypsy music. Attend a magic show, puppet show, or other children's entertainment with your kids or someone else's if necessary.

Add mind elements to spirit things:

Give your skills to the community.
Put love into your work.
Do something you love.

Do any of the relationship exercises in Part III. It's a mind/spirit activity because it gives you a new paradigm for looking at your relationship. It is a structured and logical method for uncovering the unique things about each of you as individuals. You do it in a way that encourages you to value and blend your strengths.

Mind/Body Blending Ideas

TRAVEL TO A THIRD WORLD COUNTRY

Want to know how to get rich quick? Get a new perspective by seeing how most of the world's people live. Rough it a little. You'll realize that you're among the richest 1 percent of the population!

WORK ON A FARM IN EUROPE, NEW ZEALAND, OR THE UNITED STATES

Experience a different lifestyle or culture by becoming a part of it. An organization called Willing Workers on Organic Farms (WWORF) provides a listing of farms around the world who trade bed and board for four hours a day of work in the house or outside. What a unique way to see the world!

Scientific expeditions also frequently advertise for helpers who will pay their own airfare and join the group in an exotic place. A middle-aged British schoolteacher, for example, signed up to work with a team counting kangaroos in Australia! One literary agent rides on a boat off the west coast of Canada counting whales every year. Talk about new mind maps!

Only your imagination limits your possibilities. Build a creative mind on a reality of creative adventures.

AUDIO BOOKS

Play books on tape at the gym or while gardening, driving, cooking, or doing dishes. Instead of sitting still while reading, you can move around and do things. This allows body people to fit some "reading" into their busy, active lifestyle.

For mind-focused people, it allows you to get off your duff a little more often without getting mentally bored. I listen to fiction, motivational speakers, business management authors, and other tapes while doing other things that would normally bore me. When I would rather curl up on the couch with a trashy novel than work, clean, or run errands, I feel so virtuous if I listen to a trashy novel on the exercise bike!

Caution: If you get too distracted by audiotapes, you may not want to drive, handle knives in the kitchen, or do anything else dangerous while listening to tapes.

Although taped books are expensive to buy, you can borrow them from the library or check them out from video stores. Tony Robbins has a subscription service called *Powertalk,* which sends monthly audiotapes with synopses of the latest books on management and business topics.

KENDO

Kendo is the ancient Japanese art of practicing a sport in your mind. Sit still and close your eyes. Practice your golf, basketball, or weight lifting. Whether you are a mind person trying to get better at sports or a body person trying to increase concentration doesn't matter. You'll learn both.

One prisoner of war in Vietnam played golf on his favorite course over and over in his mind during the six years of his captivity. Naturally one of the first things he did on his return home was to play this course for real at last. To his and everyone else's surprise, his game was better than before!

Scientists have found that visualizing exercise actually primes the muscles involved. Visualization makes a great warm-up for or supplement to any exercise regimen.

LESSONS IN ANY SPORT

Rather than just doing the same sport over and over, taking lessons forces you to use your mind and improve rather than just treading water. Again, this improves your body power and mind power at the same time.

TRY SEVERAL NEW SPORTS

Like travel, tackling a new sport often provides a new perspective. Volleyball, basketball, or baseball enhances teamwork skills. Skiing and whitewater kayaking can test your courage and ability to let go. Racquet sports or football can teach strategy. Scuba diving takes you into another world. Stretch your mind (and body) by trying five new sports in a row. This idea is probably more appealing to body-oriented people than mind people. But who knows? Whatever shape you are in, don't overdo it. Consult your doctor about any new exercise program you attempt.

TRY NEW FOODS

Vary your food choices or try a new recipe. Live on the wild side now and then. You may stumble on a new favorite dish!

PLAY RACQUETBALL OR WORK OUT WITH BUDDIES FROM WORK

My husband turns his squash time into a mind/body experience by playing a colleague from the lab. In between sets and over a beer afterward they often mull over sticky points in their physics research.

TAPE YOUR OWN IDEAS

Make your own audiotape of affirmations, poetry, or music to use during exercise, chores, or driving. You could record a set of questions about who you are (e.g., what you are learning, what you admire most about yourself, what makes you laugh) that will remind you to ask yourself these important issues regularly. Leave your personal tape in your car. When you have long drives or get stuck in traffic, you can do some work with your mind and spirit.

Another good personal tape idea would be a goal/vision tape. Think of a goal you are working toward like finishing a degree, successfully handling a project at work, or even finding a mate. Spend a few minutes with your eyes closed imagining what it will be like when you succeed. Describe on a tape very specifically what is happening to you when you reach your goal. What are you wearing? Who are you with? How do you feel? How does your day-to-day life change?

Playing a goal/vision tape over and over has an incredibly powerful effect on your motivation and thus your ability to succeed. If you knew it would more than double your chances of success, would you give it a try?

BREATHING AND RELAXATION EXERCISES

Look up Deepak Chopra's *Ageless Body, Timeless Mind* to find breathing exercises and a host of other mind/body activities.

DESK-ERCISES

Periodically break up sedentary desk work with simple stretches, stomach exercise, or isometrics. A list of these is included in appendix B.

I'd been preaching the virtues of this for a long time before I could actually get myself to do it. I knew the studies claimed that a stretch every forty-five to ninety minutes boosts mental productivity, but I always wanted to keep working "just a few minutes more!" However, once you try it for a day or two, even the most hard-core workaholic will be converted because you get more work done!

DESK-ERCISES ON DISK

The hardest part about desk-ercise is remembering to do it. You can order a program from my company that pops up on your computer with a new desk-ercise every forty minutes. Grant wrote the program for me!

READ *THE INNER GAME OF TENNIS* BY TIM GALLWEY

Whether or not you play tennis this book can help you master the mental side of any sport or athletic activity. It transformed my ability to learn and compete in skiing. It shows you step-by-step how to turn your subconscious away from sabotage to support. Exercises for concentrating, changing bad habits, and mastering competition are included. You'll enjoy this book whether you are a mind person dabbling at sports or a body person seeking to strengthen your game.

PHYSICAL AFFIRMATIONS WORKOUT

Take five minutes before your regular workout to answer three questions.

1. What is something you are proud of having accomplished?
2. What is something you are embarrassed about that you need to forgive yourself for doing?

3. What is something you are excited about that is happening in your life?

Tape these questions to your sports bag or racquet case to remind you to do it. Think of a good answer to each of these questions.

During the inevitable dead mind time between sets or while you lift weights or do aerobics, let your mind wander over the answers to the questions. Think about what made you proud. Why did it make you proud? How did you feel? Did anyone else notice? Savor the moment in your mind as you work out. In the same way, let yourself dwell on forgiveness and then on what you are excited about for your future.

You are using the free "mind space" during your workout to give your mind a positive workout at the same time. Like a strong body, a positive attitude doesn't last forever unless you maintain it.

YOGA, T'AI CHI, KARATE OR OTHER MARTIAL ARTS

Physical training systems from Asia often incorporate a component of mental training as well. Find a teacher who takes an interest in the mental and/or spiritual side of the training.

The national karate champion of the United States once told me, "Black belts seldom get mugged or killed by random attacks. We carry a sense of strength and confidence that discourages would-be assailants." Although the hour was late and he was catching the subway to a less than safe part of Washington, D.C., he wasn't worried. He knew it was the mental side of his training that protected him more than the physical side.

Body/Spirit Blending Ideas

EXERCISE OUTDOORS

Have you ever heard someone say, "I know I should exercise in a gym, but I just can't stick to it. I have to be outdoors"? Listen for a while and you'll hear this tipoff that you've got a body/spirit or spirit/body person on your hands. Maybe you've said it yourself.

Stop right now and give yourself permission to avoid gyms for the rest of your life! Run by the ocean, climb mountains, go dancing on Saturday night instead. Work in your garden, go bowling, or sail a boat. Push a baby carriage, play tennis, bicycle, walk for miles on a golf course and revel in who you are.

You'll probably have more success sticking to an exercise routine if you go with the grain of your personality rather than fighting it.

DO WHAT YOU LOVE

It's the only life you've got. Take out your calendar now and cut out one activity you hate and add one activity you love.

BLEND GIVING TO OTHERS WITH SOMETHING YOU ALREADY HAVE TO DO

Donate some of your products from work to charity. Offer your skills or speaking ability to schools or charity groups.

BLEND SPENDING TIME WITH YOUR CHILDREN AND GIVING TO OTHERS

You need to spend a certain amount of quality time with them. What better way to show them how well off they are? Just telling them never sinks in.

Plan an afternoon of volunteering at a local homeless shelter with families or a daycare center for disabled children. Ask the shelter for advice on what you and your children can do to help. Be prepared to answer a lot of tough questions from your children! Explaining ahead of time how to behave may prevent some embarrassing moments. Make sure your child has an opportunity (if they want to) to actually help other children or adults rather than just tagging along.

BLEND EXERCISE WITH SOMETHING
PERSONALLY SPIRITUAL FOR YOU

Make or buy a tape of bible study or religious teaching to listen to on a Walkman during running, weight lifting, or a stair-machine workout. Take ballet class in beautiful tights with wooden floors and practice barres. Organize an annual family baseball or touch football game. Exercise in whatever way brings you closer to the God in you.

Susanne, my colleague, is a terrific example. She has switched her gym membership to the Jewish Community Center where she can not only exercise and swim, but also attend cultural discussions, live music, and other enriching experiences for the entire family.

BLEND EXERCISE WITH GIVING TO OTHERS

Enter a run or walk for your favorite charity. Walk precincts for a politician. Chaperone a group of Girl Scouts selling cookies door to door. Volunteer to help an environmental group or a community park.

JOIN A PARENT-CHILD EXERCISE CLASS OR SPORTS TEAM

I know one mother who has enrolled herself and her five-year-old twins in a karate class. Many community centers have toddler gymnastics classes for "Mommy and Me." What a perfect spirit/body activity!

EAT NOTHING THAT IS NOT BEAUTIFUL, HEALTHY, OR BOTH

Food, when beautifully or lovingly prepared, is spiritual. There is a fast-food restaurant near us called Daily's, where all the meals have less than ten grams of fat, yet are wonderfully flavorful and presented with flair. Can you add more beauty, more flavor, and more health into your eating routine? The next few items in the idea inventory build on this theme.

INJECT A BIT MORE BEAUTY INTO YOUR FOOD

Think about the colors of the food on your plate. Use garnishes like raspberries, lemons, or fresh parsley. Don't make it burdensome or time consuming. Just try to add or change one thing from time to time.

If you don't do the cooking, ask if you can set the table. Put a small pansy or geranium from the garden by each plate. Find a centerpiece —a doll, flowers, a statue. Serve a weekend breakfast on your finest china for a change. Buy some unusual, bright, or patterned napkins. Serve coffee on a silver tray. Even if you are eating McDonald's takeout, you can serve it beautifully as a picnic or even with your china! Dare to have flair.

Don't feel pressure to do all these things at once. It would be too much work and might appear excessively fussy. One or two changes can be fun; too many changes may drive you crazy.

INJECT A LITTLE MORE LOVE INTO YOUR FOOD

In the story *Like Water for Chocolate,* a beautiful woman cooks sensual food to express her love for the man she loves but cannot marry. Whenever her wicked sister asks for her recipes, she says simply, "I cook with a great deal of love." Like the wicked sister, I used to be frustrated with that sort of answer, but I have since learned the truth of it. If you love what you are doing and *why* you are doing it, you can do it with greater attention, energy, and creativity than anyone else.

INJECT MORE HEALTH INTO YOUR EATING HABITS

Traditional American meals involve a big piece of meat, a starch, and some vegetables. To serve healthier meals I sometimes try to think of making the green vegetable the centerpiece of the meal and relegating meat to a supporting role. For example, a stir-fry, pasta primavera, pizza, or stuffed potato puts vegetables into the limelight. Giving fresh fruit a higher priority, either as a side dish or a dessert, helps, too. Eating healthier, more attractive, more loving food gets you into the body/ spirit zone!

COOK A MEAL ONCE A WEEK IN HONOR OF A PARTICULAR PERSON IN THE HOUSE

Think about the foods he likes and the health content as well as the appearance of the food. Make it a total body/spirit experience.

Don't forget to honor yourself, too! If you don't do the cooking, you can plan a night out for your special someone for no reason other than to serve him or her all their favorite foods.

ATTEND A LIVE CONCERT

Jazz, rock, chamber, or opera music has an electric, life-giving force when heard live. It doesn't have to be a big-ticket item either. In my town there's a music library with free lunchtime concerts with trios and quartets. Plus coffee houses, bars, public parks, etc. Get one of those weekend-scene papers to find out where to go. Better yet, start asking people in the know.

MUSICAL EVENINGS

New Zealanders have this great tradition of inviting musical friends around for dinner with their guitars, flutes, voices, or whatever. The usual effort to keep the after-dinner conversation flowing is replaced by singing, laughing, and listening. Dare to do it!

EXPRESS YOUR PERSONALITY THROUGH YOUR APPEARANCE

Think about the clothes in which you feel comfortable as well as attractive. What is it about those clothes that makes you feel good? Make a decision to get rid of something you wear because everyone else does. Treat yourself to a piece of clothing that is very *you*.

INJECT MORE OF YOUR PERSONALITY AND LIFESTYLE INTO YOUR PHYSICAL ENVIRONMENT

Does your living space reflect how you live? My husband and I recently converted the biggest room in our house, the living room, into half play-space for Darcy and half work-space with desks and computers. It didn't make sense to keep the best, most accessible room for company when we don't spend much time entertaining at home. Our space reflects what we do most: writing, working, and playing on our computers as well as spending time with Darcy.

MEANINGFUL AND GIVING SEXUAL INTIMACY

We can't talk about body/spirit activities and miss this one! Plan a special time together when the main point is having time, energy, and space to give pleasure generously. It may be a weekend away or just an early night. See chapter 16 for more ideas.

BEST SPIRIT/BODY WEIGHT-LOSS SYSTEMS

The Jenny Craig program gives you lots of support through counselors, workshops, exercise clubs, and ready-made food. It isn't a perfect system, but it is the only one I know that gives you so much human contact. Weight Watchers provides a lower cost version of a support group for healthy eating.

FIND AN EATING BUDDY

You can do it without any official program by finding a healthy-eating partner as a support system. Having someone with whom you work to meet for healthy food or take turns preparing lunches could help keep you on higher ground. Your eating buddy might also be your exercise buddy.

My husband, Grant, gets an "eating buddy of the year award" for the time he joined Jenny Craig with me, went to all the classes, ate all the food, and suffered alongside me as my eating buddy. He lost seven pounds; I lost fifteen.

A DIET WITH A PERSONAL STORY

Also try video tapes or books by Susan Powter. She has a simple, effective system for healthy weight reduction—with an attitude! Her book, *Stop the Insanity!* is one of the few books I would recommend in this body/spirit section because it is so easy to read. It is about her life as much as about diet and fitness. It will change your life!

DO ART

Instead of going to see or hear music take a painting class, a piano lesson, or a singing lesson. *Do* art, don't just watch.

USE SYMBOLS TO ENHANCE SPECIAL MOMENTS
OR FEELINGS IN YOUR LIFE

Susan Taylor lights a candle in the morning as part of her starting the day routine. A friend of mine wears a special talisman around his neck to symbolize serenity when he feels he needs a reminder. Another fellow keeps an ice chest with champagne in the trunk of his car to celebrate anything that arises. Do you keep physical symbols on hand for the feelings that are special to you?

CREATE A SPECIAL PLACE

Create a place (or find a place) that makes you feel special, nurtured, or at peace. Whether it is a special nook in your house, a section of your garden, or a public beach, have a real physical place you can go to for restoring your spiritual energy.

DO SOMETHING TO MARK THE PERSONAL
OCCASIONS IN YOUR LIFE

I tend to be rushing from goal to goal without stopping to savor personal victories for myself or my loved ones. The Deane family in New Zealand is particularly good at marking accomplishments with a dinner, a champagne toast, or some sort of special recognition. You can create your own awards ceremony to mark achievements in your circle of friends or family. Create a tradition of going to a certain restaurant or buying a particular brand of champagne.

Whenever someone passes a milestone at work, gets a raise, or reaches a personal improvement goal, you can have a little celebration of your own. I categorize this as body/spirit because it involves doing something, taking time, and frequently using food or champagne to give the meaning of the event a grounding in physical reality.

PHYSICAL GRATITUDE

Can you express gratitude for being alive in a physical way? Some people hold hands when they bow their heads to say grace before a meal. In yoga there is a stance with arms and face stretched upward that is called greeting the day. One family who survived a car accident recently told me how they held hands to say thank you for their lives. There is something powerful about accepting the grace of life in a physical way.

MOVE GRACEFULLY, AND GENTLY THROUGH A STRESSFUL DAY

There was a day I had to speak in a high-pressure situation on only five hours of sleep after being stuck in Chicago by missed airline connections. I started getting frazzled, but after I did my LaserWalk preparation technique I decided to just relax. I decided that each step, each movement would be a prayer of thanks for being alive. Thus, I enjoyed each moment more without worrying too far ahead. I allowed myself to be part of the plan rather than feeling in charge.

Can you move more gracefully today? Relax a little more. Let your movements unfold rather than being forced. When each movement is a prayer it should be graceful, unselfish, unselfconscious—an end in itself.

CHAPTER 19

What Puts Fulfillment into a Successful Life?

At first glance, my role models seem to have almost nothing in common. They come from all walks of life. They include athletes, politicians, sales reps, CEOs, nonprofit execs, and educators. They include both sexes, all colors, and people from all corners of the globe.

Some are rugged individuals who refuse to fit into a corporate mold or a traditional marriage. Others are consummate corporate professionals with very traditional marriages. It is clear that none of the obvious stereotypes or categories provide any clues as to why some people self-destruct under the pressure of success while others do not.

As I interviewed my role models and heroes, however, certain messages were continually repeated. They told me about the same core beliefs, which helped each of them cope with success. Some of these beliefs were familiar to me, others showed me where I need improvement.

This chapter covers eight basic beliefs that were shared by the most successful and happy people with whom I talked. As I explain how they apply to my life or to the lives of others, you should be thinking about how you can apply these principles in your life to guarantee more fulfillment on your road to riches and happiness.

We're now going to take a look at the day-to-day lives of successful people and illustrate how the following eight beliefs preserve their sanity.

Eight Principles for Putting More Fulfillment into a Successful Life

HOW TO CULTIVATE SANITY THAT CAN WITHSTAND SUCCESS

1. Take responsibility for your own sanity.
2. Explore and develop your passion, your skill, and your personality through your work.
3. Turn your work into your mission by making it an expression of your values.
4. Find an organization that supports your goals, values, and style of work.
5. If you can't find a supportive organization, create one.
6. Focus your efforts and your relationships.
7. Pace yourself.
8. Cultivate your humility.

PRINCIPLE ONE: TAKE RESPONSIBILITY FOR YOUR OWN SANITY

"For many years I succeeded in a very insane way," says Peggy Cooper-Cafritz, a well-known Washington activist for the arts. "I was up at seven A.M., attended meetings back to back all day long, and then did my 'essential' reading and paper work until two or three in the morning. Day after day."

Her hard work as a founder and fund-raiser for the Duke Ellington School of the Arts in Washington, D.C., has been recognized by many in the Washington elite. At the intimate parties in her home I rubbed shoulders with Colin Powell, Vernon Jordan, Donna Shalala, and other luminaries more often than at work in the White House. As a result of her work the school continues to enroll inner-city kids and produces operatic divas, actors on stage and screen, musicians, and other artists.

Peggy, an African-American woman, resembled a stereotype in the black community of a mother figure who "does" for everyone. She raises her kids, volunteers for every committee at church, works a job and then raises her kids' kids. All-loving, all-giving, she sacrifices herself for the lives of others. Literally.

My aunt Rosie, who won awards at church for service and worked as a nurse, was still raising her youngest son when she died of heart failure in her early fifties. Although Peggy Cooper-Cafritz earned her law degree and moved up in society, she was living out Rosie's lifestyle and trying to "do" for all the children at the Duke Ellington School, without doing for herself first.

But black women have no monopoly on this lifestyle. CEOs and other executives often live the same life, jumping up with the alarm, scanning reports while dressing, making phone calls in the car, and rushing from a breakfast meeting to staff meetings. They rush from task to task acting like they have to save the world single-handedly before arriving home and falling into bed "with barely enough energy to say goodnight to whoever might be next to us," as Ken Blanchard says.

"You can use me as the 'before and after' example for succeeding sane," Peggy confided. "Now if I get up early it's for exercise or doing something fun with my kids. And if I stay up late, it is more likely to be looking for that ultra quiet time when I can reflect more deeply. My schedule is less frenetic. I try not to organize every moment of every day."

Her typical day still includes dashing in and out of a White House meeting or a political fundraisers' meeting, entertaining lists of Who's Who in her palatial home, or attending a black tie gala event at the Kennedy Center. However, it also includes taking her children to a play or a silly movie, having a manicure, or meeting with kids from the Duke Ellington School of the Arts who need advice on their college plans.

"It still sounds pretty hectic," I said in awe.

"Yeah, but there is definitely more stuff in there for me," she responded. "I finally decided that I am responsible for keeping myself sane." This realization is essential to achieving bliss as well as accolades.

Succeeding sane doesn't happen by accident. One of the reasons I was able to get interviews with so many powerful people is that my interviewees have consciously wrestled with this problem for many years. They care deeply about this. Whether I was talking to a Wall Street banker, a triathlete, or a White House official, they all had a sense of being one of the few people in their arena who worried about maintaining some perspective in the midst of all-out competition.

The first step to succeeding sane is taking responsibility for your own sanity. As in the twelve-step programs for alcoholics you have to admit your insanities. Interestingly enough, most people I interviewed wanted to argue that they are succeeding sane no matter how crazy their lives are. Everyone, including me, justifies a lot of their insane behavior. Fortunately you don't have to label yourself as totally sane or totally insane. Just keep striving for more sanity in your life.

PRINCIPLE TWO: EXPLORE AND DEVELOP YOUR PASSION, YOUR SKILL, AND YOUR PERSONALITY THROUGH YOUR WORK

When I was about fourteen my brother and I had an argument.

"I am going to have a career where I do what I love," he said. "Maybe photography or making movies."

"That's a terrible idea," I argued. "If you try to make a living doing what you love, it ruins it. Look at photographers who spend all day photographing slobbering babies instead of creating art. Even if you create art, you have to deal with galleries, framing, and publicity. Who needs that kind of pressure?" I was a fundamentally cynical person.

"I'm going to go out and make as much money as I can in business," I said proudly. "Instead of trying to turn something I love into a business, I'll just do business. After that, I can do whatever I want. I can paint, read, travel, whatever. Then my passions remain undefiled by monetary concerns."

"You're wrong!" my idealistic brother returned. "You don't have to prostitute your talents to a business. If you really devote yourself to your art, the business will follow. Other people will help you when your art is good enough. You must follow your heart."

It has only taken me seventeen years to admit I was dead wrong. Putting your life on hold while you get rich is a dangerous game. By the time you earn your freedom, you may have forgotten how to use it or why you wanted it at all. Once you have lost your chance to spend your life developing your talents, your personality, and your passion, you can't buy it back at any price.

Which is not to say that business can't be your passion. Whether you sell cars, paint pictures, or write advertising copy, someone who loves their work will have more fun, work longer hours, and pay closer attention. If you don't love what you do, how can you keep up with those who do? Finding a job that taps into your talents, your personality, and your passions is crucial for succeeding and staying sane at the same time.

But my brother was also wrong. Toiling away at your art and waiting for money to find you is not a recipe for succeeding sane, either. It's an invitation to financial disaster.

Truly putting mind, body, and spirit into your vocation means tapping into your talents, but also being willing to do the work of connecting to your customers and making sure you get paid. The discipline of the market often encourages you to listen more closely to the needs of others as well as your own heart. According to my definition of spirit power, that is a good thing.

Today I enjoy the opportunity to create art through my writing and speaking. But I also have to do a lot of paper work, contract negotiation, accounting, phone calls, and all the stuff of running a business.

I also have to take into consideration what sells, who pays, and who doesn't. But I use these facts to push my creativity to higher levels rather than drag it down. As a speaker, I put more preparation into each speech, research the audience, and weave their stories together with mine to create a unique piece of performance art for each client. As a result, I get higher fees than I would for giving the same tired speech over and over. I found a way to put more in and get more in return.

As a writer, I had to change the focus of my book several times in the process of selling it. My agent asked me to make it more personally compelling by digging deeper into my heart and my feelings. My publisher asked me to make it more practical, more useful for readers. Each time I reworked it, I built on what I had done before but reached higher in my own eyes. I let them push me, but I set a higher standard for myself.

I guess you could say my brother and I were both wrong—or both right. You have to do what you love *and* follow the money.

PRINCIPLE THREE: TURN YOUR WORK INTO YOUR MISSION BY MAKING IT AN EXPRESSION OF YOUR VALUES

Magical things happen when mind, body, and spirit truly work in tandem. Blair Saddler, CEO of Children's Hospital in San Diego, raised the ordinary task of building a new wing on the hospital to the level of a mission by working from the heart.

Tapping into his spiritual/emotional side, Blair understood how foreboding a hospital could be for children. I can confirm that staying in hospitals as a child was a dreary, depressing, institutional experience. He wasn't satisfied with just making space for more beds. He wanted to create a place that was more intimate, homey, and playful.

"We had all the usual problems associated with building a new wing on the hospital," says Blair. "We had to float bonds on Wall Street, sift through permit processes, and design issues. A lot of people thought I was crazy to make the job harder than it already was."

A team of five on the building committee forged a shared vision of what a child-oriented hospital could look like. To put the vision on paper they sought help not only from professional architects, but also from nurses, social workers, and patients.

However, not everyone supported Saddler's unusual design ideas. About six weeks before the building opened, it was as though a gray cloud had descended on the hospital. Several people were spreading rumors that the new building was excessively strange and unappealing. "That was the hardest period for me," says Saddler.

"Once the building actually opened, however, everyone who went through it had this 'Aha!' reaction. The outpouring of euphoria and support was incredible. We won five architectural awards, the employees loved working in it, and most important, the children gave it a thumbs up."

What makes the building different? Simple things make a big difference like lower windows that allow kids to see out. Smaller groups of beds per unit, chimneys, and gables give it a more intimate, homey feel. Playful aspects include picture frames in every room that can display the patient's art work or any picture from the hospital catalog. Ceilings are transformed at night into a sky full of stars with different constellations in each room.

Blair Saddler and his team drew on their spiritual side: feelings, caring, and giving. They also drew on their mental strengths: imagination, new ideas, and the decisiveness to follow through. They used body power: taking action, working hard, and persevering through difficulties. Combining mind, body, and spirit gave them insight into the importance of the physical space and its effect on working, healing, and relating to one another. They created a unique and exciting hospital wing.

"It's about putting in passion rather than just getting by," says Blair.

In the course of this book, we've talked about many people like Blair who find work that is meaningful and changes the world. Johnetta Cole, president of Spelman College, changes the lives of thousands of young, African-American women and changes the way the nation thinks about us at the same time. Bill Higgins, a senior executive at Morgan Stanley on Wall Street, recruits and places minorities on the fast track. Peggy Cooper-Cafritz spends most of her time raising money to support a professional-caliber arts program at an inner-city public school.

"What about me?" you may be thinking. "I can't quit my job and go after some grandiose cause. I have to earn a living." Or, deep down, you may not want to save the world anyway.

"My dream is owning my own coffee shop," you say. "I know it won't end world hunger or drug abuse, but it's what I want to do."

Guess what? You don't have to act as though you are saving the world to turn your work into a mission. When you apply your personal standards and values to everything you do at work, it becomes an expression of who you are.

Florence Griffith-Joyner, the Olympic runner, applies discipline, love, and perseverance to her sport. She has broken so many records that many people simply say she is "the fastest woman alive." As a result she is also a role model for others. "Believe, achieve, succeed," Flo Jo tells both children and adults. Running fast may not save the whales, but Flo Jo changes the world by holding herself to her own standard.

As Michael Jackson said, "I'm starting with the man in the mirror."

Bob Chappelle, a Saturn car salesman, holds himself and those who work with him to the highest levels of integrity in their dealings with customers and employees. His mission is creating the kind of company that is a joy to work for and a pleasure to do business with. He changes the car industry by holding himself to his own standards, not the car industry standard.

Herb Kelleher, CEO of Southwest Airlines, has created an airline company that is more on time, less costly, more profitable, and more fun than any other. How he treats his employees and how he lives his life is an expression of his beliefs. He changes the world by holding himself to his own standards, not the airline industry's.

Whether you are an athlete, a car salesman, or a CEO, you can use the challenges you face every day as an opportunity to show people what you're made of and what you believe in. Whether you are a taxi driver, a waiter, or a TV star, you can put your values into your work. You can set a higher standard for performance, treat people better, and live by your personal principles. Then your job becomes a testimony to a life well lived, not just a paycheck.

If you have the drive and desire to take on a cause or change the world, fantastic. Otherwise, changing yourself and your corner of the world is enough.

PRINCIPLE FOUR: FIND AN ORGANIZATION THAT SUPPORTS YOUR GOALS, VALUES, AND STYLE OF WORK

If I am able to succeed and stay sane at all, "it's based on a combination of who I am and what this environment recognizes and rewards," says Bill Higgins, a principal in the office of development for Morgan Stanley & Co., one of the leading investment banks in the world. "I know this is true because I worked at Morgan Stanley, then left, and came back. When I wasn't at Morgan Stanley I couldn't do the same things. I was still me, but I couldn't be as successful and sane."

Bill Higgins recruits minorities for investment banking jobs. "Not as part of a cause or affirmative action," he says. He has charities that he supports; but recruiting minorities for Morgan Stanley isn't charity work.

"We recruit a lot of very bright people who might not have thought about a career on Wall Street. We get access to a pool of talent the other companies tend to overlook. This is a game where getting the most talented, motivated people makes all the difference. Recruiting minorities is strictly good business." He isn't mixing charity with business. He is bringing business to a higher level.

Bill Higgins was willing to switch employers in order to live by his values, beliefs, and personality more fully. Those who succeed sane don't complain about the limits of their organization, they go out and find the right organization.

Perhaps the most compelling story of a search for the supportive organization is that of Bob Chappelle. As the owner-operator of a Buick dealership in Oregon, he gained a reputation as the eccentric, honest car dealer. Car dealers thought he was too soft to stay in the business. Customers loved him.

As his "new" method of using integrity, openness, and no hassles showed promise he began teaching others. Soon he had a second career traveling the country helping dealers to retrain their sales force and reorganize their selling system. For one dealer in San Diego, he suggested hiring an all-female sales force to underscore the promise of a friendly, hassle-free selling approach.

Many years later that same dealer, a man named Charles, told Bob about a new car company that employed Bob's principles of honesty and integrity in everything they did. From the way they treated the employees to offering a thirty-day money-back guarantee for customers, every rule, policy, and idea supported the backbone of values.

Bob moved his family to San Diego and helped his friend Charles set up the first Saturn car dealership in San Diego. Although it was tough going the first few years with no cars available and no track record, their rise to $50 million in sales within five years is now the stuff of legends. The customers are on fire with a passion about the quality of the car as well as the integrity of the company.

Bob, the "softie car dealer," found a home. And his family shares his enthusiasm for the way Saturn works. At thirteen years of age his youngest son began washing cars for the dealership. His biggest problem then was not being able to drive the cars around to the front when he was done. His next biggest problem was being too young for a work permit. Solution: He started his own business and let his father file a 1099 form to the IRS.

I didn't hear about Chappelle's son because I asked or because he makes a big deal about it. It just happened to come up. When I sat in on two days of Saturn's sales consultant training as part of my research for the book, Chappelle's son was attending the class, too. Turns out that all of Bob's sons have become Saturn sales consultants. I don't know whether that says more about the company or the father. But I think they found a company that lets them live their mission: honest, fun, no-hassle car sales.

PRINCIPLE FIVE: IF YOU CAN'T FIND A SUPPORTIVE
ORGANIZATION, CREATE ONE

You might as well face it: The responsibility corporations have to their shareholders to maximize value often conflicts with your desire to create a sane life. The shareholders benefit from getting as much work out of each person as possible. Even the president works for the shareholders. The system isn't set up to foster family life, no matter how many family-friendly benefits there are. Don't ever kid yourself about that.

There is only one system where you will put the interests of your children and spouse ahead of an opportunity for profit or growth: the system where you are the boss. As a consultant or independent contractor you can decide how profitable to make your business and how fast to make it grow. Since you benefit from your personal life and your monetary profits, you can trade off some for the other. Although having your own business certainly comes with a lot of other headaches, it may be the only situation where you can really create your own blend of career challenge combined with family as a priority. Many working parents are beginning to appreciate this insight.

One day, as I talked to a video producer on the phone, my daughter, Darcy, started crying in the background. "So you work at home, too," she observed. I felt an instant rapport and understanding that I get from many home-based business owners I come across. We talked about how much more acceptance there is today for professional women working out of their homes, even when babies sometimes cry.

"I used to work as a video producer for a major corporation," she told me. "I traveled on short notice, worked to crazy deadlines, and felt really proud that I could handle the pressure. When my daughter was born, I just kept working. I was gone so much the first year of her life that she became an angry child. At first I wanted to keep working, then I wanted to stop. But after my husband lost his job I had no choice.

"Finally when the whole situation became unbearable I just quit. I went independent just like that with no clients and no money. It was scary but it worked out. My husband found a job and I started getting production work, too.

"Now I have a reputation for someone who gets the job done more efficiently. I prefer to work half days, so I will bid a job as less time than other contractors. People know I do excellent work, that I charge a fair price, and that I value my kids. I get a lot of referrals.

"These days I spend my afternoons at swim practice watching my two daughters. My oldest is still angry at me sometimes, but we are working through it together. Succeeding sane? We're getting there."

Becoming your own boss is often the only way to get the slack you need to design your life around your skills and your family. The good news is that opportunities to work as a consultant or start your own business are growing faster than ever.

I wonder sometimes, when I talk to friends of mine from college who complain about the crazy life of a two-career couple cramming all their family life into a weekend: Why do you do it? If you have great qualifications and a spouse with a high salary, why would you consider getting a job? You're supposed to be smart with that Harvard degree and all, why in the world are you letting someone else tell you how to organize your life?

Many succeeding sane couples involve one traditional career and another more flexible career such as freelance writer, artist, academic, or consultant. Sometimes it is the woman and sometimes it is the man who works the more flexible job.

If you can afford it, get at least one of you out of the rat race. Grab the opportunity to be at home more and do your work for love instead of money. Be a parent, but make sure you carve out a plan for expressing your skills and passions as an individual, too. Be a consultant for the skills you have on your resume. Better yet, dare to be an artist, a musician, or a writer. Ironically, you may end up making more money in the long run anyway.

A caveat, however, is in order. Bob Chappelle's story shows that starting a business is not always the most fulfilling option. Although Bob Chappelle owned his own business as a Buick dealer and as a traveling trainer, he was happier as part of a company that practiced what he preached in everything from the production of the cars, to the dealership contracts, to the customer contracts. Joining Saturn allowed him to live his values and his purpose more fully than owning his own business.

PRINCIPLE SIX: FOCUS YOUR EFFORTS
AND YOUR RELATIONSHIPS

You can't do everything for everybody. Volunteering for ten different charities or sitting on eight different boards is not a sign of a highly blended life. When you are infusing each of your activities with more mind, body, and spirit, you don't need ten different clubs to meet your needs and serve your community.

Having a mission brings your professional life and your personal life into harmony. That's what allows you to focus. People you work with become family, and family pitches in with the work.

Those who work this way become very careful about the kind of people they choose to let into their "family." At Southwest Airlines they used to interview about twenty people to fill one slot. Today they interview as many as fifty people for each opening.

"First and foremost we are looking for a sense of humor," Kelleher told *Fortune* magazine. "Then we are looking for people who have to excel to satisfy themselves and who work well in a collegial environment. We don't care that much about education and experience, because we can train people to do whatever they have to do. We hire attitudes."

At the same time, CEO Herb Kelleher treats his employees as his extended family or his clan. He laughs at CEOs who sit on a bunch of boards and hang out with other CEOs. "My people are the fountain of youth," says the man everyone just calls Herb. "They are restorative and rejuvenating for me. I love to be around them."

Faith Popcorn, noted futurist and author of The Popcorn Report, identifies "clanning" as a major trend for the coming century. The need for a group and a sense of belonging is in part a reaction to the excess of individualism in the 70s and 80s. Yet, at the same time it is an expression of one's personality and choice of identity.

Lennart and Ginny Palme, network marketing entrepreneurs, convinced their adult children to give up other career aspirations and get involved in their thriving business. Their daughter, Pam Koenig, described for me the impact it had on the closeness of her family.

"Prior to getting started with this business I talked to my family maybe once or twice a month," explained Pam. "There was a lot of distance between us. They are in Chicago and I am in California. I'd see them maybe once a year at Christmas, if that. It was hard. We were all involved in our own things." Deciding to work together changed their family dynamics.

"By doing business together I'd say we talk at least three or four times each week," said Pam. "We meet in person at least three or four times per year at company functions as well as getting together to help each other provide training sessions." Pam acknowledged, however, that not everyone would want to work with their kin.

"I have an incredible family," Pam confided. "These are people whom I would choose to work with even if they weren't related, because I trust and respect them absolutely." Even so it took more than six years for her to decide to give up her career in corporate sales and join her father's business venture.

Pam went on at length describing the unexpected benefits of working with her family to grow their business. "We are planning to go to Thailand together this summer because our company has established operations there and we can begin recruiting distributors . . . so it is a tax-deductible family trip! As NuSkin and Interior Design Nutritionals enter more countries around the world, our dream is to travel the world together." By focusing their professional lives around family relationships this family reduces the tension between success and a fulfilling life.

You don't have to assume that being more successful means more clubs, more commitments, and more relationships. Having a highly blended life doesn't mean trying to cram everything under the heading of one business. Select quality activities and people to keep close to you just as you would select high-quality furniture for your house. Focus and be selective.

An essential difference between succeeding sane and crazy is being very clear on your mission and sticking to what matters. Focusing your relationships and activities brings together all the strengths of mind, body, and spirit. The mind discipline of making choices combined with the clarity of spiritual purpose can shape the movements of your body through time.

PRINCIPLE SEVEN: PACE YOURSELF

Among all the people I interviewed for *Succeeding Sane*, Laura Tyson was sailing closest to the edge. As the first woman to head the White

House Council of Economic Advisers since its inception in 1946, she has a crazy, high-pressure job in one of the most insane, high-pressure places in the world.

Yet, when I worked with her I sensed the calmness and sanity she carried with her down the halls of the Old Executive Office Building, in press conferences, and into cabinet meetings in the Roosevelt Room. I looked up to this woman who looked elegant, handled difficult economic issues with ease, and kept a smile on her face most of the time. My first question in the interview was, "What keeps you sane?"

"Spending time talking with my husband, Eric Tarloff, and my son, Eliot, about the right balance," she responded immediately. "Balance has always been an important issue in my life. But it never gets solved at the global level. Balance only gets solved day by day.

"Neither my husband nor my son had their heart set on leaving Berkeley and moving to Washington, D.C. When I was offered the job of leading the Council of Economic Advisers, it came as a surprise to me, too. It was like this magical gift bestowed upon me." The Tyson-Tarloff family talked it over.

Eric's attitude was, "We've gotta go and do this because it's just too good an opportunity to pass up." That set the tone of moving to D.C. as a big family adventure. From the very beginning, they were all in it together. Mission? To learn, to stretch their wings, and to have a lot of fun and excitement.

Even with a clear mission, staying sane on a day-to-day basis in the White House isn't easy. "I am very conscious," Laura emphasizes, "of trying to get close to the right balance, but feeling that I have never actually achieved it. There are not many women at my level who have young children at home. For those of us who do, it is almost impossible to find time for something other than work, child, and family. In the three years I have been here, I have never found a way to go to the gym during the weekdays."

You might think that Laura's life sounds a little crazy. Every moment of life is reengineered to maximize work hours and kid time with no time for personal sanity. Laura Tyson, however, has made some decisions about pacing herself that soften the blows from her fast-paced job.

First of all, she has only one child. Knowing her own work ambitions, she limited herself to one child with whom she enjoys quality one-on-one interaction. They go to science-fiction movies or take his friends to a science-fiction store on the weekend. On weeknights Laura may pass up an invitation to dine at an embassy in favor of having dinner at home and doing homework with Eliot.

"Doing those things helps me refill my spiritual tanks," she said. "Someday I would like to have more involvement with children. I'd work with a group like the Children's Defense Fund so that I can help more of the world's vulnerable kids. But for now, one child is all I can handle."

Another way that Laura paces herself is by guarding her weekend and evening time. "[As a top White House official] You can go out every night to great events: dinners, benefit concerts, speeches. You can see the right people and be seen. You can make trips around the world if you want and go to wonderful conferences and meetings. You can network, transact business, and develop your image.

"I realized I had to make a choice between having any personal life at all and doing those things."

Her solution is worthy of Solomon himself. She decided her basic commitment is to come home after work, do homework with Eliot, eat dinner, and be with her husband. If, however, her husband, who is a freelance writer and political commentator, is interested in going to a really fun event, they hire a babysitter and go out.

"If he wants to go, I am happy to go. If he doesn't want to go, I am happy not to go." She shrugs her shoulders at the simplicity of it. "I rarely do things he doesn't enjoy, unless I am required to go as the speaker, for example." As a result she goes to the best, most interesting events with the full support of her husband and enjoys most other evenings at home.

Perhaps the most important way in which she paces herself is that she doesn't expect to live this way forever. Our conversation was peppered with references to a saner lifestyle in the past as an academic and with references to how she expects life to be different in the future.

"A university life allows more flexibility. There were more hours in a day that were not devoted to work." Although Laura won awards for her teaching, earned tenure for her research, and founded the Berkeley Roundtable on International Economics, she still found time for a dance class four times a week and driving in the car pool for Eliot and his friends.

"Here [in the White House] the work takes up more of my time and attention than I would like. I don't think it is sustainable. It is a tremendous opportunity with tremendous costs. You can only do it for a while." Laura knows that having it all doesn't necessarily mean having it all at once, all the time.

Ken Blanchard taught me another lesson about pacing yourself, which particularly helps me as a speaker and author.

"You travel over a million miles a year," I asked him, "how do you stay so close to your family?" I worry about this question a lot in my own life.

"At the beginning of the year," he told me "Margie and I sit down with a calendar and mark off time to protect for us. Four weeks at Christmas, a week at Easter, and eight weeks in the summer and a couple of other week-long breaks. The rest of the year can be very insane, but from the very beginning we decided to get away together for four months of the year. It has helped our relationship with our kids a lot." The Blanchards have a serious commitment to pacing themselves.

"I'm not sure that you can balance your life every day," says Ken. "You have periods of insanity. You have to give yourself periods of sanity."

Laura Tyson realizes that her stint in the White House is just a brief period of insanity in her life. "I am well aware of what you're not able to do: being active in charity work, exercise, or just taking a walk and seeing how beautiful the spring flowers are. Some people just forget about all that. I could see that happening to me if I wasn't married to someone like Eric."

From the very beginning of our conversation, Laura emphasized the importance of being married to Eric for succeeding with sanity. "I didn't marry someone who was driven by ambition. Eric is an artist who cares about creativity and cares about sensitivity and cares about human relations. I knew I was doing that when I did it. He is an anchor that pulls me back to another way of looking at life.

"It is easy to get caught up in all this," she says waving her hand. "It's a very heady experience. The press and the Congress treat you like you are something important; it can cause you to lose your bearings. You have to constantly relate to what you were before and what you will be again. It is important to have people around who help you do that."

I suspect that the same is true of many driven men who are balanced out by supportive, more spirit-oriented wives. All of the married men I interviewed expressed appreciation and admiration for their wives' role as a teammate. The women in high-profile positions who I interviewed, however, made it clear that they could not be who they are and do what they do without their supportive spouses. Johnetta Cole, president of Spelman College, talked for a long time about the role played by her husband, who helps her slow down, relax, and keep perspective. Perhaps the women particularly appreciated that men do not traditionally play such a role.

Laura went on to describe how Eric helps her keep perspective. "We have developed some close friends in Washington mostly because Eric has more time in his life as a freelance writer. He has always made more time in his life for friends than I have. He invests more time in his relationships."

As a result Laura can go out to small dinners with close friends who don't give a hoot about her title or image. "That's great," she says laughing. "I find that a revival."

To succeed and stay sane Laura paces herself day by day and year by year. She has followed many of the other principles, too. You'll notice that joint decision making, team spirit, and cultivating humility are all part of her story. The fact that her husband works for himself made it easier to move across country and also allows him to take up some of the slack as she works harder than ever before.

Laura may be sailing close to the wind, but she is still at the helm. Laura gets my vote as a wonderful and inspiring example of succeeding sane!

PRINCIPLE EIGHT: CULTIVATE YOUR HUMILITY

"When I wrote the *One Minute Manager*," Ken Blanchard told me, "it was a crazy time. It wasn't even out ten days and it was on the *New York Times* best-seller list. It stayed on the list for three years. That experience was so absurd, I could have had one of two responses to it. I could get a big head or I could reflect on my spirituality and the real power behind the book.

"I realized that the hardest times in life are when you have a big success or have a big failure, disappointment or trauma. The big dips up or down are scary; the ones in between you can ride." Being highly successful makes you just as vulnerable as being unsuccessful because you can confuse who you are with what you have (or have not) accomplished. Your ego gets wrapped up in your performance.

"Ego is one of the main things that keeps people from succeeding sane," said Ken. "I define ego as putting your self in the center and responding to feedback and results on a personal basis. It's exhausting to always be worried about how you are coming across. It's also harder to do anything when you are overly attached to the outcome. When who I am is wrapped up in the game, it is much harder to play. You perform better if you are less uptight about it."

"So how do you keep your ego in check?" I asked Ken.

"Old friends," he said without a pause. "It makes me wonder when people only have new friends. I have dear old friends who don't give a damn about 'Dr. Blanchard, Ph.D.' They'll be honest with me. They'll go for the jugular."

Almost every one of my succeeding sane role models had a specific technique for keeping their ego in check. Bob Chappelle, the Saturn car dealer, cooks burgers on an open grill for his staff and the customers on weekends.

"I don't wear a special name tag saying 'Head Honcho' or anything like that. My tag just says, 'Bob.' Often customers give me a hard time; they treat me like the hired help.

" 'Hurry up with that burger!' or 'Where's the #%$! catsup?!' " they say.

"I like to serve others, it cures my sense of self-importance," says Bob smiling that Cheshire grin of his. Later I found out that cleaning all the toilets in the building was another of his methods for keeping his ego at an appropriate size.

Wayne Dyer, a multimillionaire and best-selling writer, has a foolproof method for keeping his ego in check. "My children, all eight of them, are brutally honest with me. The other day my ten-year-old, whom we misnamed Serena, put her hand on her hip, looked up at me and said, 'I can't believe you wrote a book about raising children.' "

When Wayne Dyer asked the famous psychologist Abraham Maslow, "What do you mean when you say self-actualization?"

Maslow answered simply. "Two things: (1) learning to become independent of the good opinion of other people; and (2) mastering the art of being detached from the fruits of your labor."

"Of course this is easier to preach than practice," Wayne Dyer said. "I was the expert on self-actualization. I wrote books about it. Then I read my reviews, deeply stung by any words of criticism."

Comments about keeping ego in check came up over and over in my interviews. Both Dennis Kimbro and Lebron Morgan said their wives keep their egos in check. When I went back to cross check in my notes exactly what each person had said, I realized that only the men had commented on reining in their egos. None of the women mentioned it.

Women, in contrast to men, may have a greater need to build self-esteem rather than to hold their ego in check. But in the end it amounts to the same thing. Low self-esteem is also a case of worrying too much about yourself. Oversized egos have an identity wrapped up in praise while undersized egos are too much affected by criticism. When you keep your ego at a healthy size you feel special, wonderful, and unique, but you also feel that everyone else is special, wonderful, and unique as well.

I can now admit that low self-esteem was part of what drove me to be an achievement junkie. As an amputee, an African American, and a woman I continually tried to catch up with others and prove that I was just as good as anyone else. Yet, my low self-esteem couldn't be cured by outward acclaim. The truth is, I never felt comfortable with awards ceremonies, fanfare from the press, or seeing myself on TV.

I don't tell many people this, but I actually missed the biggest award ceremony of my life, the one where the queen of Denmark would have put the silver medal around my neck marking me as the second-fastest woman in the world. I was up on the mountain skiing with my sister, and I didn't really try very hard to make it. At the time I thought I had a healthy sense of humility. Now I know that I was suffering from a low self-image that made me feel uncomfortable on a stage with people cheering for me. Just describing it now makes me remember the feeling of awkwardness. All the prizes in the world can't fill you up if you feel unworthy.

Part of my spiritual journey as a speaker and author is to finally become comfortable with the attention I receive and move on to other things. Slowly my sense of self is healing in the process of looking back over my life instead of continually looking forward to my next achievement fix. Every once in awhile I get a fleeting sense of enjoyment from being the center of attention on stage and in the media. I

Reference Page:
Eight Principles for
Sane Success
(photocopy and post this page)

1) Take responsibility for your own sanity.

2) Explore and develop your passion, skill and personality through your work.

3) Turn your work into your mission by making it an expression of your values.

4) Find an organization which supports your goals, values, and style of work.

5) If you can't find a supportive organization, create one.

6) Focus your efforts and your relationships.

7) Pace yourself.

8) Cultivate your humility.

can see the day coming when my ego is healthy enough to need a leash.

When I explained my ideas about succeeding sane through mind, body, and spirit, Ken Blanchard immediately connected it with his work on self-esteem and coaching skills. He frequently asks groups of people, "If you love your children, raise your hand." The audience laughs. Hands go up. Then he asks them, "Would you stop loving your children if they weren't successful? Raise your hand." Of course, no hands go up.

"You give unconditional love to your children," Ken points out. "What would happen if you accepted that same unconditional love for yourself? What if you woke up one morning and you realized you can't get enough power, you can't sell enough, you can't conquer enough to get more love than you have now. You've got all there is.

"If you truly knew that the goal didn't matter, you could concentrate on the quality of the journey. Succeeding sane," he observed, "is about having perspective on both winning and losing."

Exercise: Practicing the Eight Principles in Your Life

Answer the following questions to help you put these principles to work in your life.

1. Have you decided to take responsibility for the insanities in your life?

_____

Do you blame them on others or deny your insanities?

_____

Write down at least one of the activities that makes your life crazy.

_____

What can you do about it?

_____

What can you do to add a few moments of serenity in your life?

_____

2. What would you be doing with your days if you didn't have to work? How would you explore and develop your passion, your skill, and your personality?

_____

What could you do in your job now that would help you prepare for that challenge? What could you do in your job now to develop your skills, etc.?

_____

3. If you applied your values in every little aspect of your job, how would tomorrow be different from today?

_____

What would your mission be?

_____

4. What would an organization be like that supports your goals, values, and style of work?

_____

Do you know of a place more like that than where you work now?

_____

5. If you can't find a supportive organization, could you create one? What would it look like?

_____

6. What would you like to be doing five years from now (in an ideal world)?

_____

Do you spend a lot of time in groups, alliances, or activities that do not bring you closer to that ideal?

_____

Could you eliminate some "off-course" activities and save time?

_____

7. Are you trying to do everything at once? Can you let go of some goals or give yourself more time to get there?

_____

8. Are you more likely to err on the side of too much ego or too little self-esteem?

_____

What are you doing to combat this problem and take your attention off of yourself?

_____

CHAPTER 20

How to Tap Your Hidden Time and Energy Resources

lorence "Flo Jo" Griffith-Joyner's success is indisputable. In the
1988 Olympics, she won three gold medals and in 1984 a silver
medal. Her world records in the 100 meters and 200 meters earned her
the title "World's Fastest Woman." She's so far ahead of the pack that
she comes in first and her long, flowing, black hair comes in second.

Successful? No question. But was she sane, too? That's what I wanted
to know.

The way she went out of her way to be nice to my mother when we
met her in Atlanta told me she might be a good candidate for succeeding sane. At the beginning of my interview with her, she told me
about all the projects she had on the go. In addition to training for the
Olympic Games in Atlanta, she is writing children's books, cochairing
the president's council on fitness, designing new products for her nail
company, and raising her five-year-old daughter, Mary.

"How do you do all that? What is your life like?" I wanted to know.

"Five or six days a week we go to the track for two or three hours.
I'm training my husband now, too. We train each other." She made
training for the Olympics sound simple. "We run three to six miles in
the evening.

"On Wednesdays I try to fit in photo shoots, interviews, and letters. Of course, that's when I'm not traveling to give speeches for youth groups and corporations."

"You must have a staff to help you—a secretary, a nanny, and a housekeeper—right?" I asked, trying to get a feel for how her life stayed together.

"Right, but I don't have a nanny."

"You *what?*" I felt tempted to clean out my ears.

"We don't have a nanny," she repeated. As one mother of a toddler to another I found this information, well, shocking. I like having Darcy around me during the day, but I can't write, travel, or even work out at the gym without someone to keep an eye on her.

"What does she do while you are training?" I asked.

"We take her with us to the track. She plays in the sand pit, rides her bike, or she runs around."

"What about your speeches?"

"She goes, too. The three of us just got back from Japan. Sometimes, though, she stays with my mother who lives about five minutes away."

"And when you work in the office, doesn't she get bored?" I thought about my fifteen-month-old, Darcy, pulling out my paper files, shutting off the computer, and trying to play with the electrical plugs whenever she manages to get into my home office.

"She has her own computer. She does phonics or reads a book while I work. I also teach her for two and a half hours a day."

Initially, Flo Jo was my idol as a great athlete. What I was learning about her commitment to her child showed me that she is a truly phenomenal human being.

That's fine for Flo Jo, you may be thinking. She has enough money and freedom to do whatever she wants. But I am trapped in a corporate job, a big mortgage, or the partner track at the firm. Whatever. Flo Jo doesn't see herself as trapped because she doesn't get caught up in the usual celebrity lifestyle. She forges her unique path as you should forge yours.

"Mary didn't like Kindergarten because she had never been to day-care before," Flo Jo explained. "So I agreed to teach her for a while." She states these amazing facts as though every superstar athlete and celebrity would naturally give the same quality time to their child.

What is remarkable about Flo Jo is that she has exercised her choices to create a life close to her child, her husband, and her mother, yet she still achieves in many public arenas. So few people who seemingly have money and freedom make these choices to design a life based on their values. Flo Jo's mixture of choices is unusual among superachievers.

She admits that some of her goals have had to stay on the back burner. "I haven't had my children's books accepted by a publisher yet. I haven't put in enough work to make them really good enough." Perhaps after the Olympics are over she will have more time to create a set of books for children based on her world-class ability to care.

Florence Griffith-Joyner's life is highly blended. Training is not just a physical job. She has the new intellectual challenge of training her husband while he is continuing to train her. She also has the spiritual element of being with her daughter and husband. Her time at the track is enriching on all three channels.

One of her favorite ways to give outside her family is by acting as a role model for youth. This, too, has become a multifaceted activity. Through their youth foundation, Flo Jo and Al Joyner help disadvantaged kids in the LA area to train for Olympic competition and seek the best in themselves. In addition they host large get-togethers with motivational speakers, workshops, and training for the mind as well as the body.

Flo Jo lives life in "3-D" along the dimensions of mind, body, and spirit. The resulting depth creates an almost visible radiance and makes her the fastest woman in the world.

Blending Mind, Body, and Spirit Is the Secret

In this chapter we're going to take a closer look at the day-to-day lives of the supersuccessful. When I researched my supersuccessful role models, the articles and résumés told me all the fantastic things these people do. None of the articles, however, explained how they fit it all into a twenty-four-hour day.

I decided to find out by asking them directly. My personal interviews with over thirty people—from Wall Street executives to White House appointees and Olympic athletes—confirmed my ideas about blending mind, body, and spirit to make it all fit.

Tapping Hidden Energy

For example, Michael Osheowitz, a financial consulting executive from New York City, uses his comfort zone to make his exercise regimen more palatable. Like many mind-centered people Michael can't stand wasting time and needs to be challenged intellectually. "I'm incredibly compulsive," Michael confessed. "I can't just sit down and relax. I have to be learning something all the time."

✿

The secret to tapping into hidden energy is blending the pleasant with the unpleasant. As Mary Poppins said, "A spoonful of sugar helps the medicine go down in the most delightful way."

✿

"My perfect exercise regimen was running up and down the seven flights of stairs in my brownstone building. Why waste time going to a gym in the morning? I started at about twenty minutes, then thirty minutes, and finally got up to nearly an hour. Every morning I did this while listening to NPR (National Public Radio) on my walkman. It was the ultimate."

Unfortunately surgery on his knees forced him to change his routine. "Now I ride on a stationary bicycle, which is terrific for my knee. At least I can read the newspapers in the morning on the bicycle. My wife has also gotten me involved in yoga. I find it difficult to meditate, but I try. I do between an hour and a half and two hours of both yoga and the bicycle every morning that I can. I shoot for seven days a week, but end up at four or five. That gives me what little sanity I have.

"The recovery of my knee was supposed to be poor, but because I have worked so hard on the therapy, I can do almost everything now. Except the stairs. Running on stairs is out."

Without some kind of mental activity, Michael would probably find a daily exercise routine too boring. When your comfort zone skills play a supporting role to a weaker skill, the task feels easier. Reading or listening to news while exercising helps mind-focused people tap into their physical energy and have fun at the same time.

Spirit-motivated people, on the other hand, must sugarcoat their body and mind activities with a more meaningful, beautiful, or inter-personal dimension.

Spirit-motivated people often dislike exercise because it seems emotionally boring and without meaning. My mother, also a spirit person, used to say, "Look at those joggers! They should use that energy to do something constructive."

Another spirit-centered friend of mine can't bear going into a gym. "It's smelly and ugly. Why doesn't everyone walk on the beach or in a park like I do?" My friend Penny needs the spiritual beauty of nature to sugarcoat her exercise experience.

(If body power is your comfort zone and you would like to read an example of a body person using the technique of "sugarcoating" a mind activity, look up Diane Buchta's story on page 124.)

We all like to stay in our comfort zone, whether it's mind, body, or spirit. However, staying inside your comfort zone and relying only on the strengths that come to you most easily will either leave you mediocre at what you do or wear you out trying to compete.

Giving it all you've got means going beyond your comfort zone and tapping the skills that don't come so easily. I don't know who said it, but it's true that "If you feel warm and comfortable, it's because you're in the middle of the herd."

Sugarcoating the things you don't like to do helps you to extend yourself beyond your comfort zone with less stress. By blending something you like with something you don't like, you develop in areas you normally avoid.

Exercise: Sugarcoating Your Medicine

The area in which you scored lowest on the quiz in chapter 6 tends to be your most hidden resource. You probably hate having to use it. You may systematically underutilize, avoid, or dismiss the contributions of either your mind, your body, or your spirit. Some people avoid exercise; others avoid family gatherings while others avoid school. Do you avoid development of your discomfort zone?

Using the left side of the worksheet below, list some things outside your comfort zone that you know you should do. On the righthand side of the page, list ideas for sugarcoating the activity by adding an element to it from your comfort zone.

Activities outside my comfort zone	Ideas for sugarcoating this activity

Tapping Hidden Time: Three Tracking!

❍

The secret of tapping hidden time is developing your mind, body and spirit simultaneously.

❍

Imagine that you are a sound system with three audio tracks. Most of the time we play our lives in mono rather than three-track stereo. We read a book, eat a meal, exercise, work, take a class, whatever. By making small changes such as reading together, exercising outdoors, or working the skills you love you can bring the power of mind, body, and spirit synergy into your life.

The best way to illustrate this principle is to tell you about my last Father's Day gift to my husband, Grant. Being such a great father and this being only his second father's day, I wanted to get him something he would really like. While we were walking to the corner coffee shop I asked him, "Do you want me to tell you my idea for a Father's Day gift or surprise you?"

"Tell me," he said. "I'm not in the mood for surprises right now."

"I thought I would buy a series of karate lessons for you. You have been saying you'd like to study karate for a long time." I watched for his reaction. It wasn't what I had hoped. I shrugged my shoulders. "Okay, what would you really like, then?"

"It has to be something that doesn't take up any time," he said. "I'm so busy at work. I come home early to see Darcy, then I have to go back after she goes to bed. I just can't fit in anything else." He threw up his hands and smiled. "Ideally, I'd like a gift of extra time. But that's impossible."

"Actually," I told him, "I'm writing about tapping hidden time resources. I should be able to think of something using the principles in my book." I pictured his life running on three tracks: a body track, a mind track, and a spirit track. I thought about the things he did: going to work, spending time with Darcy, eating, playing computer games, and watching movies.

There were many ways to blend activities and save time, but not all of them would appeal to Grant. I had, for example, been saying to Grant that I wanted Darcy to have her own electronics bench in his lab so she could work along with him the way she works alongside me in my home office. Giving him more parenting work, however, was probably not the best way to reward him for his fatherly devotion.

Finally, I thought of a blend that could actually save him some time. He'd been saying that we should join the local arts and music library so that we could enjoy borrowing their extensive range of classical music. We never seemed to get around to it. I had wondered when he thought we would be sitting around listening to music anyway.

However, I figured he could enjoy the library's collection during his late-night stints at work if I bought him a CD player for his office. They say that the part of the brain that registers music adjoins with the part that does math. Maybe this blend of music at work would enhance his productivity and give him that extra time. In any event, the quality of his work time would certainly rise.

I pitched this idea as my best time-saving alternative gift. He liked it. In fact he liked it so much, he often calls me to tell me so when he is enjoying classical music in his office. Ironically, he called just now while I was writing this section!

Using these principles, you can find simple changes that add to the quality of your life without taking up extra time or energy. Rather than making his life more hectic with a karate class, I gave a gift that uplifted his spirit without taking extra time. Since spirit is his comfort zone, he found the gift particularly revitalizing and refreshing. We added more spirit into his day.

Seeing your life goals as blended rather than balanced is a crucial principle of succeeding sane. Balancing implies giving up some of this for that. You see your time like a pie. Cutting one piece larger means another piece is smaller. Blending your mind, body, and spirit into the fabric of your life, on the other hand, enlarges the size of the pie.

Blending, however, doesn't mean you can do everything for everyone. Not all blends are good. Not every moment of your life should be blended. It isn't the "having it all" ideal of the seventies. Nor is it the other extreme of downshifting or cutting back on your goals, which is the bandwagon of the nineties. Succeeding sane is not about having more or less of anything. It is about enriching the quality of your time at work, at home, and at play.

No activity in our lives is too small or insignificant to be enriched. Your work time, your exercise, your family outings, and your bedtime habits could all be interwoven with bits of specialness for your mind, body, and soul. Some of these ideas are listed in the idea inventory in chapter 18.

In particular, many of my role models talked about changing the quality of their morning wake-up routine. "Start your day slowly," says Ken Blanchard, coauthor of the *One Minute Manager*. High achievers tend to hit the alarm, get dressed, and race to a series of meetings starting with breakfast and ending after dinner. In the rush of appointments and tasks, there is no sense of inner perspective and purpose. Awakening our internal, reflective self requires a gentler, deliberate process. Ken says he plays with his dog or takes a walk to wake up his spiritual self in the morning.

Wayne Dyer, author of *Your Sacred Self*, recommends waking early, between four and six in the morning, to meditate and connect with one's inner wisdom. Johnetta Cole, president of Spelman College, walks a brisk four or five miles alone or with friends. She calls it her "Mobile Meditation." Sarah Ban Breathnach, author of *Simple Abundance*, takes her coffee mug and cat up to her special nook for an hour of journaling. Starting your day slowly was such a common theme among those who are succeeding sane that it must be a critical factor for success.

The best example of enriching your time and starting your day off right comes from Susan Taylor, editor in chief of *Essence* magazine, who turns her morning routine into the following ritual for nourishing mind, body, and spirit:

- "After the alarm goes off I stay in bed for an extra five minutes. I don't push the snooze alarm because that just creates more stress. I lie on my back and count the blessings I have in my life. I start every day with a smile on my face and a thankful heart. I affirm that I will not hassle, hustle, fuss, or bother. I affirm that I will take everything off my calendar that doesn't need to be there. Then I get out of bed.
- I spend about twenty minutes exercising. Either I run in Central Park, or I go to the gym in my building. Sometimes I just march in place while I watch the news.
- Next I run a bath with aromatic herbs and bubbles. I light a candle. And I soak for ten glorious minutes.
- By the time I get dressed and head for work I am in the right frame of mind for a day of wonders."

If Susan Taylor can pack so much sensuous enjoyment and nurturing of her mind, body, and soul into an hour of getting ready, just think what you can do by making small changes throughout your day or your week!

What To Do

The three exercises that follow in this chapter will help you develop a long-term plan for increasing your total power. The way in which we go about designing this plan is based on the following assumptions:

- *You need to design a customized plan for succeeding sane.* Getting from where you are today to becoming joyfully successful is a very personal journey. What you have to do may be the exact opposite of what someone else should do. Some people need to wrestle with their conscience and destiny while others may need to become physically stronger. Either way, you'll enjoy developing these hidden resources more if we carefully design a program that fits your schedule, your personality, and your needs. A one-size-fits-all plan won't make you stand out from the crowd.

- *Your customized plan shouldn't take up much extra time, if any.* According to this philosophy radical changes are unnecessary, even damaging, because they wouldn't be "you." Small adjustments that bring your life into focus, however, ultimately transform. Picking the right, small changes is the tricky part.

In the exercise below, you'll make small changes in what you already do or substitute different, more blended activities that serve the same purpose. Thus, with little or no commitment of extra time, these seemingly minor adjustments will deepen your mind, body, and spirit resources.

Before you begin the exercises, make a note of your strengths and weaknesses. If you haven't taken the quiz on page 80, you may want to go back and do so now to help you identify your comfort zone. At a minimum you will need to understand the definitions of mind, body, and spirit power as described in chapters 7, 8, and 9 in order to complete the exercises below.

Make a note of your resources here:

My Comfort Zone:_____

My Backup Resource:_____

My Most Hidden Resource (discomfort zone):_____

Exercise One: Examining the Days of Our Lives

Whereas success is determined by the way you do a particular thing like skiing, banking, or politics, succeeding sane comes from the way you live your life, the way you do the little things every day. According to Aristotle, "We are what we repeatedly do. Excellence, then, is not an act, but a habit." Thus, we are going to look at the way you do the things you do.

❍

Sketch out a "typical" day in your life. Base it on an actual day by looking back in your calendar or by remembering what happened yesterday. Write down what you were doing throughout the day. If you can't remember every hour exactly, don't worry. Make up something that you might have been doing or what you usually do.

❍

Live one day at a time . . . and make it a masterpiece!
                              —*Posted on the fridge in a bed-and-breakfast inn where*
                              I went to work on my book.

6:00 A.M.

9:00 A.M.

12:00 noon

3:00 P.M.

6:00 P.M.

9:00 P.M.

If you had to live thousands of days like this one, would you be happy with who you were becoming and what you were accomplishing?

• • •

Look over your daily activities on the list above and designate which ones are primarily mind-oriented, body-oriented, or spirit-oriented.

Which type of activity dominates your day? Mind? Body? or Spirit? Is that typical?

Are you spending your day primarily in your comfort zone or mostly out of it?

Either way, spending too much time in one zone weakens our potential for greatness. Use the next exercise to think about ways to create a day richer in the mind, the body, and the spirit.

Exercise Two: Enrich Your Day, Enrich Your Life!

HOW TO BUILD MIND, BODY, AND SPIRIT STRENGTH WITHOUT TURNING YOUR LIFE UPSIDE DOWN

1. Write down one thing you do during the day on the line below. Choose something from Exercise One if you like. Some good candidates are your morning routine, your exercise activity, dinnertime, or a frequent task at work.
   Your current activity:_____
2. Try to think of ways to add more facets to this activity that will rejuvenate your mind, body, or spirit. Think of a role model for succeeding sane like Susan Taylor. How would she do this activity?
3. Write down all your ideas on the chart on page 258 no matter how silly they seem.
4. If the activity is not in your comfort zone, make sure you write down ideas for adding comfort-zone dimensions. (For extra ideas, use the ideas in chapter 18. For example, if your comfort zone is mind and you are analyzing a body activity, look under the body/mind section.)

Here's an example of how to fill in the chart.

Pick an activity and brainstorm on ways to expand the mind, body, and spirit content.

Activity: Lifting weights three times per week

Challenging Your Mind	Using Your Body	Nurturing Your Spirit
Listen to an audio book	Set physical goals that you can be proud of reaching	Listen to an audio book with a spiritual message
Start a networking group at your gym for people in your line of work	Match your exercise to the physical power you need in your job	Find a gym with a group of people you know
		Find a cleaner, more beautiful gym
Take lessons or enter a competition	Find exercises that make you feel more *comfortable* with your body	Get an exercise partner or a personal trainer
Try ten new sports in ten months (scuba, golf, ski, line dancing, etc.)	Train aerobic capacity, flexibility, and agility as well as strength	Ditch one of your regular sessions and do something more fun like dancing or playing tennis
		Take karate, yoga, or something with a more spiritual element to it

✿

Tip: Use the ideas inventory in chapter 18 for more help.

✿

Pick an activity and brainstorm on ways to expand the mind, body, and spirit content.

Activity:_____

Challenging Your Mind   **Using Your Body**   **Nurturing Your Spirit**

(See page 257 for an example of how to fill in this chart.) When you have finished writing ideas, circle the ones you would actually like to use. In exercise three, you'll learn ideas for incorporating these changes into your life.

Exercise Three: Designing Your Own Map to Succeeding Sane

Use the following steps to build your personal bank of succeeding sane ideas and begin blending them into your life.

(A) Create a personal idea bank for succeeding sane.

Decide which aspects of your life to enrich. Do exercise two several times for different activities you want to enrich in your life. Your morning routine, exercise routine, work day, or dinnertime are a few good candidates.

As you generate more ideas for enriching and deepening your life, you are building your personal bank account of resources for succeeding sane. You can do exercise two as many times as you want over the next few months or years. There is no limit!

Collect the pages together in a folder or notebook. These are the small ideas that will have a big effect in your life and no one else's.

(B) *Choose a few minor changes from your idea bank to use immediately.*

Choose one or two regular activities to change so that they include more mind, body, or spirit. Try these new ideas in the coming week. Schedule them into your calendar. If you don't want to continue them, don't feel obligated. If the new activities are not more rewarding and fulfilling than your old way of doing it, move on or go back! It has to feel right.

Try adding or changing your activities a little bit more each week for one month. Experiment until you find a comfortable routine that engages your mind, body, and spirit.

(C) *Narrow down your idea bank to the best ones.*

Sift through your brainstorming lists. Cross out the really dumb ideas and circle the ones that appeal to you most. If you want neater copies, rewrite or type up the revised list to keep as a reference. Don't throw out the ideas you can't implement right away. You may use this list for years as a guide toward succeeding saner.

If there are certain ideas you never want to use, drop them off the list. For example, if audio books sounded like a good idea, but in practice you don't enjoy them, let that idea go. Enriching your life on all three tracks only works if it feels good. It isn't meant to be a forced march.

(D) *Be patient with yourself.*

Incorporating these new dimensions of mind, body, and spirit into your life is a slow process of changing your habits, so let it happen in a gentle, long-term fashion. You'll need plenty of small, gentle reminders so try these methods of jogging your memory:

- **Words.** Choose a piece of paper you would like to hang in plain sight—perhaps an attractive color of paper. Write one word to remind you of each change you are implementing to enrich your life. Hang it where you will see it often.
- **Sounds.** If you are not visually oriented, maybe you want to talk into a tape recorder and describe your new and improved activities with more mind, body, and/or spirit. Playing the

tape in your car, your Walkman, or at home will reinforce
your shift to a more blended mind, body, and spirit lifestyle.

• **Pictures.** Visualize yourself integrating one or more changes
in your life. Close your eyes and imagine in detail how it
feels. Visualization can help you to accept the changes on a
subconscious level—or to decide that a certain change just
isn't right for you.

(E) Go at your own pace. You may want to try changing one activity
at a time and getting the feel of it before moving on to the next
activity.

Alternatively, you may want to color in your whole day or
your whole week with more physical activity or more spiritual
connectedness. Do whatever appeals to you most.

I would encourage you to take your succeeding sane idea bank
and look for teachers and role models who can help you implement the changes you have decided are right for you over the
period of time with which you feel comfortable.

Armed with your own bank of ideas that will fit into *your
lifestyle* and will make the most difference in *your life,* you are well
equipped to steer your own course through the vast array of personal development literature and self-help seminars. Look for
classes, tapes, and books that are not entirely inside or outside
your comfort zone. Subjects that provide a bridge to ease you
gently out of your comfort zone are best.

CHAPTER 21

Conclusion: Pulling It All Together

I am always a work in progress, but nevertheless a whole person.
—*Johnetta Cole, former president of Spelman College*

Last night I stayed up until four A.M. making the final manuscript changes such as spell checking, finding references, and tidying loose ends. It has been difficult to finish because the demands of my speaking career are rising. I love the pressure, though. Driving myself hard to meet a self-imposed deadline feels familiar, even comfortable.

Staying up all night to finish was the culmination of a month in which I have spent less and less time with my daughter, gotten totally out of touch with my husband, and probably burned out my nanny. As we all do, I retreated to comfort zone. Under stress my habits of isolated self-discipline and hard work emerge, leaving little or no energy for nurturing anyone. Especially not myself.

My personal care dropped to a ridiculously low level. I only curled my hair or went to the gym if I was preparing for a public appearance. Otherwise I wore jeans and a baseball cap day after day. I did so little cooking and shopping for my family, I felt like I forgot how. All of my energy was being pulled out of the here and now, out of my spiritual work, and poured into the mental landscape of creating this book. I don't know whether this behavior was really necessary for finishing the book, but I know it isn't sustainable.

Although I have improved my ability to put spirit into my goals and to nurture myself and others, under pressure I still return to my familiar habits. I retreated almost completely from the spirit dimension.

You may think that just because I wrote the book I should be the master of blending. In fact, I am only interested in the subject because I have so much to learn. The real masters would never write a book like this because blending comes so naturally to them. I, on the other hand, still have a lot to do. I'd like to share with you my personal "to-do" list for succeeding sane.

I want to follow the lead of Bob Chappelle, Michael Osheowitz, and Florence Griffith-Joyner who are building a sense of family mission. Already my husband and I have started discussing how our talents fit together and when we might start projects that blend our talents and values. It may take ten years before we find and fuse our life work together, but we have begun the process by looking each other in the eye and asking the question, "What would you like to do together someday?"

From Ken Blanchard, Susan Taylor, and Sarah Ban Breathnach, I've also learned that starting my day more gently wakes up my spiritual self and puts more sanity into a hectic pace (see chapter 20). A joyfully successful life is made up of calm days in which I am making better decisions, and I am more productive and more fulfilled. Whether I swim with Darcy, take a walk, or rise early and meditate, I can change the quality of my days by the way they start.

To let my spirit power bloom I need to find out more about my authentic self. I need to live not only in the world of writing, personal discipline, and ideas but also in the here and now. As Joanna Field did, I need to keep a diary of the little things that give me a jolt of pleasure during the day such as sunshine, visiting schools as a role model, Darcy's laughter, or a bubble bath. Blending more of these moments of joy into my life will help me grow.

I see now the importance of little things I have been denying myself like frivolous clothes, time to spend decorating my house, and manicures. I need to learn to rejoice in myself for who I am, not just what I have achieved. I need to give love and attention to myself as well as others. Only then can I genuinely connect with people and show them how to rejoice in themselves. Only then can I be the role model I would like to be.

In the months and years to come I know that I will be focusing more than I used to on how to support others through mentoring, advice, encouragement, and true inspiration. I will be thinking not only about my company's business strategy but also about my deeper sense of purpose and how they fit together. By maximizing my value to others, my company will prosper.

In addition to learning to extend myself spiritually, I see the need to blend more body power into my life. Although I have been an Olympic athlete in the past, I still need help fitting body power into my life as it is today. After my business associate, Susanne, reviewed the final draft of this book, she suggested a new blending idea: "Can we move some of our business discussions into the gym?" she asked.

"Let's go!" was my immediate response. Our stair-stepping meetings have already produced amazing, more creative business discussions. Perhaps you, too, can add more blending into your life by giving this book to friends, colleagues, and family with whom you would like to be blending more mind, body, and spirit. Then they can give you blending ideas that never would have occurred to you!

Susanne, who is a body/spirit-centered person, has also encouraged me to invest in high-quality vitamins and continually improve my eating habits. Both of these changes allow me to survive my challenging schedule of work, travel, and parenting with a lot less wear and tear.

I may have begot this book, but like my child it has a life of its own. It has grown in ways that continually surprise and amaze me. The ideas are so much bigger than me; they challenge me to grow as well. The book leaves me with as much work to do as it should for you.

The philosophy of living that it teaches is not new and not mine in the sense that many people already live by it. Many people live by it much better than I do. What is new about this book is seeing a new ideal and getting step-by-step directions to get there. It helps you identify the small changes that will work in your life, and yours alone, to nudge you toward a deeper *wholeness* that naturally makes you successful. I am proud of bringing these ideas to light and showing others the way.

Be patient with yourself. Learning new ways of seeing the world and acquiring the habits of blending takes time. In the process of writing I have often reread and rethought the basic principles. Retracing this ground causes me to reflect on whatever is simultaneously happening in my life. Each time I get valuable ideas that immediately improve my life. I encourage you to recycle through this book as I have. It's worth it.

Living the blending philosophy has become clearer to me in the process of writing. We never get done because mind, body, and spirit become more interrelated as you develop them. Every time you work on one area and improve it, it forces you to pull yourself forward in other areas as well. To reach a higher level you have to build on all three legs of the stool. That is why reading this book over and over is so important.

Maybe someday I will instinctively do all the right things. For the foreseeable future though, doing the exercises presented in this book still helps me to keep pulling my life on to slightly higher ground each day.

To sum it up, the philosophy of blending gives you permission to have joy mixed into your success as well as success mixed into your personal joy. This book shows you how.

I've told you some of the things that I have changed and plan to change in my life based on what I have learned about the philosophy of blending. Take time now to think back over how the exercises and ideas are improving your life. Which changes in your life will make the most difference? Can you build bridges into your discomfort zone? How will you align your success and fulfillment so that both are easier to accomplish?

The most important conclusion that can be written about this book is the one that you write. Take out a piece of paper now and summarize the most important changes you have made or will make to bring the power of blending into your life. The conclusions of this book are, in reality, up to you.

The LaserWalk: Unleashing Your Peak Performance in Seven Steps

Winners give their peak performance at the right place, at the right time.

You don't win Olympic medals by being the fastest on the day before or the day after the big race. You stand at the top of the hill with a timing wand at your shin and a set of blue and red bamboo poles on a white hill. How do you guarantee that you will do it right? You have to ski your absolute best, then and there. Then you have to do it again. Flukes are eliminated because it takes the combined time of two runs in order to win. What is the secret of unleashing your peak physical performance at will?

There are no second chances for the Rhodes scholarship, either. I received a letter on Monday in Boston requesting my presence in LA on Wednesday. The Rhodes committee didn't care how (or if) I got there. It's one chance: Take it or leave it. No show, no scholarship. Once you get there, it's just like the ski race. If you have a bad day, get sick, or get your period, then you lose. If you sparkle, dazzle, and appear to be brilliant you can win the prize, the trip, the money, and a place in history. That is, if you can do it again at the regional interview.

What is the secret of unleashing your peak personality and intellect at will?

Isn't it the same way when you have a job interview or a big sales presentation? You perform beautifully then and there, or you go home and lick your wounds. Every kind of winner has to be able to pull a peak performance out of his back pocket when it counts: Game show contestants, movie stars, firemen, football players, newscasters, politicians and you. To win, you must bring out the best in yourself as easy as turning on a light switch. You do it consistently.

What is a peak performance? I call it the dance. One feels reverence when watching years of practice, knowledge, and experience being used by a master. Like a football player putting together all the right moves at the right time to score the impossible touchdown, he is not just playing football; he is dancing and it is beautiful. Watching someone achieve peak performance inspires a response in us whether it is a fireman rescuing a family, a fast taxi driver in rush hour or a receptionist who is great on phones. Can you imagine living life mostly in the state of the dance? Some people do.

The LaserWalk is the secret for unleashing your peak performance at will. I have a technique for focusing all your knowledge and energies so that you can achieve the inner state that precedes the dance. I call it the *LaserWalk* because it harnesses your energies like a laser beam harnesses light. Lasers are made up of light that is coherent, which means the phases are synchronized. Just by taking light waves and making them all pull in the same direction, an ordinary light beam can be converted into something that cuts through metal, performs surgery on the human eye, or even plays music on your CD. That is the same power that you can have by learning to synchronize your own thoughts, feelings, knowledge, and energy. Here are step-by-step instructions for turning on your mental Laser.

LaserWalk in Seven Steps

To prepare yourself, you must stand on your head against a wall. While upright, bend your legs into the fourth variation of the lotus position. Just kidding. Actually it is so easy, it's almost embarrassing to describe.

Don't be deceived; easy things can be very powerful. It's amazing how easy swimming can be when you stop flailing.

> *Life wasn't meant to be a struggle.*
> —Stuart Wilde

Step 1: Sit down in a quiet place where you will not be distracted or interrupted.

Step 2: Close your eyes and imagine yourself walking down a long staircase. Count backward from one hundred as you tread each stair.

Step 3: When you get to one, the stairs will end. Imagine two doors at the bottom of the stairs.

Step 4: You may enter the door at the right. Behind it is the place you would most like to be. It is a pleasurable place, the fulfillment of your dreams or whatever you want to see.

Step 5: After a suitable length of time (ten seconds or five minutes, whatever you are comfortable with), leave this place and enter the left door. It is your inner self.

Step 6: Give yourself suggestions once you are in this place. Repeat what you need to do in order to achieve peak performance. You will probably experience joy and relief as you feel the forces of your inner being lining up in support of your desires like tumblers falling in place to unlock a safe. You will become King (or Queen) with loyal armies gathering in the valley.

Step 7: Open your eyes, feeling the LaserEdge, a readiness to do your best. Try it a few times in minor situations to get the feel of it.

○

Question: Is this just "positive thinking" in a new wrapper or is it supposed to be some kind of hocus-pocus?

Answer: Positive thinking is part of the LaserWalk, but there is a lot more to it. By relaxing, putting your mind in a pleasant and receptive state and then focusing on your inner self, the positive thoughts that you place there become supercharged. Your critical success factors are no longer lost among grocery lists, silly conversations, stray visual cues, and the rest of the flotsam and jetsam blocking up your brain. Suddenly, it's as though Paul Revere has ridden around your whole body waking up all your cells to say, "This is important, really important. Everybody pull together."

No, it isn't hocus-pocus. It's really just common sense. If you can't spend five minutes clearing your mind and thinking about what is essential to your peak performance, it isn't really important to you. If you want to spend the last few minutes before the big moment joking around with friends instead of marshaling your concentration, go ahead. That is what most people do. That's why most people aren't winners.

○

Next, I will share with you a bit about my personal experience of the LaserWalk. I'll tell you how it feels and looks to me. Then I will give you some tips that I have picked up from years of experience with this technique. Before continuing to read, you should try the seven steps a few times. That way you will develop your own style and your own experience without making it a carbon copy of mine.

Okay? So go away and try it. But make sure you finish this section later because the tips at the end will help you to master the LaserWalk more quickly.

Here's what my own LaserWalk is like. When I go down the stairs I see a dark winding stone staircase, as in a castle. I don't usually spend much time behind the door on the right. I should probably work on that because it is linked to increasing the power of visualizing your goals. I quickly move to the place behind the left door. Inside there is a girl. When I began using this technique she was a small, blond girl with blue denim overalls in a plain room. I would take her on my knee and give her encouragement. I would ask her to be confident, warm, and charming for an interview. I would imagine that she nods and smiles.

Over time she has grown up to look a lot like me. The room has expanded to a house with several rooms and large windows. Often when I walk in, she is lying down on the couch relaxing. I ask her to help me. I say, "Will you listen closely and give them a presentation that touches their souls?" She repeats what I said to show that my inner self is committed to the task. Thus, the thought is planted.

I have always felt kindly and loving toward her, but as time passes I grow to like her more and more.

So that's my LaserWalk experience. Yours may be completely differ-ent. You may see a mirror behind the left door. Maybe you will come to blows with your inner self. Maybe you will shape your inner world more consciously than I have. It is your own personal journey.

Here are some tips I have picked up that could help you to master the LaserWalk:

1. You can use this method for everyday things as well as great mo-ments. I used it regularly to get the most out of my three-hour ski training sessions. Use it at the start of the day to put yourself in a positive mental framework or to be very productive at work. I have even tried it at night to get the most out of a few hours of sleep or to suggest that I will wake up refreshed and ready to face a big day. Explore your own applications.

2. There are natural limits to what you can do with the LaserWalk. It won't make you sing like Tina Turner if you can't carry a tune. You can only induce your own peak performance—not someone else's. This method gathers up all your subconscious energy and knowledge, not things you have never learned or can't physically do. If you tried to use the LaserWalk to live on only two hours of sleep every night, your body would likely wear down and get sick. The LaserWalk cannot make you do more than your own peak performance.

   On the other hand, what are the limits of human achievement? I tend to use this method only haphazardly, whenever I remember to use it. Maybe if I used it in a strict routine, ten times daily, I would be ten times the woman I am now. Who knows? When you find out, write to me first! Anyway, doesn't it make you feel more inclined to build skills when you know that they won't fail you in crucial moments?

3. I get maximum effect when I focus on actions and attitudes that are about to happen. Platitudes like "I will exercise regularly" have not worked well for me. "I will enjoy exercising today" is the sort of approach that has been more successful.

4. Decide on the essential elements of your peak performance before starting down the stairs. If you hash out your statement once you are focused it's a bit like waving a laser beam all around the room or trying to perform surgery while brushing up on your anatomy. Spend-ing a few minutes in your fully awake state deciding what will be the

key factors in your success makes the LaserWalk much more power-ful. Take aim carefully before lining up all your energies in that direction.

5. *Important:* Give yourself a positive message. If you say, "I won't be nervous or say stupid things," your brain will focus on nervousness and Saying Stupid Things. The result would be worse than if you hadn't done the LaserWalk at all, because all your energies would be focused on the reverse of what you want! Turn the statement to a positive one such as, "I will be calm and confident, saying meaning-ful things in an eloquent way."

I often forget this maxim or find it difficult to state something positively. Take fat and eating, for example. Instead of thinking about eating less, suppressing hunger, or losing weight, one must try, "I will eat healthy, light meals today," or "My metabolism will speed up today." Sometimes trying to find a positive restatement can be like wrestling with a monkey. That shows that you really don't understand the essential elements of your objective. Pin the monkey and your true objective is revealed.

6. As you become more confident, try doing it faster. I can project myself down the stairs and into my inner self within seconds. Once you know what it feels like to be "there," you can start getting there more quickly. Although it isn't as good as a full LaserWalk, there may be times when jumping downstairs and unleashing the Laser-Edge in a few seconds comes in handy. I have done the LaserWalk on chairlifts, buses, or planes, and standing up. Sitting in a bathroom stall is a favorite place because so often in a crowded office building it is the only quiet place where you can sit down with your eyes closed and not attract attention.

7. *Explore!* Imagine different things. Experiment with statements to achieve your goals and try to find patterns that work for you. Buy books on affirmations and positive thinking to incorporate with your LaserWalk. Write to me and let me know how it goes. You can also try the LaserWalk course on an audio cassette. Or give the audio cassette to a friend as a gift.

Use the LaserWalk to achieve the inner dance every day at work. You will enjoy your work more when you do it well. The days will pass faster and easier. I would also be willing to bet that you will start getting promo-tions or find better work, if you can dance daily through life.

○

Question: If this is so powerful, why isn't everyone doing it?

Answer: Part I. Winners *are* doing it. All winners have their own rituals, routines, or habits that put their inner forces in gear when they need to be there. (They may not know how to transfer this ability to other areas of their lives, as you now do.) Not all winners go through steps like the LaserWalk, but rest assured that they know how to flip the switch deep down inside that unleashes their power, full force, at will.

Part II. Losers *won't* do it. If they ever read the LaserWalk, they will try it once and then forget about it. Their minds regularly toss diamonds and emeralds out the window absently as they curse at other drivers during rush hour. Furthermore, if they have no direction, no passion, and no skill, what would they say to their inner soul anyway?

Others may read this and not believe it. Imagine telling a scientist in 1890 that a beam of light could cut through metal. He would laugh at you, because he doesn't even understand light very well.

You, however, read this because you wanted to achieve something. You know that there is greatness in you. Given the key to your soul, you will learn to use it effectively. You are one of the few people who can fathom the riches available through the LaserWalk. Practice it wisely and make it your own.

○

Desk-ercises

Try the following exercises, which you can do at your desk. They will allow you to work more efficiently and improve your fitness by tapping hidden time resources.

To help you remember to do them, tape a note to your computer or your desk that simply says "Desk-ercise." When you see it you'll remember to do one of the following. You may want to photocopy these pages and keep them at your desk to give you lots of ideas.

Alternatively, make up your own! Write to me and let me know your favorite desk-ercises from this list or your own creation. I'm sponsoring a contest to find the best desk-ercises and the best stories about desk-ercises. If you submit the winning story, I'll send you a special prize, then put your picture in a magazine article about desk-ercise!

Here are a few ideas for a little physical activity at your desk, on the phone, or in a waiting room.

- *Relax your neck:* Drop your chin to one shoulder. As you count to ten, slowly roll your head so your chin is to your chest and then around to the other shoulder. Repeat in the opposite direction.

- *Seated relaxation exercise:* Tense every muscle in your body as you breathe in. Hold for five seconds. Release your muscles as you breathe out. Feel your body relax.
- *Stretch your neck:* Turn your head slowly to the left and look over your shoulder. Then turn your head to the right and look over your other shoulder. Let your head droop down and forward as you move it from one side to the other. Repeat two or three times. Do this again occasionally or whenever you think of it while you work.
- *Exercise your stomach muscles:* Pull in your abdomen, tighten your muscles, and hold for ten seconds while breathing in and out. Let go and relax your stomach muscles completely. Repeat ten times. Do this again whenever you think of it while you work.
- *Stretch your back:* As you take a deep breath, stretch out your arms in front of you and clasp hands. Round your back and drop your chin, pulling your stomach in tight and reaching your arms forward. Breathe out.
- *Stretch your legs and feet:* Back your chair away from the computer so you can stretch your legs out in front of you. Point your toes and hold for five seconds. Flex your toes and hold for five seconds. Circle your feet one way, and then reverse for ten seconds. Click your heels together and say, "There's no place like home!"
- *Stretch your body and do an attitude check:* Take a moment to stand up and stretch your arms up to the ceiling. Look up and think of one thing you can be grateful for.
- *Cleanse your body to help you stay healthy:* Drink eight glasses of water a day. Notice a higher energy level, smoother skin, less water retention, and an overall sense of good health.

Scoring the Quiz

How to calculate your score:

Determine the point value for each of your answers using the answer key below.

Add up questions 1–4 to find your Body Score:_____
Add up questions 5–8 to find your Mind Score:_____
Add up questions 9–12 to find your Spirit Score:_____

What does it mean?

Your *highest* score shows you which area is your Comfort Zone.

Your *lowest* score shows you the resources that you use least.

If your high and low score are very different, you may be relying too heavily on one thing and not giving it all you've got!

1. Do you do any physical activity on a regular basis?
    0   Frankly, no. I am a couch potato.
    2   Yes, but not regularly.

3   Yes, I do regular, low-impact exercise (walking, gardening, etc.).

4   Yes, lots! (gym, tennis, basketball; two or three times per week)

5   Yes, and every year I set an increasingly challenging goal.

2. How do you feel about your physical activities?

0   I hate it: It is boring, sweaty, and sometimes even embarrassing.

3   I have fun doing what I do (running or lifting weights), but it's not what I would call intellectually or spiritually challenging.

5   I feel intellectually challenged by classes, learning new aerobics routines, etc.

5   I feel spiritually involved as in karate, mountain climbing, or gardening.

3. Do you like your appearance?

0   I don't like the way I look.

0   Other people don't like the way I look.

2   My clothes and hair support my professional goals.

2   I strive to meet other people's standards of beauty rather than finding my own style.

4   I like the way I look.

5   I really enjoy the way I look!

4. Do you feel drained, tired, and exhausted?

1   Never

5   Rarely

3   If one of the last three checked

2   If two checked

1   If three checked

5. How often do you read books that challenge you with new ideas? (Not just newspapers, magazines, or TV!)

5   Daily

2   Monthly

0   Once a year, whether I need it or not (or less)

3   Weekly
1   Twice a year

6. Do you use any subconscious mind techniques? (Count Prayer, if you like.)
   5   All four checked
   4   Three checks
   3   Two checks
   2   One check
   0   No, I don't use subconscious mind techniques

7. Do you use subconscious mind techniques to improve
   5   All four checked
   4   Three checks
   3   Two checks
   2   One check
   0   None

8. How would you rate your abilities in terms of time management?
   1   Help! This is my weakest link.
   3   I'm good, but I could improve.
   4   I have a great organization system, but I still never seem to have time for me!
   5   Time management allows me to enjoy life more!

9. Do you live by your values?
   1   I'm not sure. I don't really know what my values are.
   0   I don't live by any code of ethics. Like Nietzsche, I have no regrets.
   2   I know what my values are, but I *often* fail to meet my own ethical standards.
   3   I know what my values are, and I *sometimes* fail to meet my own standards.
   4   Yes, I know my values and follow them rigorously.
   5   Yes, I have a written personal mission statement and/or a code of ethics which I live by and update regularly.

10. Do you like your job? (Try to pick the most accurate statement.)
   0   I hate my job. I dread Monday mornings.
   1   It pays the bills.
   2   I have learned to love it.
   2   It's a good job, nice people. I am lucky to have a good job.
   3   I haven't figured out yet what I want to do when I grow up.
   4   This is one step in my plan to have the job of my dreams.
   5   If I won the lottery, I'd still do the same job!

11. Are you generous to strangers? When and what do you give to
   whom? (Omit this question if you are not comfortable with it.)
   money = 3
   hours of time = 5

12. Do you renew your spiritual strength (circle one or more)?
   1   Hardly ever.
   2   Some, but not as much as I would like.
   3   Regularly, but still not as much as I would like.
   4   Enough to keep me going strong.
   5   Enough to inspire me to do great things!

Index

ABOUT THE AUTHOR

Bonnie St. John Deane is an international speaker, executive coach, and president of SJD & Co. As an Olympic medal-winning skier, author, Rhodes Scholar, Harvard honors graduate and former White House official, Bonnie specializes in high performance under pressure. Having been an amputee for most of her life, she knows how to adapt when conditions are less than ideal. Bonnie has been featured by *NBC Nightly News* as one of the five most inspiring women in America. Her greatest challenge? Succeeding in business while staying sane with her family in San Diego.